A WALK WITH AN IRISHMAN

By Terry Robinson

FOREWORD

Before you join me in my walk I should like you to put your hand in mine so that we can feel each other's vibrations. I say this because I want to encourage you to write your own story - I'd like to read about your walk. And, if for some reason you cannot write it, maybe you can commit it to tape or find some other way to set it down.

For each and every one of us our greatest need is to be able to express our feelings without fear or hindrance. The beauty that lies dormant within us calls out to be expressed in whatever ways we can find to do it.

Remember, your greatest friend or enemy is yourself. Your constant struggle through life is you competing with your own self. And the moment your self-expression and your self-growth are arrested you've got nowhere to go. You're a prisoner within yourself.

In writing this book I leave a lot to your imagination in much the same way as Jesus did. 'Whoever has will be given more. Whoever does not have, even what little he has will be taken away.' A ladder of cautious courage is a difficult one to climb - you're bound to be frozen stiff before you can reach the top. Anyway, that is how I am presenting this book to you.

As I travel to talk about the things I do and write about I

use my voice as another means of expression, as I love to sing. I am an unaccompanied singer, but always appreciate musical backing when I can get it.

What we find in each other is always well worth exploring. And when we meet I am always open to a hug as well as a handshake. That way I believe our vibrations can be felt not only around this earth but throughout the entire universe.

This book is dedicated first to my lovely mother Annie for giving birth to me and for supporting me as only a mother like her could do. The values my mother gave me I have tried to hand down to my beautiful children and grandchildren and to those who have crossed my path: and if I have failed her in any way be assured that is no reflection upon her.

Secondly, this book is dedicated to all those mothers who have made every possible sacrifice to give their children a head start in life, and to mothers in general.

And this book is also dedicated to those who were scarred like me, and in many cases a lot more than me. My heart goes out to you for having to walk along that path. And to those who have weathered the storm, and to those who fell by the wayside, I salute you.

PEMBROKE STREET

I was born in a nursing home in Pembroke Street in Dublin. You might gather, from the fact I wasn't born at home, that my father was not as poor as were so many of my long-suffering countrymen and women. Things were to change later, however, and our family had its taste of hard times - the breeding ground that can break a family or hold them together, make or break a man or woman.

One of my earliest memories as a child was sitting on a pot with my mother encouraging me to do the deed. Strange as it may seem that one thing remains in my memory as if it were only yesterday. We were living then at Sandymount, close to the sea. I remember my lovely dark-haired mother taking me to the beach in the summertime. And I remember how graceful she was as a swimmer and I'm very happy to say that my two daughters are blessed with the same grace both in and out of the water.

From Sandymount we moved to the upmarket Victorian seaside resort of Bray, about twelve or more miles from Dublin. This is where my first real memories as a child come into focus, around 1933. By now my brother Gerald was also a member of the family. Gerald was three and I was six. Now I had someone to play with and annoy. Gerald was quite delicate in his younger days though I was never told why. Little boys were conditioned like puppets for the later guidance of the Church and politicians who worked hand in hand when it suited them.

Our father rented a two-storey house in Galtrim Road which ran straight down to the seafront. I loved Bray with all its touches of heavenly scenery. But Bray also had its mixture of sad and happy times for me just like everywhere else we lived. I guess your first learning experiences in your growing years have the most profound effect on you.

When a child's confidence is undermined his growing years can so easily become a story of unfolding miscalculations. My past experience led me to write this poem:

> *Laugh with your children*
> *and they will laugh with you.*
> *Cry with your children*
> *and they will cry with you.*
> *Experience with your children,*
> *and they will experience with you.*
> *For if you miss this time of sharing*
> *you can so easily miss them.*

The front garden of our house was full of standard rose trees. In the rear garden there were trees with fruit to fill our jam jars. But the house had two frightening things about it that I can clearly remember.

When my father came home on dark winter's nights he would send me to his bedroom to fetch his slippers. The hall light would be on but when I entered his bedroom I couldn't reach the light switch. Though some light did penetrate the gloom it wasn't enough to rid my child's mind of the monsters waiting to claim me.

The second was even more terrifying. My mother would tuck me into my bed after my prayers. When I asked her, she would leave my door open for me, but my father always insisted it be closed. Yes, he knew my fear of the dark and thought he knew best how to counteract it. This, in all probability, he'd learnt from his own father. Some of the traditions fathers hand down to their sons are full of unsolvable problems.

To this day I remember that room. It contained two chests of drawers, a wardrobe and my bed. The ceiling was white, and the wallpaper a yellow shade with red flowers on it. My window looked out onto the back garden. In the dark when I couldn't get myself off to sleep I would imagine the room growing larger and larger, and me getting smaller and smaller. I'd lie there terrified until at last sleep claimed me in its loving arms.

My father's brother Percy lived with his wife Babs and children Brian and Doris in a house facing the seafront. Babs would take me down to her house on the back carrier of her bicycle, her blond hair flowing out behind her. I remember well the day my foot wandered between the spokes of the back wheel. For a few weeks I had a very sore foot. On other occasions Doris and Babs would take me to the swimming pool on the seafront to try and teach me how to swim. One of them would go into the water, and the other would throw me in, I loved the way they both shared their precious time with me. And even if I slipped through the hands of whoever was waiting to catch me, I never felt afraid. Sure, from time to time I swallowed more water than usual but it never bothered me. When a child trusts someone, that someone has the power to create or destroy.

I saw very little of my cousin Brian — being a lot older he ran on a different circuit. My Aunt fussed over me and fed me with her homemade scones. She walked with a bad limp, and I was told she had broken her leg earlier in life and it had never been set properly.

Though Uncle Percy was a good family man I was never at ease with him. He was hard to get close to, a lot like my father in that way.

My father owned a four door Ford. No idea of the model. A car was a major requirement for his profession — he was a motor vehicle engineer working for a number of insurance companies. He travelled around the country assessing vehicle damage for insurance claims.

On certain summer weekends Da would take the family on picnics into the heart of beautiful Wicklow, the Sugar Loaf, Glendalough, Glencree and Roundwood being top of the list. Unfortunately I developed car sickness after a number of outings, so later stayed behind with a lovely couple, friends of my mother who lived at the top of the road. I spent many happy hours playing with their amazing Hornby train set. They were always very kind to me, something a child rarely forgets.

By now my brother Ken had arrived and we were a family of five. Shortly after Ken's arrival we moved to a bungalow in a close by suburb. I can't remember the name of the street. Though I didn't know it at the time, money was starting to become a problem due to my father's drinking, and in general living beyond his means.

My mind is still very confused about my schooling. I was more often out of school than in it, the way of life for so many in my country at that time for so many reasons.

By now I had seen a big change come over my father. The gulf between us was becoming wider by the day. The affection that many fathers express towards their children was to pass me by. Dad had turned to heavy drinking, whiskey being his constant companion. Life was becoming hell for both my mother and me. I would hear her piercing screams as he used his hands on her. Sometimes I would dig myself in under the blankets in an attempt to drown them out, crying out to God to stop him.

And what caused the fly in the ointment? You won't be too surprised to know it was religion. That man-made serpent that God sent us to free ourselves from, or destroy ourselves with. The truth lies within ourselves if we take the time and the effort to look for it.

My mother began locking herself in their room when my father became violent. Usually three quarters of a large bottle of whiskey would set him off. There was never a shortage of money when it came to buying whiskey. I well remember breaking one of the Ten Commandments by stealing a penny off the mantelpiece to buy to buy sweets and being caught by my father. He took me into his bedroom, tied me to the bedpost, and thrashed me with a belt until my mother intervened. That beating gave me food for thought. I knew I'd have to be a lot more careful next time. We never seem to repent until someone has the loving or unloving ability to show us how.

I was now somewhere between nine and ten years old. Because my father could not reach my mother when he was drunk as she locked herself in their bedroom, I became the target on which he vented his frustrations.

Many were the cold winter's nights he'd call me from my bed in my nightshirt to the sitting room with the fire gone out. Following a grilling on my participation in the Catholic Church I would be subjected to one of his sermons. To my child's mind the look of drunken frenzy twisting his face made him appear almost beast like. Yes, you're right, I feared no one as I feared my father.

Some of the worst times for me were those when he came into the bedroom late at night and woke me up by twisting my arm till I was fully awake. But even that silent torture wasn't as hideous as the times he spat on my face. That would turn me almost inside out. I had no answer to that. I could, though, live with him calling me a sissy, a mama's boy knowing that my mother loved me.

There is a lot more I could say but I think I have made

my point. We need to guard against over-dramatizing when we are talking about abuse in our lives. I do understand that others have suffered far worse abuse than I have, but some kind of a line needs to be drawn somewhere. Maybe these words of Eugene O'Neill will convey my meaning better than I am able to. 'None of us can heal the things life has done to us. They're done before we can realise what is being done, and then they make you do things all of your life until these things are constantly coming between you and what you'd like to be. And in that way you seem to lose yourself forever.'

My father would only release his hatred when he was pretty well oiled. When sober he could be quite charming and humorous. I often asked myself in later life what caused this build-up of hatred. I did hear that he had been baptised a Catholic but was later rechristened a Protestant. The reason for that I was led to believe, was that his mother had died at an early age, and his father had married again. What followed from there only God knows. And you could also ask why did he marry my mother, a Catholic, knowing his family and friends wouldn't approve?

Mind you I didn't know much about love at that stage of my life. How could I? Besides not getting much from him, little did I know about the implications that love placed on the shoulders of both men and women. I would have to wait till I got the first bite of that apple.

At that time the gulf of distrust and fear between the Catholic and Protestant churches was huge, and I'm sorry to say there is still a certain unhealthy fragrance lingering in our atmosphere to this very day. The damage it has done in the name of man's philosophy of religion is a price we all have to pay in many ways. People spend so much of their precious time seeking what they already have.

One of the greatest highlights of my life growing up was the time my father bought two bicycles. A half size one for Gerald, and a three quarter-size for me. I'd never ridden a bike before but believe me I learned fast. That bicycle became a very big part of my life as well as becoming my second best friend after my mother. Apart from bringing me into this world, that bicycle is something I shall remain grateful to Da for.

Many was the time, after helping Ma in the house, I'd take off for Bray Head to play Cowboys and Indians with a few boys I got to know. And wherever possible I'd take Gerald on the crossbar. There wasn't much to me, but there was a lot less to Gerald.

More important, however, that bike gave me the opportunity to accomplish many things. First, it gave me the freedom I so badly needed. As I grew older, so long as my mother knew where I was, I could stay out reasonably late. In that way I played for time. The more Da drank the less of a problem he was. Mind you, he soon caught on to my little scheme and would lock me out, but Ma, bless her soul, was on top of that. Her bedroom window was always available to me and from there I could sneak into my bedroom when the timing was right.

The things I enjoyed most of all on my bike were the wind in my face, the sun and rain in my hair, the pleasure and excitement as I took corners at high speed, and all the clever and stupid tricks I learnt. Some were more stupid than clever because I collected plenty of cuts and bruises when I hit the ground. When I look back it still amazes me that I never broke an arm or a leg. Maybe God in his fantastic wisdom said to Himself this young fool needs a bit of support. He might be useful to Me later in life. I wonder what God's thinking now? I haven't changed much in that regard. I still take risks because I believe that's what life is all about.

Because of Da's drinking and the way we moved around I had no long-term friends when I was growing up and missed out on the education that youngsters give one another.

Probably the most embarrassing period in my life was when Da decided to send me to Wesley College in Dublin. Da was educated there himself and became a champion boxer in his division. However I heard little of that unless he was drunk and then it was only to embarrass me. I was a disappointment to him because I was so skinny and went to Mass. He said 'you'll never make the boxing ring'. He was right, I never did. Unintentionally he saw to that.

But the sorry fact was that he wasn't around to see the positive things I did when I got the freedom to make my own choices, apart from joining the R.A.F. I'm sure he would have been proud of me in some way. But who knows, maybe he is.

MALAHIDE

The little I learned about Da came to the surface when he was drunk, and from other little corners I can't really put together. It would have been far more enlightening and valued if we could have had a real father to son relationship. He'd served in the British forces in World War 1, patrolling the seas for U Boats from airships. He was shot down in 1916 and sent home to recuperate. While at home the Easter Rising took place, and he decided to help out by driving an ambulance. On what turned out to be his final trip he was driving two women along with a priest who was giving the last rites to one of them. She was pregnant and had been shot in the stomach. Six men with guns stopped the ambulance, the man in charge being none other than Éamon de Valera. When de Valera found out that Da was serving in the British forces he ordered his execution. The priest got out of the ambulance and pleaded with de Valera to allow Da to continue the wonderful work he was doing in the name of humanity.

As you can well imagine Da took a very strong dislike to de Valera after that episode. On a number of occasions I remember Da saying that had Michael Collins lived de Valera would never have got his foot in the door of Irish politics to do the damage he did. Da also held him responsible for the assassination of Michael Collins. I myself form no judgement in my presentation of this statement. Just giving you the facts as they fell on my ears.

Though he wouldn't let me close to him there was a lot of good in my father. He was well respected, charming, generous and obliging when sober.

Wesley College turned out to be a disappointing option for both of us. Because I had received so little previous schooling, I really hated the place. To add to that embarrassment my mother asked me not to attend morning prayers as they were laced with Protestant addictions that were capable of destroying my childlike soul. Poor Ma. She had been educated in a convent, and there I'll leave you to work it out for yourself rather than add or take from it, other than to say 'Oh God, What fools we mortals be.'

Not attending prayers made me as much a figure of ridicule among the boys as did my inability to keep up with them in class. I stood out like a sore thumb, an open target for those who had no idea where I was coming from. How could they know with their upbringing? As children most of us are screwed up in one way or another because our parents or teachers don't in so many ways have their own answers. Children can so easily become their victims as they look or don't look for solutions at some stage in their lives.

I am very happy to say that I attended Wesley College only for a period of three months. Da never came up with the fees. That is the one and only time I could salute his whiskey drinking — it got me out of a very embarrassing situation.

From Bray we moved to Malahide, about ten miles from Dublin. Da rented a small chalet just above the seafront. Though it was run down it was a magic place for me. It was somewhere around late May or June, with summer knocking on the door. Mind you, summer is always knocking on the door in Ireland, but before you can get it open it's usually gone again. But not so that year I'm so happy to say.

Almost every morning for the three months we lived there I would run to the beach with Gerald to play in the water or among the golden sand dunes. My mother allowed Ken onto the beach only when she was able to come with us, which doesn't say much for my sense of responsibility.

Ma well and truly warned me not to venture any further into the sea than the area she had mapped out for Gerald and myself. Across from where we lived there was a small island with a channel separating it from the mainland. At the mouth of the channel was a very treacherous patch of water named the Short Deep which, I was told, had claimed a number of lives. Many a time I wandered down to the Short Deep to watch the water in constant turmoil with itself, sufficient deterrent to keep me away from trouble there.

Soon after our arrival I was down playing in the water on my own when a voice behind me said, 'Would you like to learn how to float young man?' I turned to see who was speaking but couldn't make out the man's features. Somehow the sun seemed to be playing tricks on my eyes. I said, quite shyly, 'Thank you Sir, I would very much like to learn'.

The man put me gently on my back and supported me with his right hand. He told me to relax and put my head well back in the water. Then in what seemed no time at all he took his hand away and I was floating on my own. What that did for my boyish sense of confidence was one hell of a boost. I felt about ten feet tall. When I got up to thank him a little later he was nowhere to be seen.

At the time I thought little more about the man's kindness but was hit by its full force when, on two occasions, my ability to float saved me from drowning. I wrote the following in memory of this man's kindness, and I believe God's mercy for me.

Was it an Angel

We went to live in Malahide
In a chalet by the sea
The roof had many a hole in it
But we had many a pot, you see
The summer was at its pleasant best
The sand was soft and gold
Oh how I loved that untamed beach
Where the birds sang joyous songs
Each morning to the beach I'd run
When all my tasks were done
With a hop and a skip and a jump

The water and I were one
As I stood looking out to sea
A voice quite startled me
From nowhere it seemed to come
Yet it changed my destiny
A voice so soft and tender
Spoke these words to me
'Young man would you like to float?'
Was the challenge it flung at me
I shyly replied with a nod of my head
And a quivering 'Thank you Sir, I would'
He guided me gently to float with ease
Then like a gust of wind was gone
But he left behind a happy boy
who shall never ever forget
Not only did he save my life
But another one as well.

From the beach at Malahide we moved to Yellow Walls a couple of miles away. The three bedroomed bungalow we were to live in had just been finished by a lovely man named Tom Holiday. Tom had designed and built it, but it seemed the effort had proved too much for him and shortly after its completion he suffered a breakdown. Periodically he'd sink into a depression and would need to be hospitalised. I quite clearly remember one occasion when it took four of us quite a while to coax him down from a tall tree. But Tom was always very kind to me. He would listen to me when no one else really would. He could be both man and child at the same time, a rare gift. Tom's mother was a lovely lady. She lived in a house about two hundred yards behind our bungalow, and her other son John and his wife lived in a lovely little cottage about the same distance behind her place.

Beside John's cottage was a small barn where Tom's mother's turkeys and hens were housed, so there was no shortage of eggs or Christmas turkeys.

When I had finished helping my mother I'd do little jobs for Tom's Ma. She was forever baking brown bread and soda bread. And boy could she cook — anything and everything. When she took to you you'd never go hungry. She knew my weakness - brown bread straight from the oven with lots of homemade butter and jam on it, washed down with a big glass of milk. I remember her once boiling me a turkey's egg. I thought I'd never finish it.

On one occasion I was allowed to watch Tom's mother kill a chicken for dinner. Before she'd managed to sever its head cleanly it escaped with its head hanging half off. I didn't know whether to laugh or cry. Then there was the time I was strolling down the lane to see John and his wife and was met halfway by a gang of Mrs Holiday's turkeys. I paid them no attention until they flew at me with their wings spread out uttering deafening turkey language. That day I learned the meaning of the saying, 'Discretion is the better part of valour'. I was back home in no time.

Below our bungalow was a piece of land called the Marsh, a tidal inlet which looked like a river at full tide. When the waters receded Gerald, Ken and I would go down to see what was left behind. At first we would carry home frogs and tadpoles until Ma spotted us and told us nature could look after itself a lot better than we could. A wise woman was our mother.

My sister Ann had arrived by now so we were six in the family. Ma had a little girl to dote on and worry about. The bungalow had no electricity so cooking had to be done on a coal range. Money was getting scarce, with fuel and food our first priorities after my father's whiskey needs. On a cold winter's evening, early to bed was on the cards.

The long-drop toilet was a first for us. At first I was fascinated by the big hole, but as it began to fill up the fascination wore off. The newly experienced aroma assaulted my nostrils. We noticed Da had stopped taking his newspaper out in the mornings. On a cold winter's night I wasn't too impressed with the walk either. When I saw Da watering the flowers I soon took a leaf out of his book.

By now Da's drinking had reached its peak. I feared him more now than ever, not so much for myself, but for my mother and my baby sister. Many was the time I had to grab Ann out of harm's way as he floundered around the room. I remember him picking her up out of her cot and falling on the bed with her. Had the bed not been close she might not have been with us today. I rushed over and grabbed my baby sister, shouting 'you crazy fool, you'll kill her'. Mind you, I had to make a quick exit with Ann in my arms.

It was only when Da was so drunk he could scarcely move that we had little to fear from him. That was the time to raid his pockets. I could be quite brave at those times. I knew I had the strength to hold him should he move while Ma was going through his right pocket where he stuffed his legal tender. He could have some small change in his side pockets, but we were after the big fry. There was one time when he wasn't as drunk as we thought. We started to do the deed when he grabbed my arm, but I just managed to get away from him. He then lurched over for Ma. She ran from the room. I struggled with him, pushed him back into his chair, and then took off. After that we were a lot more careful.

Then there were all those times when I would stand at the bedroom window waiting for my father to arrive in his car at the front gate. If he had a bottle in his hand or was staggering I knew what to expect. Even when I thought everything was going to be okay he'd often go out again to tank-up. I lived in constant fear of the evenings.

We did once have close to a full week of tranquillity after Ma had given Da a taste of his own medicine. I can't remember how it began, but it ended up with Ma throwing a pot of very hot water over him. That was the first time, and the last time I ever heard my father scream with pain, and I must have been more than a little sadistic at the time as I enjoyed every moment of it.

Da ran an account at the grocery shop in Malahide. Ma would often send me down on my bike to collect things she needed. I didn't mind running the errands for her, but what I did mind were the near refusals because the account was so large. I found that very embarrassing indeed.

I attended Malahide public school on the usual on and off basis, more off than on at the time because Ma wasn't in the best of health. I wasn't good at cooking but boy I could change nappies and clean bums. If they'd had a university degree course on that subject I might have had rooms in Harley Street today.

Mind you, I was so far behind in my school work, I must have stood out like a Priest saying mass in an Orange Lodge — it didn't bother me to stay at home. The headmaster frightened the living daylights out of most of us when he was annoyed. Still, there were a few more idiots like me there so maybe I'm being a bit hard on him seeing he's not here to defend himself. For those who got on the wrong side of him it was his three-pronged leather strap we feared most. He could do anything with it but make it talk. You get the picture of what teaching used to be about. Then again it didn't kill any of us, but did give us food for reflection.

For those of you who are wondering why the authorities

didn't come down on Da for not looking after my education here are the only answers I can come up with. They did, on a number of occasions but nothing came of it, the reasons probably being that we moved around a lot, and that Da had drinking friends in what our society calls the right places. That, along with his gift of the gab. After that it's pure speculation.

And if anyone could get away with anything it would have to be my father. How the hell he didn't get pulled up for drunk driving, or for what he put my poor mother through is beyond all belief. Though I wasn't in the car very often, I do remember him coming home on certain occasions after a picnic, stopping at pubs along the way getting tanked up, then driving home like crazy, cursing and swearing, and us all praying like there was no tomorrow. I've had many wild experiences in my time but they had to be in a time-zone of their own. I could well believe that he was behind that saying 'The luck of the Irish'. Da was awarded an OBE for driving that ambulance around in 1916, but I think he was more qualified to receive it for the luck of the Irish.

As there was no running water to our bungalow my daily chores included collecting the water from the pump down the road. Friday was a busy day because Friday night was bath night. We needed lots of water to wash away the odours of the week. Ma did see that we had a rub down at night so I guess we were possible to live with, but not up to today's standards where one or two showers a day are always on the cards for those who can afford them, or deem them necessary. Makes you wonder how we all managed to live together in those times of necessity.

One Friday night I remember Da staggering into the kitchen and falling into the big steel tub in front of the fire. He looked so funny struggling to escape the rising tide. From a safe distance we laughed our heads off. He didn't bother us for the rest of that night so it was well worth the big clean-up afterwards.

The picture I've painted of my father's drinking and the bad times he created for our family when I was growing up is, I think, a reasonable one. I have no wish to destroy his memory in the eyes of my family or anyone else. My story is about me, not my father. Also, my story is not about looking for sympathy, more an attempt to explain how ill-equipped some of us are to face life. It's not the beginning or the end of life, just what I'd call an unnecessary hurdle.

THE DUNNS

Now for another highlight in my life. Our neighbours on the left of our bungalow were two elderly ladies and their two brothers. Their surname is all I remember them by. They were farmers and had a good sized piece of land that included their cottage, a cowshed, a stable, a chicken run, and a barn, and a shed that housed all their equipment.

One day I took the liberty of wandering into their yard to have a good look at their lovely farm horses. I've always had an affinity with horses, ponies, and donkeys. One of the ladies spotted me and came over to ask me my name. She said 'I've seen you around. You live next door in Tom's house, don't you?' I said yes and told her my name. She invited me into their cottage and sat me down in the kitchen. She was wearing a long black skirt with a grey sack tied around her waist. On her head was a long pointy grey hat and her straggling grey hair covered part of her face. But what drew me to her were her kindly eyes and her smile. They were welcoming and made me feel safe.

When inside other people's homes I was never one to take stock of what they had or did not have. I simply felt comfortable or uncomfortable, so I cannot describe the Dunns' kitchen for you.

The lady put a large glass of buttermilk before me and some homemade bread with jam on it. It was the first time I'd tasted buttermilk and I was hooked. When I finished eating she took me on a tour around the buildings. That was the beginning of four wonderful friendships for me. The other sister, who looked much like the first, treated me with the same kindness, and the two men couldn't do enough for me.

I asked the Dunns if I could help in any way as I wished to get involved in their lives and learn something of value for myself. I was learning nothing from my hit and miss schooling. I wanted to feel useful and appreciated instead of just being put down by my father. I know Ma did what she could but that wasn't enough for my boyish needs.

The Dunns told me if I got the okay from my mother I could start by cleaning out their cowshed. I ran all the way home and told Ma. Without hesitating she said, 'Find the oldest rags you have to wear and off you go.' That was one of the very special gifts my mother had. She could look into your eyes, read your needs and without a moment's hesitation fill them. And I am very fortunate to tell you besides my mother, three other people have also filled that gap for me -- my daughter Rachel, my uncle Harry, and Sister Yvonne Heffernan.

As you walk this walk with me, you will I'm sure be touched by their beautiful natures.

Though cleaning out the cowshed was a messy chore I enjoyed every moment of it. Later I was allowed to clean out the horse stables, a job I really loved because I could get close to those great bulky farmyard animals who may not have been graceful like racehorses, but more than made up for it with their friendly nature.

In the summer holidays the two men would take me with them on the hay bogies to pick up the hay they had stacked in their fields. Each bogey was a made up of a large wooden platform mounted on an axle with two wheels, and it had two long wooden shafts to which the horses were harnessed. On the driver's side was a device which allowed a rope to winch the hay stacks onto the bogey when the platform was tilted towards it. I loved winching these peaked hay stacks up onto the bogies. One day I got the thrill of my young life when one of the men, who I dimly remember as being called Pat, handed me the reins and let me drive the bogey back to the yard. There wouldn't have been a prouder twelve year old boy in all Ireland that day. Our family did quite well from my little job, never going without eggs and vegetables. And the only damage I ever did was to rip a gate post out of the ground with the side of the bogey.

During my stay in Yellow Walls in Malahide I made two friends, Kevin Fitzgerald and John Kennedy. Kevin, who was older than me, took me under his wing until he was sent down the country to work. His family lived beside an area called the Cross Roads. I liked Kevin straight away after meeting him, and also his family because they all made me feel welcome.

Kevin soon got to know about Da because he called to see me one evening when Da was ready to give us and the Catholic Church another roasting. Da was in the hall when Kevin knocked, so he opened the door to him. Kevin introduced himself as they hadn't met before and Da took him into the sitting-room and called me. To my relief they were having a reasonable conversation when I came in. Da was fairly drunk but cute enough not to put a foot wrong. He had taken an instant liking to the well-built sixteen-year old with his soft voice and gift for words.

After Kevin had met the rest of the family he and I went for a walk. He said, 'You have a nice family, and I really liked your mother. Your Da was very pleasant but I sensed that everything is not as it should be'. I then told him about Da and what the family was going through. From then on I felt close to him, as though I had a big brother to look up to.

Kevin taught me a lot of things - like how to get in and out of an orchard without getting caught, how to make a sling and catch a rabbit, how to ride a bicycle backwards and how to dismantle it and put it back together again. This last teaching enabled me to keep my wheels on the road as long as I did even when my legs were getting too long. He also taught me how to ride a horse and how to row a boat. I shall never forget Kevin. Friends like him are a joy to behold, and lay a sense of positive reinforcement in your mind to face the future with more equipment than you already had. When he had to leave for the country there were a few tears in my eyes. He gave me a big hug before he left. I've got a strong feeling that's where this need to hug people originally developed, looking back once again over my life as I rewrite my book. And in doing this I have remembered the Christian names of two of the Dunns. One was called Pat, and the other Kate. I wonder what else will come to light as I continue.

After Kevin left, John Kennedy appeared on the scene. His family lived on a small farm not far from us. John was the reverse of Kevin, cute as a fox with no idea what the word truth meant. His old man gave him a hard time, as my old man did me, so that could explain it. Fear has a wonderful way of turning us into liars. The lies I had to tell when I got the third degree about my participation in the Catholic Church were almost too much for absolution. But I was one of the lucky ones, I went to the Catholic Church - they'd forgive you anything as long as you didn't change your religion. And I don't believe anyone of my age could have prayed so hard to God to let his father be sober when he came home. I gave the Hail Marys and Our Fathers such a bashing it's a wonder they're still with us.

John was younger and smaller than I was. He was in my class at school and fitted in much better than I did. Now the subject I feared most was Irish. I was far enough behind in all the other subjects, but trying to learn Irish was nearly as bad as some of the sessions Da put me through. I was given the strap a number of times which made me shudder at the very thought of it. One day I was given this Irish essay to write out for my homework and was shitting my pants at the very thought of it. I told John and he said he'd write it down for me to copy. I can still remember being very impressed with his handwriting and thinking his efforts might do the trick.

John, I soon found out, was not the literary genius I hoped he was. When I handed in my essay to the teacher my mind got a taste of what it needed, but my hands were not so impressed. I said nothing to John about his handiwork, even though he gave me some nervous looks, because I knew the responsibility lay in my court. As one could say about life, it all comes down to choices.

A week later I had just finished playing handball after lunch when John came up to me crying and holding his ear. He said one of the boys had smacked him for no reason. Had I known John better than I did, I would have thought no more about it and eventually saved myself a lot of humiliation. But as I didn't I allowed myself to be manipulated into defending his honour without realising at that time he didn't have one to defend.

So next day the whole school came at lunch time to watch this chap and I do battle on the village green. That day I learned another sharp lesson - a bleeding nose, a black eye, a sore jaw and some painful ribs.

The fight was all over in the first round much to the disappointment of the onlookers. I wasn't very impressed either. As my adversary helped me back to my feet he held out his hand, smiled, and said 'Sorry, the odds were against you from the start. My father is a boxer in the police force and he's taught me to handle myself.' I didn't tell him that my father too was a boxer but the same consideration hadn't come my way. To add insult to injury, when my father asked me how I got my injuries and I told him, he said 'next time be quicker on your feet'.

The great lesson that came out of that for me was that ignorance makes use of what it has to work with. Even twelve year-olds must put their thinking caps on when faith shows its hand of necessity. Life's sharp lessons have no respect for age. But if parents and teachers take the trouble to really examine their own values before they pass them on to children, maybe not so many of us would fall by the wayside. I think R.D. Laing sums it up beautifully with these words: 'We think much less than what we know. We know much less than what we love. We love much less than what there is. And to this precise extent we are much less than what we are.'

Our family left Malahide for Clontarf in 1939, but a part of me was to stay in Malahide. I had some rough times there, but also some wonderful times. All in all, the good times outweighed the bad.

CLONTARF & RATHMINES

The one thing I remember clearly about Clontarf was that World War II broke out while we were there. I remember my father coming half-shaven into the kitchen to tell my mother that Britain had declared war on Germany. Da had just heard it on the radio.

Our stay in Clontarf was a short one due to the usual problem that kept us on the move. Unpaid rent. One thing for sure, Da never won any credibility with landlords.

From Clontarf we moved to a two-bedroomed flat in Rathmines. The building consisted of three flats. We had the middle one. My brother Tony had now arrived. This the youngest son was now to go through the mill like the rest of us, and I must say came out with flying colours. He was very special then, and still is. Mind you so were Ann, Ken and Gerald. As I write this (in 2014) my daughter Rachel has informed me that she is taking me to Canada to join up with Tony and his wife Joan at my sister's house in Toronto. I am really looking forward to the family catch up.

Soon the War was in full swing with everyone feeling the shockwaves. Da could no longer afford a car as work and petrol were in short supply - though not, miraculously, whiskey. The money for that just had to come from somewhere.

We had not long been in Rathmines when my

grandmother came to stay with us. My grandfather had passed away. I was told that a chicken bone had lodged in his throat and he'd died before anything could be done to save him. I remember visiting my mother's parents on very few occasions, but I do recall my grandfather as a kindly man. Da always spoke highly of him, while not impressed with my grandmother. I was told that my grandfather owned a pub in Dún Laoghaire at some time of his life, and was reasonable comfortable until he met my grandmother. What happened after that is anyone's guess.

But it did trickle down to my ears a few times when my father was drunk that my grandmother could spend money like there was no tomorrow. Where have we heard that story before?

One of the many scraps of information that sticks in my mind that came out not long after Grandpa's death was that evening Da came home a little more intoxicated than usual and had fallen in the hall doorway when I opened the door to let him in. Yes, he did have his own key, but you might for a moment visualize him trying to fit it in the keyhole. If we'd had the video it would have been a priceless heirloom to leave for future generations. Anyway I got him into an armchair in the small sitting-room and was pleasantly surprised by the change in his language, saying to myself 'Terry you'd better enjoy this while it lasts.'

What I was about to witness I shall never forget in all my life - my father crying like a baby. I was alone with him, everyone else having hightailed it to bed after seeing his condition. God knows I hated being the eldest at such moments. Da started mumbling about my grandfather, and after years of such drunken speech I could I could now pick up what he was saying. Pity I couldn't have made my fortune interpreting the utterings of people like my father. I'd certainly done the groundwork. You just have to be very patient with a sense of humour, and be fast on your feet. Seemingly Da had caught up with one of his old drinking buddies who knew my grandfather and they'd decided to have a few drinks in his memory. I have no quarrel with that, believing it's a nice way to pay tribute to nice people, and even some of the others. We Irish are masters at that. In fact it doesn't even need to be in memory of a man, woman or child, anything will do. And we just haven't the heart to give it up.

Observing Da's mood I thought I'd encourage him in the hope some family history might fall into my lap. At least for the moment the barrel of the rifle wasn't pointing at me. Da said Grandpa was a good man for the way he looked after interests of others. He would encourage those who came into his pub on payday to go home to their wives and families after they had a few drinks and put their money to the use it was meant for. Sometimes he would even order them out. There were two things Grandpa feared, Da said, his wife and the church. The gates of hell are never closed for us Catholics no matter how good we are. Maybe that's not a bad idea, just in case we become too complacent.

By now Da was fast losing the plot as he was still

drinking. I had the job of keeping his glass topped up. I learned nothing more after that, but was quite satisfied with the few crumbs that he had thrown my way, a little scrap of family history to leave for future generations that might help them to look at their options. As someone so beautifully phrased it, it takes courage to have tried and failed as it does to have tried and succeeded. This is what my whole walk is about no matter what path I'm on.

Something else I heard when Da was tanked was that my mother's sister Molly had been the apple of her father's eye, and was consequently spoilt. She was very good looking with a striking figure. I remember that from a photograph I saw of her in her younger days sitting in a flashy Lagonda sports car that her father had bought for her. There were other stories about her tragic life that are best left to let her memory rest in peace. There are enough judgmental people in this world without me joining their ranks.

I remember Ma taking me on a number of occasions into O'Connell Street to meet my aunt. We would find a cake shop and sit down to have tea and scones. Ma would give her some money when she could manage it. Anyway that's how it looked to me. And whatever good looks my Aunt had to my young mind's eye were no longer there. Her eyes were the saddest eyes I had ever looked into, and I've seen a few. Rouge, powder and lipstick couldn't hide the misery her features portrayed. Poor Ma, as though she didn't have enough on her plate without having to worry about her sister's troubled life.

And although my father would never allow her to visit us, Ma never forsook her. Ma was there to hold her hand on her deathbed. If you have ever seen anyone die of syphilis please spare a thought for all those poor women who got abused for whatever the reasons may have been.

The day Grandma arrived was quite a shock for us kids. This large unhappy-faced woman dressed in black standing up in a horse-drawn cart in front of our flat conjured up all sorts of ideas in our minds. We were fascinated to watch the poor driver struggling to unload her large black box and my grandmother having a fit for fear he'd drop it. It was her most important possession we were to find out, a commode - her own portable toilet. It seems that her feet and legs had given up from the lack of exercise while living the good life and her walking was limited to moving from one side of the room to the other.

In no time at all our curiosity turned to gasps of dismay when this unsightly piece of furniture began to give off odours that clashed with our noses. And we had no way of escaping from them because Grandma lived and slept in our room. Seven of us had to sleep there when Da was drunk.

That room in which we had played and slept was no longer popular with us kids. You would only find us in there when we were asleep or sick. To be perfectly honest I didn't like my grandmother. She seemed to be always fussing about or complaining, and poor Ma was always at her beck and call.

Between Grandmother, Da and all us kids Ma never had a moment's peace. There was no way I could blame her for taking a few drinks now and again. She had nothing else to turn to. But even that solace was a disaster as Ma would be unbelievably sick for days afterwards. I'd take the bit between my teeth then and try to keep things ticking over, hating it but not complaining for Ma was worth much more than that.

Da hated my Grandmother. On occasions he would raise his hand to her, then think the better of it. I remember him saying that she had been responsible for her husband's downfall with her extravagance. Seemingly she'd been a waitress in Cornwall when my grandfather met her so thereby hangs a tale. From a rough guess I'd say that about six months after she came to live with us Ma using considerable persuasion, managed to get her into a home for the aged. It was a great burden off Ma's shoulders, and I must admit we kids breathed a lot easier.

Ma and I visited her occasionally after that but nothing had changed. Life was still a bitch to her. A year or so later she died. 'From rags to riches and back to rags' would have gone well on her tombstone had we been able to afford one. And I must admit that I have no right in God's eyes or anyone else's eyes to be judgemental about my Grandmother, but sometimes you have to write it as you see it, and accept the consequences when it come for your time to be judged. And I still pray for my Grandmother's soul, as I do for family and friends.

UNCLE HARRY

My uncle Harry was now to come into the picture and play a wonderful supportive role to both my family and I. Until then I had seen little or nothing of him. Our side of the family due to poor old Da's drinking was left out in the neck of the woods. Anyway I think I've done what I could to see that it doesn't happen again on a wing and a prayer.

What I knew about my Uncle Harry I learned from Da who idolized him. From that I sensed there had been a strong bond between them when they were growing up. One night when Da was close to being tanked up he told me something about my Uncle that touched my very soul, and still lingers with me still.

Harry was sent to fight the Turks in the Dardanelles soon after World War One broke out and while he was there he took a bullet in one of his legs. He was lying alone in pain when a Turkish soldier spotted him and walked towards him. The soldier had a rifle with a fixed bayonet on it, and Harry said to himself this looks like the end of the road. Then suddenly the Turk took off his backpack, dropped it beside Harry, and walked away without a word. There is nothing I can add to this story - it speaks for itself.

The war had left its mark on Harry as it did on so many others. He contracted a bad case of malaria which later was to claim his life. Quinine more or less kept him going on that home run to his Heavenly home. God knows if anyone deserved it, it was my Uncle Harry.

However, I was told that following the war he went to France and became a race car driver. He was involved in a life-threatening accident in a race there and was hospitalised for a considerable time. I can clearly recall the scars on his face.

Harry later returned to Dublin and joined the family firm of S.T. Robinson's Engineering premises. His step-brother Sam was the central figure, though I'd heard it said that Sam's sister was the driving force behind the wheel, which later proved to be the case. S.T. Robinsons was situated on the corner of South King Street and Mercer Street. I only remember Da taking me there on one occasion, but I do remember clearly seeing a number of people using machines, and mechanics working on various makes of cars.

Like so many family firms, however, the mask of solidarity is eventually lifted to show its true face. Shortly after Sam passed away both my Uncle Harry and my Uncle Percy were shown the door with nothing to show for the dedicated years they devoted to the firm. It appeared Sam's sister had other favourites. Does that have a familiar ring to it?

But you can't keep a good man down. Jesus was an almighty example of that. Harry, being the well-liked and respected man he was, quickly managed to secure some funds, and opened a garage at 9A Lower Pembroke Street not far from where I was born, adding to the important part that street has played in my life.

Though it was not the best time to start a new venture

because of the war, that garage was to prove a godsend for my two uncles, my father's family and myself. Harry gave Percy the job of turning all manner of things on a lathe in the upstairs workshop. Percy could do anything with a lathe except make it sing. There would be few I believe who could match his skill, my father told me, but he had no head for business.

That was where Harry came in. Not only was he a good and honest businessman but also a brilliant engineer. He offered Da the use of his office to keep in touch with the insurance companies he worked for. Da had an office across from Stephen's Green but was forced to let it go. I believe that was the only place he kept the rent paid up.

There were many wonderful ways my uncle helped Da to keep food in our mouths and help with the rent as Da's insurance companies were also brought to their knees because of the war.

Harry was the kindest most generous and courageous man to ever cross my path. He was one of those natural gentlemen you would be proud to call Irish who would have made a wonderful father had his marriage produced children. One of the many lovely things I remember about him was his generosity to the old soldiers of both the Irish and English wars. These men, some with only one leg or arm, others just shadows of men, would call in to have a chat with Harry and never left without a little something in their pockets. Where this had its beginning I have no idea. My uncle didn't talk about himself, he just faced the challenges life put before him and did what he could.

Living in Upper Rathmines gave me a chance to keep up with my swimming, the Dodder Canal being within easy cycling distance. During the summer Gerald and I spent many happy hours in the water and watching the barges going through the locks. I also joined the Harold's Cross Scouts while we were living there. This all had its beginning when one day Ma sent me in to collect some money from a cheque Da said he was expecting from one of his insurance companies, as we had little or nothing to eat. Well the cheque never arrived but Harry came to the rescue - one of the many times he helped our family out without Da ever paying him back. While I was there I got introduced to Tommy who filled me in with what was required to join the scouts. I took to Tommy straight away and immediately jumped at the chance of meeting new friends and trying something new in my life. I had become very much a loner because of Da and my self-consciousness.

And I had begun to realise that I could not blame everything on Da, and the fact that it is not the years that make a boy a man, but his belief in himself. Our greatest enemy I believe I was starting to realise somewhere in my subconscious was self-pity. Mind you I didn't understand that at the time, but looking back I can see that quite clearly.

When I arrived home I told Ma what had happened and asked if I could join the scouts. My mother was only too delighted to see some happiness come my way. Da had no objection so long as it wasn't the Catholic Boy Scouts. I had only one more problem to overcome - a uniform. With seven mouths to feed, and seven people to clothe and house there was nothing left for such luxuries as a scout uniform. Well I won't deny I was disappointed at the thought of missing out on this wonderful opportunity, but as disappointment had become a way of life for me I accepted the fact with some grace.

About a week later Da came home and told me that my Uncle Harry wanted to see me, but gave no reason. I arrived at the garage the following morning with all manner of notions spinning around in my head and knocked on his office door. He called me in and sat me down. 'I hear you want to join the Boy Scouts' he said.

I told my uncle I would love to join the Boy Scouts. 'Right', he said, 'go home and ask your mother to get you fitted out in whatever you need and get them to send the bill to me, and get them to ring me if there are any problems.' Before I could find the words to thank him he stood up, laid both his hands on my shoulders and looked at me with those kindly but penetrating blue eyes. 'Enjoy your new venture', he said, 'I was a Boy Scout once.' Besides thanking him I'm quite sure that he would have been able to read my gratitude from the tears in my eyes.

About a week or so later I became a member of the Harold's Cross Boy Scouts, a major step for me lacking those tools so necessary for the discovery of my presence and my voyage. I honestly believe that the lack of confidence within us is the greatest handicap that faces those of us who have been ill-treated in some way. We are left shy, uncaring, angry, immature and vulnerable. Unwilling in so many ways to accept what life has to throw at us.

There were a few boys who spotted the chinks in my armour and exposed them as I went through my paces to become a fully-fledged boy scout but by this time I had learned to bite my lip.

Tommy Hendrick and I became good friends. I often visited him and his lovely family in Inchicor. They were very nice people who made me feel at home. I would have liked their hospitality in some way, but that was out of the question and Tommy and family understood that.

At last the day arrived for me to experience my first weekend in a tent. Ma put together a loaf of bread, two eggs, a slice of bacon, some cheese, and rice to tide me over the weekend.

Full of excitement I joined up with Tommy on the Rathmines Road around five on that Friday evening and we headed for the camping grounds at Powerscourt Domain in Enniskerry. For those of you who feel as I do about nature I would suggest you go to Powerscourt should you pay my country a visit. As I remember it, Powerscourt House, was built in 1740, and the only thing to detract from its beauty was that it was later destroyed by fire, though it has since (in 1996) been rebuilt.

Within the Domain's fourteen acres there was a beautiful waterfall that gave us scouts many happy hours dancing in its arms, along with all the other high jinks we got up to whenever opportunities presented themselves. Being human we all bend the rules from time to time. Even the scoutmasters had their moments of weakness when it came to enjoying the extra bit of fun. They, and the assistant scoutmasters slept in a log cabin, while we, the rest of the tribe, slept in tents. Having to put up with us during the day was one thing, but having to sleep with us would have been too much hard work for them. I learned that the first night. A noisy lot we were, and as silly as they come. One of the guys knocked a kerosene lamp over onto some newspapers and if one of the senior scouts hadn't been quick enough to smother it with a blanket I might not have been writing my story today.

The three things I valued most out camping was getting away from my father, and the freedom and comradeship it brought to my soul. Two whole days and nights without having to worry about Da, and the responsibility with being the eldest in the family, and also the sharing values it brought to all of us. Because times were tough not many of us had enough food to last the whole weekend, yet no one went hungry.

THE STEAM PACKET COMPANY

Apart from the usual mishaps with my bike I had only one real painful and embarrassing accident. Coming home from Powerscourt one evening I was gathering speed to get up the hill on the other side of the cross roads that lay in front of me, when fate decided I should have a rendezvous with a young maiden coming down the hill on my left on her bike. Because of the trees and a wall we had no chance of seeing each other until the damage was done. Fortunately for her I took the full impact. She fell on me as we hit the road. At another time I might have welcomed her calling card for she was a nice looking girl as I remember.

There were four witnesses to this accident who had me tried and convicted the moment it happened. This judge and jury were all elderly gentlemen who happened to be sitting on a wooden form with a good view of the accident. Seeing the fair maiden spread-eagled upon me and showing more leg than was customary was enough in their eyes to convict me even though I did have the right of way. They rushed over to assist the maiden, calling me all sorts of names while I struggled to my feet with blood streaming from my head and knees. A number of people soon gathered from the surrounding houses as well as the village policeman who had been on duty nearby.

My four accusers continued to give me the hard tongue but were told by the policeman to bite their lips and let him deal with the matter. After checking us out to ensure no serious damage had been done, the maiden was taken into a nearby house, and I was taken into another. There a very kindly couple dressed my wounds and made me a cup of tea. They took my sorry-looking bike into their backyard. When I examined it later I saw the front wheel was badly buckled and there was a slight bend in the crank pedal. The man suggested I take the damaged wheel off and take it home with me on the bus. He told me to pick up a second-hand wheel and salvage anything I needed from the buckled one. He asked me if I had money for the bus. When I replied that I did not he put his hand in his pocket and produced the fare. He said they'd look after my bike until I returned for it. I thanked them both and managed to catch the last bus home. My friend Tommy had been in front of me when the accident happened. As there was nothing he could do I told him to go home because his bike had no light.

Ma was waiting when I got home, and when she saw the condition I was in, and the wheel in my hand, she said 'God what war have you been in?' and shot me into the bathroom to check my injuries.

Tommy rang the Scoutmaster the next day from work to tell him what had happened. The Scoutmaster called immediately to see me. After satisfying himself that I was ok he told Ma he would take some money from the scout fund to buy me a new front wheel for my bike. Three days later he appeared at our door with the new wheel. All I had to do was to change the tyre and tube over.

On the following Friday I caught the bus to Enniskerry with a letter of thanks Ma had given me for the lovely couple who had taken care of me after the accident. I had with me the bus fare to repay them. They very kindly told me to buy some sweets with the money and to drop in and say hello whenever I had the time, and this I did.

Before we left Rathmines I was to have another soul-saving experience. As I had never been confirmed to become a foot soldier in God's Catholic Army Ma had to dig into her purse to pay a tutor to prepare me for this last and final hurdle to become a fully-fledged Roman Catholic. My feelings with regard to this were very mixed indeed. At that stage in my life I didn't know if I was coming or going. Coming to Heaven or going to hell. When it came to religion I wondered who was trying to save whom from what. I used to think to myself what a lot of mixed-up people these so-called grownups are, talking about Jesus and love one minute, then pulling each other apart the next. But I loved my mother for all she had taken on board for us kids, so I let the question lie.

Twice a week Ma and I would take a bus to the end of Rathmines Road nearer the city centre, and there we would enter this three-storied house to further my religious education. With Ma waiting outside in a chair I was taken into a small dark room with only a desk and a few chairs in it, as far as I can remember. Behind the desk sat a large women who directed me to sit in front of her and began to test my knowledge of the Catechism. I don't need to tell you that she wasn't very impressed, saying 'it's boys like you that give our faith a bad name.' I felt like saying I think you've got that the wrong way wrong way round, but for Ma's sake I said nothing. 'Your mother tells me your life has not been too easy for you,' she went on to say, 'but that does not excuse you. Never mind, we'll soon set that right.'

Two months later, with Ma out of pocket and me none the wiser, I was drafted into God's Catholic Army with no chance of ever getting a commission. The teacher said that I was one of her worst students. 'You'll never get anywhere in life' she told me, and she was right. I never found out where that anywhere was, and what's more I would have been afraid of bumping into her there had I ever found it.

Soon after that we moved into to small damp and rundown three-bedroomed house in Kilmainham quite close to its famous, or infamous jail, depending on how you view Irish history. Because of my lack of education like so many who came before me and after me, I did not have an in depth understanding of my country's history.

Not long after we moved I found myself a job in The British and Irish Steam Packet Company office which was located at the North Wall. I was just about to hit fifteen years of age and had been looking around for work for some time with little expectation of finding any. The firm needed someone to run errands between their office and the Custom House with the idea of later training them to become an office clerk. As you well know by now I had no qualifications for that position but I did have one ace up my sleeve, my bike.

That's what got me the job. My best friend apart from Ma. But there was one stipulation, I would have to further my education by going to night school, and that was a challenge I was not looking forward to. But I said to myself, I've got to start somewhere so I'll cross that bridge when I come to it, or failing that there's always the river to take me somewhere else.

Ma was delighted for me but Da said that there was no future in a job like that. But I didn't care what Da said. At least for the present I'd feel useful and it was a boost to my already shaken self-confidence.

When I handed my first week's wages to Ma I felt as proud as punch. For the first time in my life I was able to give her something instead of always taking. Ma opened my wage packet, took out ten shillings, and then handed me back five saying 'Well done.'

And what did I spend my money on? No it wasn't girls because I'm quite sure I wouldn't have got far with five shillings a week in my pocket and me so shy as well. I settled for my sweetest delight, Mars Bars when I could afford them.

We were well into the war by now. Black bread and dripping, though also rationed, was often on the menu, and very glad we were to get that though I still allowed myself the luxury of complaining about it. Occasionally, however, the dark clouds would open up to show a silver lining. Now and then one of the ships that docked beside the wharf sheds near our office would offload along with its cargo a number of freshly- baked loaves of white bread. Boy did our family relish that loaf when I could get my hands on one for the price of sixpence. First come first served. Ma was very impressed when I brought the first one home. She said what a clever son I have.

But once again life was to change for my family and me quite dramatically. Ma had to go away for almost a year. I will not say any more on that because that was a very personal issue for her. Anyway, I had to give up my job to look after the family. My brother Gerald could have done this equally well but he needed the education I had missed out on. As it was, I could not have kept the job much longer because my bike had finally come to the end of the road. And I can tell you there were a few tears in my eyes that day, for we'd been through a lot together.

About two months later we received our marching orders once again so Da found a room on the North Circular Road. There was one thing you could say about my father, he was never a social climber. The house we moved into was occupied by four other families we never got to know because of Da's drinking. The walls were thin and his ungraceful language passed through them loud and clear. The room was quite large with two windows looking down on the street below. The wallpaper didn't bear speaking about. The gas stove could have been something that came from the Ark. The sink was large enough to wash a two year-old in as long as you weren't fussy about the stains and cracks. Least said about the fireplace the better. I thought to myself 'I hope this is rock bottom as I wouldn't like to fall any lower.'

Once again my lovely Uncle Harry came to our rescue.

He and his wife took to looking after my young sister Ann, and my baby brother Tony while my mother was away. That was probably one of the greatest blessings that could have been bestowed on our family at that critical time in our lives.

A few weeks later as far as I can remember Da came home one evening with a whiskey bottle in his hand and started to give me a going over with his tongue. About an hour after I'd finally got to bed he came staggering over to where Gerald and I were trying to sleep and grabbed my arm and began twisting it. When I couldn't stand the pain any longer I managed to escape and took off out of the room wearing just my shirt. I heard him following me so I made a beeline down to the basement where nobody was living.

Among the rubbish in there I found an old mattress, a blanket and something that looked like a sheet. Talk about home away from home. No, I certainly wouldn't have looked twice at them today, but under the circumstances I classed them as a gift from heaven. And who knows? The weather was still warm for late September and there was enough daylight for me to organise myself. I curled up and went to sleep with a prayer of thanks.

Next morning I waited until Da had gone to work then went back to our room and got myself something to eat. When the others asked where I'd been I said, to my new hideout out. Then we all hugged each other and had a good laugh. I realised, however that I was a sitting duck in that one room with Da. He'd eventually corner me by locking the door when it took his fancy. I couldn't get through the window because there was too big a drop to the basement below. I needed a spare key and a few clothes stowed in the basement to tide me over the emergency times.

I took the key out of the door and walked to my uncle's garage in Pembroke Street. After making sure my father wasn't there I went upstairs and asked my uncle if he could get me a spare key. He sat me down and asked what was going on. I told him, but begged him not to say anything to Da because I'd get in hot water. Harry said 'I knew your father had a drinking problem but didn't realise it had gone this far.' 'You look pale', he added, 'take this half crown and go down the road, get yourself some bread and soup. I'll have the key for you when you return, and also a proposition to put to you.'

When I returned feeling the benefit of the bread and soup I handed my uncle the change. He told me to put it in my pocket. He then put his hand on my shoulder saying, 'Would you like to come and work for me, as your friend Tommy Hendrick has found himself another job and I'm in need of an apprentice?' I jumped at the chance to work for this kindly uncle of mine, and to be useful again.

He said 'I'll talk to your father and get back to you.' A week or so later Da came home and said 'Your Uncle Harry needs a new apprentice. Would you like to work in the motor trade? I'll work it out so the kids can take care of one another while we're out.' I was waiting for him to ask me what took me to see my uncle but he didn't say a word.

The next day I was up early and made my way on foot to see Uncle Harry. After he sorted out the paperwork he supplied me with overalls. He said to eventually become a motor mechanic I'd have to attend night school to complete my studies and for that I'd need a bike. He told me that they had one there that they used from time to time to collect small spare parts, and deliver messages on. 'You can use that to get to and from work, and also use it for night school. I mentioned nothing about what you told me, but should things get any worse for you, you must let me know and we will take it from there.'

I thanked my uncle for his kindness as he gave me a hug and sent me on my way saying I could start working as soon as I wished to. It was only as I started to make my way home that the effect of that hug really hit me as a tear or two ran down my cheeks. Someone else really cared for me apart from my mother. I whistled and sang I believe all the way home. I still sing as I walk the streets of Auckland and other places.

I started my new job the very next day. It felt good to be working again and earning a little pocket money. When I handed Da my first week's wages he gave me back five shillings out of the ten. I gave my two brothers a little something, but can't remember how much.

The mechanics who worked for my uncle were very helpful though they did give me a hard time with their practical jokes which I accepted as part of my training, like it or not. There were two jobs that didn't turn me on. Running messages on the bike, and scraping and cleaning the garage floor. My friend Tommy Hendrick still had four weeks to go before he took up his new position so he was a great support to me as both companion and teacher. Though our scout days were over their valuable lessons and comradeship would always remain a fond memory to both of us.

For the first couple of months in my job Da didn't bother me too much, but something told me that the storm clouds were gathering. God knows how much we all missed Ma, but at the same time I dreaded the thought of her having to put up with Da in that one room when the drink exposed that fury within him. Many times later it crossed my mind that God in his wisdom and compassion thought that that she needed a break not only from Da, but us kids as well.

Then we all got a dose of the scabies due to the poor food we were receiving. We had to go to the hospital a number of days a week and be soaked in baths that contained something that looked like milk.

I was right about the storm clouds, but never in my wildest dreams did I expect they would eventually force me to make the first major decision of my life. Da was up to his old tricks again and I could no longer take refuge in the basement as it was being cleaned up. I had to take to the streets at night when he was in an ugly mood. When I could afford it I would go to the cinema and stay until the last show, something you could do in those days thank God.

I didn't mind staying out so much when the weather was fine, but in cold wet weather it was a bitch. I'd spend many hours in the underground toilets in O'Connell Street reading cowboy stories or whatever else I could get my hands on. You used to have to put a penny in the slot to open the toilet door, so I got more than my pennyworth. And if I was quick enough to catch the door before it closed behind someone, then I was richer by a penny. My reading improved, but I don't think educating oneself in a public toilet will ever really catch on.

I kept very much to myself, so ashamed was I at having to wear a pair of Da's old trousers. They were too long and too big around the waist, and his old shoes that I wore were a size too big, and the soles were just about worn through. I was forever cutting cardboard to put in them when it was wet. You're right if you gathered that I didn't have any girlfriends. And for that matter didn't have any young male friends either.

Around five to six months after I had started at the garage I arrived at work feeling rotten with an awful cold. My uncle spotted me and came over to speak to me. He took one look at me and said I should be home in bed. 'Come into the office,' he said, 'I want to talk to you.' He sat me down and asked me how things were between Da and myself. I broke down and told him what was happening in my life. 'Right, go straight to my place and ask your aunt to give you some hot soup and to make a bed up for you on the settee in the lounge. I'll talk to your father. You're going to stay with us for a while.' My eyes started to water up, and quick to sense my emotions, Uncle hugged me and sent me on my way.

My Aunt and I had met on only one occasion but she made me welcome after hearing my story. I was soon tucked up in bed after my bread and soup. Before I go on I must admit that there is a blank space in my mind because I did mention that my sister Ann, and my younger brother Tony had gone to stay with my Uncle and his wife. So where they were at this particular time I have no idea. But I am going to Toronto to visit Ann in July, so we will get together and try and sort that one out.

When my Uncle came home he said he'd had a long and heated talk with my father, but in the finish Da had agreed to allow me to stay a while. Then my Uncle looked at my clothes lying on a chair, 'I'll take you shopping this weekend before you end up walking on your bare feet and your clothes fall off you. If you are willing,' he said, 'I'll buy you a tailor-made suit and you can pay me back at five shillings a week. Now that you've had a rise you will still have ten shillings in your pocket.'

Imagine how I felt on hearing all this!

My Uncle took me on a shopping spree the following Saturday. We went first to his tailor to have me measured for my first ever suit, great excitement I can tell you. I was given the freedom to choose whatever material appealed to me, and when I did the tailor said I had good taste even if somewhat on the expensive side. But laughingly he said to my Uncle 'because it's his first suit and there's that gleam in his eye I'll stick to the five pounds I quoted you.' Then he got me a pair of shoes, two shirts and some socks and underpants.

A week or two later after a few fittings I collected my new suit and thought I'd never get home fast enough to try it on. When my Uncle and Aunt saw me in they said what an improvement the old clothes I came to them in. 'Now you look like a young man with a purpose in life' said my Uncle, and he gave me a shilling to go to the cinema. 'But watch out for the girls,' he said, 'you look quite handsome in that new suit.'

I can't express in words what a wonderful uplifting experience all this had been for me at a time when I was being forced to cross borders before I was prepared for them. But then again life and living have no set patterns for us at any age. No matter what our circumstances may be, we are forever being tested to expand our horizons. This I believe will be made very clear as my story continues. We should in some way be vision seekers.

One day I asked the foreman if he would give me some driving lessons. I was nearly seventeen now and wanted get into driving. He said to me give another three or four months and then he'd look at it. The answer did nothing for my pressing needs so I came up with a brain wave that I could either sink or swim on.

I started coming into work an hour earlier than usual. My Uncle gave me two spare keys. To get into the garage you had to first come through double doors on the street front, then walk about ten metres down an alley to the garage's main doors. One of the street front doors had a small door fitted to it, which I could slip through and lock it behind me. I was then able to walk down and open the side door that that led into the main premises. I then opened the garage doors, and began to drive the Morris up and down the alley way. I did that for about a week for a period of twenty minutes at a time, then tried to cool the engine down as best I could in the hope no one would spot it, and thank God no one did.

Then the big day arrived. I came in on this particular morning, opened the street front doors, then the main garage doors, and took myself on my first driving lesson out in the real world. With chattering teeth and my hair standing up on the back of my neck I drove up the road to a place called Fitzwilliam Square. I drove around and around changing gears until I felt it was time to return and try and cool the engine down. I did this until I felt confident I could drive on the open road. I'd say in all it took about seven days. I didn't want to push my luck too far. And if you should ask how I felt about what I was doing the answer was, shite-scared.

Then a few days later Jimmy McGill the foreman asked me to collect some gaskets on my bike in the rain, so I plucked up the courage to ask him if I could use the workshop car. He said, 'You can't drive. Away with you!' But I stood my ground. 'Yes I can,' I said. 'Right' said Jimmy, 'let's find out. Take me to Fitzwilliam Square where it's not too busy in case you kill us both.' I said to myself, 'Terry this is your lucky day. You should be able to drive around there with your eyes closed.'

When we got back Jimmy asked me where I'd learnt to drive, who taught me. I said a very good friend of mine had given me some driving lessons. I wasn't lying was I? He said 'Okay, you can drive for a week and we'll see how you go.' That was a feather in my cap and well worth the effort I'd put into it.

Two months or so later I received a rare compliment when I drove my father and a friend of his to a meeting in Abbey Street. Da's friend passed the comment that I was a good driver and Da said 'yes, he's a natural.'

Living with my Uncle for the period of time that I did had shown me yet another side of his beautiful nature. The basement flat below us was occupied by my Aunt's niece and her family. The husband was a bookie's clerk who like my father was very good at supporting publicans but not his family. I can't remember how many children were in the family, but I felt very sorry for them living in that small dark and unhealthy place.

But a beautiful thing that came from it was the way those children would gather around Harry after he'd gone to bed around eight. He would take up the Bible that lay on his bedside table and give them his own charming interpretation of the gospels. I did mention in my last book, which I am now trying to correct, that he was a

Presbyterian, but from some information which I can't find, it seems more likely that he was Church of England. But I also believe that he had little time like myself, when it comes to man-made religion. The way this wonderful man reached out and touched those children was something else. Their faces glowed as he spoke to them with his enchanting voice. I was only in that room to see this on a couple of occasions, but the scene touched my soul. I wonder how many of you have been privileged to have someone like that in your life.

It was a very happy time for me working and living with my Uncle and my Aunt till that terrible day malaria took its final toll on him. Uncle was walking home as usual after work when the final attack occurred. He collapsed and died I believe almost straight away. Tears flowed hard and fast that day. A few days later we all paid our last respects to a man who had lived his life, for the sake of life.

Two weeks later my Aunt asked me if I could find somewhere else to live. She had problems of her own which I won't mention. She had always been good to me even though she could be critical at times. My Uncle Harry had many crosses to bear.

As much as I loved my brothers I decided that I would not go back to live with my father. The taste of my new found freedom was too good to give up without one heck of a fight.

A week or so later Da came to see me at work and said I'd better get my things together and come home. He said he'd got a letter from my aunt telling him she'd asked me to leave. You should never have gone there in the first place, he said.

For the first time in my life I stood up to my father. 'No - no way am I coming back for you to put me through the hell you've been putting me through all these years.' Da was sober now, but for a moment I thought he was going to hit me. This was the first time I'd ever stood up to him, and I could well see that he didn't like it. 'Until you're eighteen you'll do as you're told, that's the law,' he almost shouted, but I turned around and walked away even more determined than ever never to return to live with him on his terms.

I got talking to my friend Tommy Hendrick on the phone the next day about my situation and he said that he would have a word with his uncle. A day later he took me to see his uncle and I explained my situation to him. He said he could put me up for two or three weeks if that would help. Then Tommy's uncle introduced a further option to me. He was a corporal in the Irish Army and said you could join up. I wasn't prepared for that step, but at the same time was in no position to turn my back on a rope thrown my way. So I bowed to the inevitable. Two days later I moved in with Tommy's uncle and his wife who seemed who seemed to welcome me. A week later he took me to Collins Barracks to attend an interview he had arranged for me. I was given a written examination which I believe put paid to me becoming soldier material. I was given no reason for not being accepted into the Army, but was happy enough to leave it at that. With a huge sigh of relief I made my way out of that cold grey building and dreary courtyard, which seemed to me to lack both heart and soul.

I was beginning to find that God never closes one door without opening another. That very same evening as I queued up outside the Savoy Cinema in O'Connell Street I got talking to a guy named John, the same age as me. He'd had to leave home because of his old man. After John heard my story he said 'This is your lucky day. When the film is over I'll take you back to a Boys' Home where I am staying, I'm sure they'll take you in when they hear your story.' You can be quite sure that I had no idea what the film was about. Finding somewhere to stay was the only thing on my mind that night. Apart from having only a week left in my temporary digs, things were not going too well for me. The lady of the manor turned out to be a right bitch and was blaming me for not taking her husband's advice and joining the Irish Army. Her husband understood what happened when I explained, but she maintained that I sabotaged the interview. I thought to myself God help this man having to live with this women, but thank God I don't have to. After the film was over I went with John to the Boys' Home near the corner of Middle Abbey Street. I was greeted by a very friendly Christian Brother who after hearing my story didn't hesitate in offering me a bed in their dormitory.

This Brother was certainly far removed from those I'd known who thought they could educate you by jumping over desks and beating you with black leather straps. I thought to myself no wonder the devil doesn't need to advertise for labour when people are falling over themselves to work for him.

The Brother said to me 'As a general rule we would check your story out but no one could have made up what you have told me. You can move in tomorrow.' When I moved into the Boys' Home after work the following day I was given the rules. Number One, you could only stay there for four to six months as it was classified as temporary accommodation for young people with family problems, or maybe some other reason I was not aware of. If it was discovered you'd lied about your circumstances, John told me, you were out on your ear.

Number Two, if you were working you paid the home two shillings and sixpence a week. Number Three, you had to be in bed by ten o'clock and up for breakfast by seven. The meals were basic but I was very glad to get them, and nobody was on your back unless you got out of line.

John and I became great friends. John was the first person to introduce me to snooker which I still play today. When we could afford it we would spend hours playing together in a saloon at Fairview. Naturally John with previous experience was better at the game than myself, but I soon learned to give him a run for his money.

Together we did some crazy things, but managed to stay out of trouble. A few days after moving into the home Da asked me where I was living. I told him. His only remark was 'See you behave yourself.' I felt that somehow he respected me for the stand I was making though he would never admit it.

Now at seventeen, time was once again running out for me. My Uncle Percy was managing the garage and things were never to be the same again. Percy didn't have the head or the manner for business that my Uncle Harry had, but don't get me wrong, he was a good man.

So once again desperate measures were being called for as I could see that the garage as I knew it was falling by the wayside. Also my time at the Boys' Home had almost run out. It was like I was being told 'Llook further afield Terry, God hasn't taken you this far for nothing.' As Jonathan Winter says, 'If your ship doesn't come in you swim out to it.' And that's what I believe I did. I put the word out among my workmates who knew my problems with Da and once again another door opened for me.

A workmate named Jack who had served in the R.A.F. gave me the answer I needed. 'The R.A.F.' he told me, 'is looking for young people like yourself to sign up for five years, and it would be a great experience for you as well as getting you well away from your old man.'

My mind jumped into top gear, and that very evening I wrote to the recruiting office in Belfast with the help of Jack. The reply arrived about a week later. They sent me a form to fill in, and it also had to be signed by one of my parents. So I contacted my mother who would be returning soon to re-join her family and got her to sign it for me. My mother said 'I can forgive your father for what he has done to me, but it will take a while for me to forgive him what he has put you through.' I took her in my arms with tears flowing from both our eyes and said, 'It's okay Ma, I don't feel anything for him, but I don't hate him. You have been my inspiration and the guiding force in my life. Because of your devotion I now realise the winning or losing is not the test, but the loving.'

Ma gave me her blessing as she handed back the signed enrolment form and hugged me. Then she said, 'Go do what you have to do and walk tall as you do it.' I pray I shall never forget those farewell words of hers.

Three days later I was gathering what belongings I needed and giving the rest to my good friend John to do what he wished with them.

John came down to the train to see me off. 'See you write to me or I'll have your hide,' he said, laughing. I said 'You can rely on that John and if I get accepted into the R.A.F. we'll see each other when I get home on leave.' We gave each other a big hug as we said our goodbyes.

On the journey to Belfast many questions were running through my mind. What was I walking into? Would I be accepted? What would happen to the ones I was leaving behind? Had I betrayed them? Did I have the guts to see this through?

The day was fine as I remember when I alighted from the train, but nothing much else about Belfast registered with me. My mind was far too obsessed with questions and doubts as I made my way to the recruiting centre. The thought of being turned down weighed heavily on me.

At the centre as I waited for my name to be called I felt as jumpy as a mouse fiddling a piece of cheese from a mouse trap. 'Pull yourself together Terry' I said to myself, 'you really need this one.' My name was called out at last. I leapt up to the table where the interviewer sat and eased myself into a chair facing him.

Well, what a refreshingly different attitude this man had to that of the man who interviewed me for the Irish Army in Dublin. Had that man been here in Belfast with me he might have learned that only God is in the position to look down His nose at anyone else. Maybe this poem adds a little something to that:

> *We struggle every single day*
> *It's just a way of life*
> *Confused alarm bells ringing*
> *And visions full of strife*
> *Man needs to share his lot*
> *Knowing it won't make him rich*
> *But he'd rather see his fellow man*
> *As miserable as himself*

After the interview I was taken to a large room where

there were others around my own age, and was given a written educational test. I couldn't even begin to describe my feelings as I tried to answer the questions on that paper they put before me. I'll just let you use your own imagination, something you'll be doing a lot of as you walk this walk with me. In part the motivation behind the telling of my story is to say that there is hope beyond a mistreated past if you are prepared to look for it. Anything learned can always be unlearned. I have met so many people as I pursued the challenges of both pleasure and obstacles that have been presented to me, some of them I'm so sorry to say literally dying of loneliness. I see it written on their faces, or observe it through their actions. But in no way am I trying to put them down because I have been there myself.

Even before the written examination papers were taken away I knew I had failed the test. I had a very empty feeling as I joined the others in a nearby room to await my call. When my name came up I reluctantly returned to my interviewer to hear the bad news. He said, 'I'm sorry we can't offer you a trade but we will take you on if you are prepared to do general duties, all sorts of tasks.'

I couldn't believe my good luck as I grabbed his hand to thank him. 'As bad as that?' he said, noticing my watering eyes. I nodded and he put his hand on my shoulder and said 'You'll do just fine.'

I passed my medical with flying colours, and a while later was on my way to Long Kesh. The date remains with me just as my service number does — the Twelfth of July, Orangemen's Day. I was ignorant of the full significance of that day in Irish history but was starting to learn fast.

Be it true or not, I remember reading in a book a number of years ago that the Battle of the Boyne was not the full event that gave birth to Orangemen's Day, but it was in fact the Battle of the Diamond sometime around 1795. And, what's more, it had nothing to do with politics but the Linen Trade.

Mind you, whatever the motivation force behind it was, I am really sorry for the havoc and suffering it has brought to our lovely little Island.

When we arrived at Long Kesh we were taken to the clothing store and given our first service issue. I was told when I received my first pair of boots to make sure there was plenty of room for my toes otherwise I would be in trouble. Well at my age trouble was something very few of us escaped, and once again I marched painfully into it. Three days later I was just about screaming in agony yet to ashamed to say anything. But pain ultimately overcame shame. With remorse written all over my face I told our sergeant-in-charge my problem. After hearing a few words I won't repeat, I accepted my piece of humble pie with as much grace as I could.

Something else that lingers with me in a humorous fashion was my introduction that evening on the Twelfth of July. Out of the quiet of night came the beating of drums that seemed to come in all directions. One of the lads from Cork said 'They're playing silly bastards again. We won't get much sleep tonight, this will go on for hours and hours.' A little more of my country's unhealthy culture came my way that evening, and it was the reason we lads from the South were confined to camp that evening. But anyway it wasn't our kind of music.

About five days later we were on our way to England, a very pleasant crossing from Larne to Stranraer and then the overnight train to London. We were well looked after on the journey. From London were taken to Burtonwood to receive the rest of our service issue, and from there to Wilmslow to do our square bashing, the drilling we needed to knock some discipline into us. The camp was well laid out and the food good. When I received my first thirty shillings I was told that I could make an allowance of seven shillings to my family in Ireland, or to anyone else if I wished. I asked if it would be possible for just my mother to receive the seven shillings and they agreed. That small contribution to my family helped ease my troubled mind after leaving them to face Da.

I felt at peace with myself for the first time as long as I can remember. I was now free of my father, and was on that long trail to find myself, and hopefully do something with it eventually.

But as I lay on my bed the first night I felt a surge of hurt and anger. All those years of fear and frustration that I'd gone through to get here. Refusal after refusal when I needed help most. I believe I felt a lot like Jesus when Peter denied Him three times. First my Aunt. Then a priest that said he would help me. Then last the Irish Army. Tears came hard and fast that night as I took my first step into manhood.

My new home was basic but comfortable – a large Nissen hut with around twenty beds in it. To the left of the entrance was a small room that housed the corporal in charge of the hut. Now, just as in any walk of life for those of us in the services, corporals come in two categories, nice guys, and frustrated ones. We, I am so grateful to say, had a nice guy, tough but fair. We gathered around him on our first morning while he told us that he and the rest of his crew had exactly eight weeks to get us into shape, but get us into shape was what they would do come hell or high water. 'The next eight weeks of your lives belong to me and mine,' he said. 'You can make it easy or hard for yourselves, and if you don't come up to scratch we'll keep you till you do. Come and see me if you have any problems and we'll take it from there.'

Most of us accepted what our corporal had to say with a certain grace, but as always, there are those smart alecs who won't stretch their minds to any reasonable degree. There were seven or more English lads in our group who were conscripts so like it or not they had to do two years of compulsory military training. This caused a certain amount of friction in the group because these lads had other ideas of what they wanted to do with those years of their lives. On the whole, though, our two cultures blended well, the English guys having the upper edge on us in education, but our dare-devil exploits helped us to keep our end up. Learning to live together was an education in itself.

A day or two after we had settled in I got talking to a guy named Sean Brassell who came from Kilrush in County Clare. That was the beginning of an ongoing friendship that was to last until we were demobbed from the R.A.F. Sean was around my height but more solid built with curly red hair and a firm jaw to match his strong features. What appealed to the humourist in me about Sean was that mischievous grin of his, and the twinkle in his blue eyes. Sean's bed was next to mine, and I shall never forget that first night when the two of us knelt down beside our beds before lights out and said our prayers. We had discussed this beforehand. Though we both knew we'd stand out like rosary beads in the hands of Ian Paisley our faith was still strong enough to lead us to this plan of action. God knows our religion had been well and truly grilled into us and we did need something to hold on to being away from home for the first time in a strange country at such a tender age. Well, stand out we did. But we must have taken the others in the hut by surprise because you could have heard a pin drop. Feeling very self-conscious, but comforted, we climbed into bed as the lights went out. We continued in this way until our training was finished.

As you can well guess we were a raw bunch, but then as the non-commissioned officers got stuck into us we began to settle down into serious training, and gradually the rough edges were trimmed away. I never had any real problem with the all-over training except kit inspections. Having to lay out all our service issue in certain order in double quick time was not good for my nervous nature. I never really mastered getting my boots shining for inspection like most of the others, and was pulled up over that a few times. I put it down to the university education I'd missed out on. Life's a bitch for some of us, isn't it?

In spite of a certain amount of nervous tension and stupidity I managed to get through my training without killing anyone. Mind you, it could have been otherwise when a group of us were taken out on the firing range for Sten gun practice one day. That day I unintentionally added a few grey hairs to the head of the sergeant instructing us. Around ten of us were standing in front of the rest of the group and were about to discharge our weapons when the instructor called out my name for some reason I have never been able to work out. Anyway too eager to respond I turned around to face him with a fully loaded Sten gun in my hand. I don't believe I've ever seen anyone move so fast, or utter so many nasty phrases in one breath. After that I was nicknamed Danger Man by most of the guys, and was none too popular with the instructor. We all got through our training and the passing out parade to become fully-fledged airmen ready to be posted to our units. Much to our delight Sean and I were both posted to Barnwood in Gloucester. We arrived there bubbling with excitement and were shown to our billets and told to report to the hospital at eight in the morning to be given our duties. Then it was off to the Airmen's Mess for something to eat.

Next morning at the hospital we were met by a corporal. John I think his Christian name was. He marched us into the office of the medical officer in charge of the Hospital. I was struck by this officer's yellow skin and his thin frame. Where had I seen that sickly colouring before? Then in a flash I remembered, my Uncle Harry bore some of those features. Not so pronounced as this poor man, but quite a similar skin pattern. The bones stood out on his face and neck, the smart uniform that must have once fitted to a tee now sat tragically from his shoulders and hips. With a far-away but kindly smile he put us at our ease straight away sensing our rookie nervousness, a man I sensed with the hallmarks of a gentleman like my Uncle Harry.

The officer informed us of our duties, and the boundaries we must stay within. There were a number of airwomen stationed just up the road from us who frequently used the hospital's facilities so we were expected to be on our best behaviour at all times. 'Like a church,' he said, 'this hospital is a place of comfort for those in need and I will not tolerate any of my staff abusing those privileges. Do your duties to the best of your ability and we'll get along fine.'

We were then marched off to meet two lovely ladies in the kitchen who provided meals for the hospital staff and those hospitalised, who would soon be spoiling us. Phyllis came from Dublin, and Kathy from somewhere in Scotland. From the moment John introduced us to them the brilliant sense of humour of the Irish and Scots opened all sorts of doors for Sean and myself. And I believe it did something of the same for Phyllis and Kathy. Our corporal with his dry sense of humour could see that he was out of his depth and pleaded that he had paperwork to catch up with, saying he'd be back shortly to show us what was required of us as hospital staff.

That day began a beautiful friendship between the four of us that would last till Sean and I were posted overseas. For Sean and myself it was the spoiling with good food whenever we needed it, and for Phyllis and Kathy it was the tasks we would do for them that that cemented our friendship. All those wonderful times when the four of us would sit over a cup of tea and talk about our lives and our feelings. Both ladies had around six months to go before they were due for demob. Kathy was going home to marry her childhood sweetheart, while poor Phyllis was caught up in one of those hit and miss relationships that seldom satisfy anyone's needs. Had I been older and more mature I could have easily have fallen for Phyllis myself. She was so easy on the eyes and had that strong mixture of Irish culture that characterizes so many of the women of my country. Outspoken and honest, willing to tackle most things with no expectations of anything in return, gentle and passionate in her beliefs. But like most of us Phyllis had chinks in her armour. Man's concept of religion had blinded her to her own needs. The man she cared for, and who cared for her came from the side of religion's many faces, he a Protestant, and she a Catholic. God help them both I said to myself, knowing from my upbringing that fate was ninety-nine percent against them at that particular time.

What happened to them I know not. I'm only happy to have shared some of my time with Phyllis and still hold her dear in my memory. She reminded me of my lovely mother, a special kind of woman a good man would be proud to have at his side in good times and bad.

Our work in the hospital wasn't hard. It involved cleaning the floors and wall, maintaining the restroom in good order, and cleaning the kitchen floor. All the staff ate their meals in the kitchen except for the Medical Officer-in-Charge who had a tray taken to him in his own quarters. I was used to this kind of work through helping Ma, as was Sean, though he wasn't quite as particular as I was.

When we had time to horse around Sean and I would wrestle in the restroom and he always got the better of me. But I was putting on weight and his reign was coming to an end. I had been an underdog for far too many years. One evening after dinner a few months later from the start of our wrestling bouts I got the upper hand and was able to keep it that way. However, there were other areas I could never match Sean in - mixing with people, drinking and gambling.

After lunch one day when Sean and I were clowning

around in the restroom I told if he didn't shut up about something I'd throw the nearby bucket of coal over him. He said you wouldn't dare. Before he could take another breath I had him looking a Black and White Minstrel. Sean didn't dare me to do anything to him again and I really enjoyed myself, even the cleaning up I had to do.

I also became friends with one of the medical orderlies who looked after the men's ward. Norman was a lot like me in build, but not quite as tall. He liked to read and play chess, and I believe I helped him to develop a sense of humour. He'd come from a stuck-up English background. One evening after payday Norman got this bright idea about furthering my drinking education and challenged me to a drinking contest. 'I'm going to drink you under the table' he said. 'That shouldn't be too hard' I thought. I'd never taken a drink in my life as my father had done enough of that for the whole family. But my pride wasn't going to let him get away with it without a fight. And on a more serious note I needed to know if I would be anything like my father after I had ventured into that arena. If that proved to be so I vowed I would never touch liquor again after seeing what it had done to our lovely family.

Off we went into town the next evening to do battle. The name of the pub eludes me but I still remember the table that he was going to drink me under. It was dark with bevelled edges and one of its legs was a lighter shade than the other three. I said to Norman, the guy who painted this table must have been drunk, or run out of paint. That gave us a laugh.

We started drinking beer, then switched to rum and coke, brandy and coke, finishing up with a whiskey, with me thinking to myself as I downed the whiskey 'Are the sins of the father about to visit themselves upon the son?' That would be too much for society. But the thought was only a fleeting one. I was too busy enjoying this new habit I'd been introduced to. I felt on top of the world as the liquor fumes danced out their crazy ideas in my brain. And, much to my relief, I was only more stupid than I usually am and not like my father at all.

At the finish I had to almost carry Norman back to base by stopping and starting when it got too much for me. But I was well satisfied with our little drinking spree. Another lesson to tuck under my belt. I still remember that silly grin on my face as I helped Norman into bed. Poor Norman spent most of the next day in bed, while I had few after effects. Norman never asked me to go drinking with him again.

I also made other friends in the hospital. David the ambulance driver and Gwen, one of the orderlies in charge of the women's ward. We didn't have a lot of contact but when we did the crack was good. I would do odd jobs for them, and in turn they would invite me to have tea or coffee and share something of our lives. They were both looking forward to getting on with their lives in Civvy Street. They were to be married about six weeks later so I got an invitation to the wedding. In my first book with all its topsy turvy misplaced words I stated otherwise, but in rewriting my story the fog has cleared a lot more to give me a better picture all round.

I find it quite amazing that I am able to fill in a lot more missing pieces that had escaped me before, so now I'm trying to make the most of it before the brain storm hits.

Anyway I jumped at the chance of a wedding invitation. As might have seen from my story to date I'd never been to a wedding, only the odd funeral, and I felt this would be a lot livelier.

Gwen told me her parents would be delighted to put me up for that weekend, so I applied for a 48 hour weekend pass the very next day, and this was granted without any problem. All the staff chipped in for a wedding present.

On the Friday, the day before the wedding, Gwen and I caught the afternoon train to Birmingham, then a bus to her parents' home in Small Heath.

This was a whole new ball game for me as you will well realise. I was both excited and nervous. Gwen's parents tried to make me feel at home, but with my lack of education and social skills I was feeling way out of my depth, a feeling that was to follow me around for the greater part of my life.

The wedding went off without a hitch, the bride and groom looking the picture of happiness.

At the reception I hung back feeling shy but Gwen's parents spotted me and brought me well and truly into the picture. Then, right out of the blue, I fell deeply in love for the first time in my life. Gwen had introduced me to a lovely young lady named Jane. I was gone. We spent the rest of the occasion in each other's company.

Jane, with her good grip on life, did most of the talking sensing my shyness and awkwardness. But we did have one thing in common, chocolate.

Well, as love, or perhaps fascination knows no boundaries, and I had been invited to visit Gwen's family again I came up with a brilliant plan to impress Jane. Though chocolate was rationed I knew Sean and Norman didn't bother with it, and I thought to myself I'll buy them a few drinks in exchange for their ration of chocolate. Everything went according to plan and three weeks or so later I travelled to Small Heath with my bag of seduction goodies in my hand.

After a lovely meal that evening with Gwen's parents I got talking with a very good friend of her father. He asked me did I like soccer and if so, would I like to join him and a few others who were going to watch Aston Villa play Blackpool the next day? I jumped at the chance to see two top teams in action, plus the invitation to party later that night. More and more excitement.

The day was fine as I remember it, and the game brilliant, but what put the icing on the cake for me was watching one of the legends, the outstanding Stanley Matthews, known as Twinkle Toes, treat us to a wonderful exhibition of football along with the other players. I have forgotten what the score was, but I shall never forget how privileged I felt to be watching a soccer genius in action.

Full of excitement I joined the others at the party that night with my bag of chocolates for the young woman of my dreams. Well I waited and I waited but she didn't turn up, so I never did get to play my trump card. I ate it instead.

Not long after this first romantic heart wrench Sean and I were informed we were to be posted overseas for two and a half years. We weren't told where to, but that we were to get twenty eight days leave before we left. We made the most of our last few weeks in Gloucester with all sorts of notions running around in our heads about where the future would take us.

On arriving in Dublin for our leave Sean agreed to come home with me to say hello to the family. Ma had now re-joined the family in a Corporation house in West Cabra. 82 Fassaugh Avenue. I knocked on the door. Ma opened it and threw her arms around me. There were tears in her eyes. I introduced Sean and we went into the lounge for my brothers and sister to bestow their feelings on me, and for me to bestow mine on them. Then came the moment I had mixed feelings about. You could have knocked me down with a feather when my father put his arms around me for the first time I can remember in my life. There seemed to be a glassy look in his eyes as he said 'Welcome home son.' I said to myself, going away must have been the right move. I no longer feared Da, but his way with words still made me a bit uncomfortable.

Da took to Sean straight away. My mother invited him to spend the night with us if he didn't mind sleeping on the couch in the lounge. Ma had just bought a new lounge suite on the hire purchase. This new trend was to help hire purchase firms get richer, and people like ourselves get poorer. But having said that, it did make life easier as long as we could keep up the repayments.

Sean said he'd be delighted to stay the night, and would catch the bus home to Clare in the morning. We had a great evening with Sean entering the family with his lively lifestyle. My brothers and sister really took to him, and so did Ma and Da.

Around 9.30 the next morning Da took off for work. Now that the War was over things were beginning to pick up. My brothers had been given the day off school to celebrate my homecoming. When I came down for breakfast my brothers and Sean were chatting in the lounge. Ma was putting the pan on the stove to cook our breakfast when I put my arm around her and asked how things had been since she came home. She said, 'God has been good to us. The Housing Corporation allocated us this three-bedroom house, and your brother Ken has become quite a match for you father so we don't have the problems of the past. So we can breathe easily again.' A great wave of relief came over me when I heard this as you can well imagine.

Then she said 'Thank God that your Uncle Harry was there for us all when we needed him most.' Men like him are few and far between, and he'll always be in my prayers even though I'm sure he'll never need them.

I said to Ma, 'It was you in the overall picture that made it all possible, your courage and devotion have always been the guiding force in our lives. If any of us get married and have children your unselfish love will I hope be the seed we plant in them.' She turned and gave me a big hug.

I was really happy now that my brothers and sister were able to live a more normal life. I can't speak for them, but they also had to live through their own unnecessary hell. As for my beautiful sister I feel that she suffered more than any of us. Ann now lives in Canada and is a credit to her husband and family. I am going to visit her with my lovely daughter Rachel in July.

After Sean left us I got in touch with my good friend John and we quickly went through my leave money drinking, playing snooker and going to the pictures. Before I knew it my leave was over.

With a lot of hugging and a few tears I bade my family goodbye. The thought of not seeing them, especially my mother, for two and a half years brought a lump to my throat.

I caught a bus into town, and a tram to Dún Laoghaire Harbour. Sean was waiting for me on the Quay. He said he'd had a ball catching up with family and drinking.

As the boat pulled out from Dún Laoghaire he said, 'Well that's the last glance of the old country we're going to get for two and a half years.' He put his arm around my shoulder and said 'We're on our own from now on.' I put my arm around his shoulder and said, 'What's new?'

CHAPTER 4 —OVERSEAS DUTY

In no time we were standing on the pier at Southampton waiting to join our troopship. I think it was the Arundel Castle but I'm sure you'll forgive me if I'm wrong. If not, I'll forgive myself. What human being is more qualified to do so than myself on this earth? And I also allow everyone else the same privilege.

The weather was fine but cold as we were given orders to board the ship and then directed to our living quarters which were quite spacious. Soon after we were on our way though still in the dark about our destination.

After a light lunch and a wander around the unrestricted areas of the ship we were assembled for our first boat drill. We went along with it reasonably cheerfully as night was approaching and we headed for the Bay of Biscay. Rain and wind soon drove all but the hardiest of us to the mess deck for the evening meal. Then the threatening storm decided to give us a hard time. The ship behaved quite well at first but the wind velocity increased and so did ship's antics. She seemed to do everything but talk, and the further we went with our meal, the greener grew our faces. One by one we made our exit. Sean and I were among the last to leave, and I'll never forget my envy of the remaining scavenger, a huge Kerryman, eating his heart out on what remained on some of our plates.

There were soon queues outside the toilets and guys

throwing up before they could get inside.

Sean said let's go down below, and I said lead the way. We eventually reached somewhere round the bottom of the ship and found our own corners to empty our stomachs out. And we were not alone in this un-sanitized emergency toilet. Apart from the discomfort, which remains very vividly in my memory, there was also a funny side to it all. While we were lying in that helpless state of sickness a young flying officer appeared on the scene. He ordered us back to our sleeping quarters only to hear a rich Irish voice saying, feck off and leave us alone to die. He must have got the message because we never saw him again that night, nor anyone else. I'm sure it must have been one of those rare occasions when senior rank capitulated to lower rank without retaliation.

The big ship was sailing along quite smoothly by the time our stomachs settled down, so we made our way back to our quarters to shower and change our nauseous clothing. I gasped in wonder at the brilliance of the sun, and the blueness of the sea as we came up on deck. All I could do was wander from side to side drinking in the scene as we passed through the Straits of Gibraltar and out into the Mediterranean Sea. As we progressed along the coastline, Morocco, Algeria and Tunisia seemed to be waving to us over the glittering water bringing to life all those films I had seen of the Foreign Legion, and all the intriguing stories that held a breathtaking fascination for this young mind of mine.

Sean and I had missed breakfast, and lunch seemed a lifetime away. My stomach demanded I sell a folding camera I had with me to buy us some food and a nice cool beer. After being so sea sick there was an even greater hole waiting to be filled.

So I managed to get 30 shillings for it and off we, and another friend, went to replenish what the sea had taken from us. Then as we approached the Island of Malta I had my first close encounter with a school of porpoises. They charmed us with graceful acrobatics in the in the sun shimmering Mediterranean Sea.

After boat drill that evening we were informed we would be leaving the ship early the next morning after we'd docked at Port Said. Our mystery destination was beginning to unravel itself with our arrival in Egypt. My mind started to wander on its travels to the Pyramids and Pharaohs' tombs. I'm sure you can well imagine what was going on in my mind?

After disembarking at Port Said trucks took us to a nearby R.A.F. camp which was comprised of tents and buildings. We lined up in four groups on the parade ground for a roll call. Then, after being assigned to our tents, we reported to the cookhouse where my taste buds got a rude awaking, one of the many things that were to change my whole outlook on life as the boy in me was slowly being taken into manhood.

Four mischievous Irish lads on the Mediterranean bound for the Middle East. The author is back left.

Next morning we received our first issue of khaki uniforms and boy were we glad to get into something light. It was so damned hot. Once outfitted we were marched to the Paymaster's tent for our first introduction to Egyptian money. I commented to Sean that we'd be a bit disorganized till we got used to it. He said 'It's just like English money. You spend it when you've got it, and when it's gone you do without it.' Bright boy our Sean.

Shortly after we'd been paid we fell in again to receive our first weekly ration of cigarettes. Fifty Players Navy Cut in a tin. I did mention in my crazy mixed up last book that it was a hundred. The fog's still lifting.

This gullible young Irish Catholic was on the way to becoming hooked on nicotine. Nearly everyone was doing it, and I've got to say it seemed the thing to do to keep up with the Joneses. It wouldn't do to be lagging behind this new society structure we were walking into almost blindfolded.

About five days later we received our postings. Sean and I were to go to Palestine, and the next day we were taken to the station to begin our journey. The station platform was lined with men selling all manner of goods to us as we leaned out from our carriage windows. One guy bought a watch that stopped about an hour later. One of the guys who knew something about watches took off the back and declared it to be a makeshift job. We were learning that how to make a buck is any way you can along with the rest of the education that lay behind it.

At another station we stopped at, near our destination, one of the guys had his arm dangling out the carriage window and had his nearly new gold watch whipped off his wrist. To look at his face you might have thought he'd been struck by lightning. I thought to myself, there's more brain banks on this platform than on this train. No doubt in some way tomorrow's adults will be what today has to offer them.

On reaching our last station we were quickly loaded into trucks and taken to our final destination known as 104-MU which stood for a Munitions Dump, I'm told. Our mission here was to tidy the place up and ensure that no munitions were left lying around for the Israeli or Arab people to use against each other before we vacated the camp. Palestine in 1946-47 was a sharp thorn in the side of Britain and claimed a number of British servicemen's lives as they attempted to police the handover to the Jewish people. A couple of our guys, I was told, lost their lives while collecting mail in a van.

We were issued with rifles and ammunition when we first arrived in camp and were told we were now on active service. A week or so later we were taught how to use a Bren gun and how to service it.

I'll never forget, if that's possible, one night when four of us guys along with our sergeant were patrolling the fence perimeter of the camp when all hell suddenly broke out above our heads. The Arabs were raining bullets down onto the Jewish orange groves below us and that whole area we were in looked like Guy Fawkes was putting on a show for us. Talk about being caught in no-man's land. It frightened the daylights out of us I can tell you. And I don't want to put our sergeant in any kind of a bad light but shouting to us, he was first in the ditch that was beside us. He had called out to us to get down but we as green as a virgin having her first baby. And that has to be classed as green under any circumstances. That incident never ceases to amuse me whenever it flows into my mind.

Naturally we were confined to camp and had to forego the mystical pleasures of beautiful Israeli woman and the fascinating scenery our minds had been conjuring up. So we were left to the ordinary pleasures that camp life brought to us.

The Naafi canteen was a popular meeting place for our philosophies of life to be thrashed out and sometimes bashed out. Boredom brought out the worst in some of us, but being an easy-going person I began learning to play cards and table tennis. Sean was a good card player, and poker was his master card when he hit a winning streak. He tried to teach me the art of the game, but I didn't have the ruthless nerve that makes one a good poker player. I did learn to play a reasonable game of solo and whist so my venture into cards brought its rewards of enjoyment. Reading was another pastime, though I read only fiction. The realities of my growing up tended to steer me towards escapism, and I've always been a dreamer and a romantic, and still am.

One for All and All for One

One day another chap and I were restacking ammunition boxes in one of the sheds when to our horror as we lifted the last box of its wooden platform and then lifted the platform itself we found a long black snake curled up asleep. We dropped the platform like a sack of hot potatoes and took to our heels. Our brave corporal in charge of us grabbed an ammunition box and dropped it on the snake. I think the poor creature, sluggish with the weather being quite cold at that time of the year, got an even bigger fright than we did before it met its untimely end. That was my first encounter with a snake of the reptilian variety.

We spent around four to five months in 104M.U. and

were very happy to leave because our toilets were filling up fast. I'd never sat so close to human waste in all my life as I did that last morning before we left.

We then boarded a convoy of trucks to take us to the port of Haifa. Only those of us at the rear of the trucks got a chance to view the people or the scenery. We hadn't seen any civilians since we arrived at our camp, so it was a treat for me to see some lovely young women as we passed some built up areas to allow all sorts of romantic notions to flow through my mind and body. I did see some lovely girls but I don't think my feelings were reciprocated as none of them smiled or waved to us. Not knowing what so many of them had been going through, a few ungracious thoughts filtered through my mind. Mine were unspoken, but some of the other guys put theirs into words.

I should have dearly loved to have had a good look at that lovely part of the world, especially Jerusalem and Nazareth. Even as a boy and into today Christ's wizardry has always fascinated me even though I had some misapprehensions about Him through my upbringing. And I thought that by visiting Jerusalem and Nazareth I might have been able to form a clearer picture of Him. Would I have been ready? I doubt it. But it was a nice thought anyway.

From Haifa we were shipped to Port Said, and a few days later Sean and I were posted to Cyprus. So at last we got a taste of what it was like up in the air, and we were quite excited about it. But that soon lost its flavour as we approached Cyprus. We ran into some turbulent air pockets that had us bouncing up and down like yoyos. Most of us reached for our doggy bags as our stomachs started to react to the antics the plane was getting up to. Luckily enough I managed to get mine around my mouth quickly, but some of the others didn't fare so well, and poor Sean was one of them. When we landed in Nicosia I for one was very glad to get out of that so my stomach could settle down again, as well as escaping from the unhealthy smell lingering around those who couldn't get to their doggy bags in time.

Anyway, we were quickly assigned to our quarters and told to clean up.

The hopes and dreams of most of us had taken beating that day. We had, I believe, visualized getting a bird's eye view of this beautiful island standing alone in the Mediterranean Sea. Instead all we got was a blanket of cloud, and air pockets to screw up our insides.

But time heals just about everything. A few days later we were the same cocky young airmen eager to explore new pastures filled with wine, women and song. I would have said beer instead of wine, but the beer was too dear for the common airman's pocket. The day after we got paid around eight of us headed off with our tails up to explore the township of Nicosia with more devilment running through our minds than we could ever hope to receive absolution for. We let top drinker Sean lead us to a bar-cum-restaurant. To our great disappointment we found that beer was too pricey for our pockets so we got stuck into the Cherry Brandy. I won't bore you with what we got talking about for the more liquor we consumed, the less sense we made. I was made well aware of that trying to make sense of my father's ravings as he downed the whiskey. Mind you many secrets can surface when a person is intoxicated. All those dark alleys or innocent fibres can be manipulated in so many different ways.

As the evening wore on one of the guys from Waterford got abusive. We dragged him outside and told him to get lost before we knocked the living daylights out of him. As far as I know he staggered back to camp. The night was still young, and growing bold on the brandy we were no longer deterred by the big round signs saying out of bounds. Our appetites lusted for those lovely creatures we never fully understood because we were men. We gabbled drunkenly among ourselves and decided to split up to avoid unwanted attention. Seven of us going into a brothel together, and the Service Police patrolling the out of bounds area in their jeeps would be on us like flies.

Well, Sean and I picked our street and staggered down it with foolish grins on our faces. We were fast losing the plot. We approached this house as far as I can remember and knocked on the door. It had a red sign on it. We were greeted by three women who welcomed us in with smiles, and then money changing hands. And as odd as it may seem I can't remember anything more till I woke up next morning feeling as though a truck had run over my head. As Sean and I made our way back to camp I emptied my stomach and told Sean that as long as I lived I would never touch Cherry Brandy again. Not only had it blown my brain away, but robbed me of my first night with a women. I couldn't remember if I did or didn't. Sean just about wet himself.

Our camp base at Nicosia was pleasantly situated not far from the mountains. As memory plays tricks with the real facts I'm just hoping I'm not too far from the reality of these places my service days took me to, and what involvement they brought me. Little did I ever dream I'd be writing about them one day.

I clearly remember most of my swimming trips in Cyprus. Periodically trucks would take us to different beaches. The weather was beginning to get really hot. Famagusta, Larnaca and Limassol were our three watering holes.

Our truck broke down one day on the coast road and while we waited for another one to come from the camp we made our way down a safe but steep cliff for a swim. Wow, it was a hot day. In the inlet below us we found a patch between the rocks where you could see the sand around twenty feet beneath the water. To this very day I have never seen anything so beautiful. I felt I could have stayed there forever. Have you ever been in a place, or in a situation like that? Something that seems to stay with you forever.

The highlight of my time in Cyprus was saving the life of someone in Limassol. We arrived at the Lagoon on a Saturday morning. I can't be sure, but I do know that there were at least two man-made diving boards out in the water. So on this particular day I swam out to one of the diving boards to practice my diving when I saw this guy lying motionless on the sand below. With difficulty I managed to get him to the surface, but as I had no life-saving experience I held his head out of the water and shouted for help. I caught the attention of two guys swimming towards me, and between the three of us we got him back to shore. The Corporal in charge was soon applying artificial respiration. The guy's face was the colour of chalk and we thought he must surely be dead, but the corporal kept on working on him until finally all sorts of horrible stuff started coming from his mouth, and he began to cough and splutter. We gave a big cheer and soon the ambulance arrived and he was taken to hospital. Though I heard nothing more about the incident I was rewarded with the feeling that I had helped to save a life whilst in a service where one was more likely to take life than save it.

I enjoyed my four months on the island of Cyprus. But there were no more nights out on the town after my first experience, or what I could remember of it. I left that to the more seasoned optimists, and those whose needs were greater than mine. Snooker, swimming, reading, cards and day-dreaming, wet and dry, about the opposite sex were enough to satisfy this silly boyish airman.

KHARTOUM

In what seemed no time at all we were informed that we

were to be posted to Khartoum to join 249 Squadron. A short time later most of us that had been sent to Cyprus were flown back to Egypt to where we'd tasted our first experience of the Middle East.

I found the sea trip from Port Said through the Suez Canal and into the Red sea to Port Sudan quite enjoyable because I didn't get seasick. Just looking at a rough sea after the Bay of Biscay was enough to churn my stomach. Maybe it had something to do with bobbing up and down in my mother's waters.

What I must have looked coming into this world.

Just before we docked at Port Sudan I saw some of the biggest jellyfish I'd ever set eyes on. The sea seemed to be covered with them. I remarked to Sean I don't think swimming would be very popular around here.

We were soon off the ship and into the train that was to take us to Khartoum. Iron rations and water bottles were issued for our three day journey to Khartoum. Then we were off puffing our way across the desert, taking in the scenery, desert after desert after desert. It was quite fascinating for a time until the never changing horizon began to bore us.

The only way I could describe that journey was that it was bloody uncomfortable. Sitting and sleeping on wooden seats for three days tends to give you every sort of ache and pain where you'd rather not experience it. But there were the relatively luxurious moments when the train stopped at the man-made watering holes. Large wooden troughs filled with water in what seemed to be makeshift stations in the middle of nowhere. We stripped off in these and endeavoured to get feeling back into our sweaty tortured bodies.

Eventually we arrived at Khartoum and anyone who'd thought it was warm in Cyprus or Egypt was in for a rude awakening. Man was it hot! I said to Sean, 'Remember how the Jesuits told us where we'd be going if we didn't repent our sins. Well, I think we've just arrived!'

Khartoum was to leave its mark on me. Good, bad, and maybe indifferent. Sometimes it's not easy to put things in a way you would like to, but that's as near as it gets for me. You can evaluate it as you choose.

One evening soon after we'd arrived, and Sean and I had been to the Naafi canteen to play darts and have something to eat, we made our way back to our sleeping quarters to settle in for the night. I then decided to write one of those now and again letters to my mother. She had written to me, and an answer was well overdue. I found it so hard to write because of my spelling. I was sitting down on my bed with my back to the open window with just my underpants on as the evening was so warm. The slight cooling breeze coming through and it felt good. The letter finished, I turned in for the night but woke some hours later covered with perspiration and feeling as if the devil had at last caught up with me. I was literally burning up and felt as sick as a dog. I called Sean. He took one look at me then went straight off to fetch the corporal in charge of us. I was quickly take to the nearby sick quarters. The medical officer read my temperature and said, 'He's burning up. We'll need to pack him down with ice.' I remember nothing more till I woke up in the British Military Hospital in Khartoum.

For the first while there I wanted only to sleep, but improved gradually as time passed. One morning about two weeks later the medical officer in charge of the hospital spoke to me on his rounds. He said 'You had us quite worried for a while. That was a very bad dose of pneumonia you had. We'll take some X-rays and hope to give you a favourable report.'

I spent around three weeks in that hospital and felt something like Ma's pincushion with all the jabs of penicillin they pumped into me. My backside came in handy for them when my arms were too sore. The lovely nurses gave this shy young man a hard time, but I've to secretly admit I enjoyed the hands of those beautiful nurses with their good-natured laughter wandering just about all over me. I leave you it to your own imagination the sort of thoughts that filled my sleepless nights with the tender devotion those nurses gave me when I first arrived as helpless as a baby. If my memory stays with me, I hope to remember that till I die.

The day before my discharge I was ordered to report to the surgeon in charge of the hospital. He sat me down in front of him and I was pleasantly surprised to learn he was one of my countrymen from Cork. He soon put me at my ease and asked me what brought me into the R.A.F. I told him my story and we shared a few laughs. He said pneumonia very often leaves a calling card. 'The X-rays looked clear' he said, 'but only time will tell. Don't let it worry you though. I'd say you've got a lot of living to do to catch up with all those lost moments of your childhood. I'm granting you seven days sick leave in the holiday centre at Ismailia. Nine days in all as it will involve two days travelling.' The surgeon then strongly recommended that I give up smoking and shook my hand. I thanked him and made my back to await my discharge.

The train journey to Ismailia was unexciting until we began climbing the mountain that led to it. There were times when I held my breath from fear and fascination as we made our way round and round the mountain. And I didn't really wish to know how close to the edge the train was travelling so I sat tight to the inner corner of my seat.

When we arrived at the station in Ismailia, a small bus was there to take us to the Servicemen's Holiday centre.

Once there I settled into my room, and then went in search of something to eat. A little later I went to investigate the games room as my priorities were snooker, table tennis and darts. As soon as I walked in I bumped into one of the guys I'd done my square-bashing with in Wilmslow. John came from Waterford and was a hard case if ever there was one. His needs were more compelling than mine, and filling them more complicated. Women and gambling. He had only four days of his sick leave left.

We spent the rest of that day playing snooker and darts with a few drinks thrown in. As I had been advised to take it easy John was always ahead of me in the drinking stakes. In fact everyone was ahead of me. Drinking alcohol was not among the genes I'd inherited from my father.

The following morning we went down town, but my only clear memories of that walk were me casting my eyes on the beautiful women that took my fancy. I soon found out that John had a terrible tongue when he spoke about members of the opposite sex. But the spell had been cast, and I very vulnerably accepted his invitation to once again satisfy my sexual appetite.

Later that afternoon John guided me into area dotted with trees and mud-like houses. He'd been here a few days before so knew exactly where to go. We approached one of these houses and a lady came out to greet us. In appearance she did nothing for me, but her big ear-to-ear welcoming smile compensated for that. We were taken inside where another lady joined us. This slim young lady did catch my eye and left me in no doubt as to which lady I wanted to spend my time with. I said to myself this is the real thing this time. Now you're going to find out what it's like to be with a women.

The lady stripped off in a small room with a bed in it. I wish I could tell you it was a wonderful romantic experience with all the trimmings. But no. The lady didn't speak. She never smiled, and she didn't respond to me in any way. As naïve as I was, deep down I knew that I had used this young lady. Sure, I was going to pay her for the use of her body which she offered for sale. But what bothered my conscience most was the fact that I had given no thought to her feelings, or the circumstances that had brought her to this point in her life. Had anyone really loved her? Not used her like I did. This time if an excuse had to be offered I had none. This time I wasn't intoxicated as I had been on my first such sexual adventure. I knew exactly what I was doing.

When John left I was not sorry to see him go. Maybe my conscience felt better. Misplaced desire is always looking for something to ease its pain.

When I returned to my unit Sean asked me how my leave went. I told him. He sensed my feelings regarding my unromantic brush with the opposite sex so he didn't put the boot in.

Looking back over that four-month stay in Khartoum I must say it holds many memories for me, mixed as they may be.

Though there is great history attached to Khartoum I was only interested in the history of which I was part. My history.

One of the many experiences that crossed my path in Khartoum was being caught in a number of sand storms that hit us out of the blue. Twice I was in the swimming pool when one of those storms hit. Trying to reach the changing rooms to get protection from the sand cutting into your eyes, ears and body is something I would not put on the entertainment list. But yet I was glad to have experienced it like so many things I already had and would in the future.

As the heat was so intense in Khartoum we were told to take plenty of salt tablets to keep our pores open. If we failed to take this precaution we would leave ourselves open to contracting Prickly Heat. And guess who got Prickly Heat because he didn't listen to sound advice. For almost three months I went crazy with the discomfort. And as if the itch wasn't bad enough I came up in boils on my face and back, and even my butt. Maybe it was payback time for using that poor young lady in Ismailia.

Among the other experiences that came my way in Khartoum was a very cruel example of what man is capable of in his quest to entertain himself. Some guy found a scorpion in a hangar we were working in. The nasty-minded individual put it out in the middle of the floor, and poured a ring of kerosene around it, and then set fire to the ring. I didn't wait to see the end result, but was told that the scorpion would sting itself to death. I know that I would have killed one if I had to, but with a little more humanity. You don't need a key to the door of reason, it is always open to those who have the courage and the heart to walk through it.

MOGADISHU

So once again it was time to pack our kit bags and move on. Our next destination was Mogadishu, the capital of Somalia. Three Dakotas were used to fly out all the equipment needed to service our fighter squadron of Tempests along with all the guys who kept the show on the road, or in the air, depending on the role we played.

Again we were in the air with all those unanswered questions running through our minds as we headed for Aden, our only port of call before Mogadishu. Things were going well till we approached the Gulf of Aden then suddenly the temperature seemed to rise in the aircraft and it began to dance around and lose height. I don't know how far we dropped before it levelled out but my stomach was giving me its danger signals, and I then pleaded with it to behave itself. Fortunately we landed soon after so I managed to keep things where they belonged.

When we were assembled later we were informed that the aircraft required some repairs and that we would be staying here overnight. Bloody hot and uncomfortable as it was, at least it gave my stomach a chance to settle down.

Early next morning we were on our way again. I was lucky to have the monotony of the journey broken when a corporal seated alongside me asked if I played chess. I said yes, but that I was only a rookie at the game. He unfolded a portable chess set and I received two valuable lessons. One was how to accept defeat gracefully, and the other to look more closely at my options.

I was hungry when we eventually landed in Mogadishu. As soon as we'd got ourselves sorted out in our new living quarters we were marched to the cookhouse. Well we could hardly believe our good fortune. There was real fresh butter, fresh crusty white bread, fresh milk and beautiful fresh vegetables along with fresh fish. And the following morning we had bacon and eggs for breakfast. Mind you it only lasted a week but it was a breath of heaven compared with some of the food dished up to us. But after saying that as I now look back in this later stage of my life, we were well looked after.

I guess most of us really don't stop complaining till we're dead, do we?

Later that evening I went looking for Sean and was told that his plane had not arrived. So as I was tired and happy to have reached our destination with my stomach intact I went to bed. On looking for him again the next morning I was told that his plane had still not arrived. I felt this to be very strange because his plane was to leave shortly after ours, but there were no answers to my queries. A certain amount of apprehension then started running through my mind.

Two days later Sean's plane landed. He looked as if the banshee had sent him a calling card. I said, 'You look like someone whose coffin has gone into the ground and they're not in it.' He did look bloody awful. He said 'If you'd been through what I have with that stupid stomach of yours, you'd be feckin dead.'

105 | Page

I sat down with him and let him slowly tell the story which unfolded with a string of words I can't repeat. Not a bit like the happy go-carefree Sean but I guess we all have our breaking point.

It seems that soon after their plane had passed the halfway mark on their journey one of the engines decided to give up the ghost. I could have said it cut out, but you know what we Irish are like? Anyway, the pilot said he was turning back to make an emergency landing on a small airstrip somewhere between Aden and Mogadishu.

As the plane was carrying a large part of the Squadron's servicing equipment it soon began to lose height and the pilot realised that one engine and a prayer were not going to keep them alive for much longer unless they got rid of some of the weight. The order was given to unload as much as was necessary to keep the aircraft in the air till they reached the landing strip. I dread to think how they would have fared if they'd put the aircraft down in the wilderness we'd flown over on our way to Mogadishu. I couldn't even begin to think at what was going on in the minds of those guys in the one-eyed aircraft with the crew fighting to control the monster, and the rest of the guys on board wondering if it would have its own way in the end. With the beast dictating the terms and the ride getting bumpier by the minute the guys with weak stomachs unloaded their contents all over the floor and unwillingly gave up helping to offload cargo. The others were skating around in a mess and had to put up with the smell. Except for the very sick who couldn't care less what happened to them, I guess there must have been some very mixed feelings among the guys as to whether or not they'd ever see their loved ones again.

Then at last, the pilot announced, hold on to your hats the landing strip is just over this hill-cum-mountain ahead.

Well that's how Sean related it, thinking at the time they'd never get enough lift to clear it. But it was a very close call as they came in to land. Sean said if he ever had to pray again as he did on that flight he'd expect to be canonized.

Once settled in, after work about ten of us made our way down a winding unsealed road that led to the beach. I remember how picturesque it was with fine rushes growing along either side. It took us about twenty minutes to reach the beach. But what a beach! From the moment I saw it I was hooked. It fairly took my breath away with its soft near white sand, and the bluest of blue water I had ever seen. To top this off, there was a three-tier diving board, and a shop selling soft drinks and those treats so close to my boyish soul, chocolate bars.

Though Mogadishu was situated on the Indian Ocean and the sharks were plentiful we didn't need to concern ourselves about them because the swimming area was surrounded by a shark net.

They'd have to look elsewhere for their dinner. I certainly wouldn't have been too happy with the thought of having a shark eat me so far away from home after all I'd been through, especially when things were looking so good. I have come to realise over the years that at times I have failed to build on my God-given optimism, but I have rarely ceased to chase after it in some way or another. It is my optimism that I believe supported me in my darkest moments.

I visited the town on three or four occasions. Two visits were to watch our lads play soccer against two local teams. Boy could those Somali guys play soccer. Wonderful sportsmen with good-natured smiles on their faces. Not only did they give us a lesson, but they did it in their bare feet having no money for luxuries such as football boots. God, was I getting educated in the greatest university of them all, life itself, and not hurting my pocket either.

The first of the two evenings I spent in the town, I was accompanied by Sean. We went to a bar for a light meal and then got stuck into the wine as the beer was in short supply. We made sure it wasn't Cherry Brandy! We had a very happy evening singing and laughing in a quiet little corner of the bar till it was time to hit off back to camp.

Our four to five months in Mogadishu was coming all too quickly to its conclusion. I really loved swimming at the beautiful beach there. Anyway the day before we were to leave for Egypt, about eight of us decided to have a farewell evening in the town as we had just been paid that day. Well, I have got to say I really blotted my copy book that evening. Yes, the Devil in me once more took me very easily into Eve's garden for another bite of that apple that started the ball rolling in the distant past. A few of us decided once again to sow some wild oats after the wine fired our boilers. Well, we didn't have far to go as all the action was taking place at the rear of the bar-cum restaurant that we'd been revelling in.

I must say that the lady I was with was very responsive, but yet there was a feeling of guilt mixed in that took from the real value of the deed. I guess your conscience in the end is always going to be the deciding factor.

Four days later we were up in the air once again on our way to Aden and then on to Egypt and I'm happy to say that my stomach remained in harmony with the rest of me. We were all in good shape when we were marched off for our first meal in Deversoir which lies beside the Suez Canal, and the Great Bitter Lake. Again the water was extending its hand of friendship to me. Though I was unaware of it then, Deversoir was to be my last tour of duty in the Middle East. I had about a year to serve before I was due to be posted back to England. My feelings about my family and the distance that lay between us were very mixed. While I was enjoying this growing-up period in lands full of mystery and ideologies so far removed from those of the little Green Island where I had laughed and cried with those I loved, all sorts of feelings were beginning to surface. How was my family coping with my father? My Mother wrote regularly but I felt that I needed to read between the lines. She would take all the burden on her shoulders rather than upset me. Mothers like mine are the very salt of the earth. Their specialness never dies.

On my side I could be very slow in writing because I really hated putting pen to paper, conscious of my shortcomings when it came to spelling. There was so much I wanted to say about my feelings and the fascinating things I'd seen, but getting it down on paper could be slow torture. But at least one good thing had come of my leaving home. For the first time since I began growing up my father had come to realise that he'd driven me away from home. This had not stopped his drinking, but the pangs of remorse had taken the edge off his violence. My mother told me this in one of her letters soon after I arrived in Deversoir. When I read it I cried my eyes out.

It made me wonder how many fathers love their sons deep down, but die without been able to tell them. Or how many sons never forgive their fathers for what they have done to them. I forgave my father the moment I read that letter. My tears washed away the sins of the past, both his and mine.

About five days after we'd arrived in Deversoir when I woke one morning and went to the toilet I discovered all wasn't well down below. I put myself on sick parade and received a rude shock when informed by the doctor I'd contracted gonorrhoea. 'I'm admitting you to the hospital in Ismailia for treatment' he said, 'but don't look so worried. They'll have you fixed up in no time. But one thing I will add, I sincerely hope that you've learnt a lesson from this experience.' When I'd recovered a little from the initial shock of it all, I thanked the doctor. I then spent seven embarrassing days and nights in the R.A.F. hospital in Ismailia having penicillin pumped through my system.

When I returned to camp the lads in my billet gave me a hard time but all I could do was bite my tongue. I made a pledge to myself that I would never pay for my sexual pleasures again.

But after saying that along with the fact that I was very young, I still had to learn that everything we do has to be paid for in some way or another. Life's lessons come in all shapes and sizes to be dealt with or not to be dealt with. As you can see I have, and will be opening up my vulnerabilities to you in hope that it may provide you with the comfort to know that being honest about yourself in the end is the most comfortable bed you will ever lie in. As Christ says, 'The truth will set you free.'

Most of the area of our base was taken up by the airfield. The remainder was comprised of buildings for eating, sleeping, recreation and what was needed to supply the aircraft needs. What I loved there most of all was swimming in the Suez Canal. A gang of us would spend hours there when we weren't on duty. We could swim in safety in one long u-shaped area of the canal before it opened out into the Great Bitter Lake. And when the ships were going the turbulence would add to the fun. Once when a large liner was passing through someone shouted 'Shark!' I believe I should have been awarded the prize for reaching land first. But it was only a porpoise following the ship.

I often went to watch movies that were shown in an area that had four walls, but no roof. When a storm blew up we would have to make a quick exit. The pictures were always well patronised by the families of the married personnel who lived across the main road from our base. They used to hold whist drives in the family quarters, and from time to time us single guys would be invited to participate. The wives of the married men always made us welcome, and put on a good spread for us.

I began playing for money in Deversoir but soon gave it away. My good friend Sean said, 'Terry it's like taking candy off you when you join us at cards. Stick to what you know best.' That's what I really believe. It's only your true friends will tell you what they think of you

So I stuck to what I loved most. Snooker, table tennis, darts, badminton and swimming. Can't say I excelled at any of them, but they were a great source of enjoyment to me.

Most of my working days were spent back and forth between two large sheds used for housing aircraft parts, and the ammunition used for target practice. My job involved me in the unpacking and stacking of various items, and generally keeping the place clean. I enjoyed keeping as busy as I could, and can't remember having any major complaints directed at me. The officers and NCOs who flew the aircraft were a nice bunch of guys and treated us with respect, not pulling rank on us like some I'd come across both in and out of service life.

As we were enjoying our ten o'clock break one day we heard an approaching aircraft making a variety of unhealthy noises. We ran outside and saw a plane with its engine periodically cutting out trying to make an emergency landing on the airstrip. The undercarriage was down ready for the approach, but luck deserted the pilot. The wheels dug into the sand just short of the runway. It came to an almost sudden halt and tipped onto its nose. We were close enough to see the pilot in the cockpit so we ran to try and get him out. However, when we were a hundred yards or so from him the aircraft exploded and flames enveloped the engine and cockpit. We could only watch horrified as he burned to death. The fire tender got to the scene as fast as it could, but nothing could be done to save him.

My real education in life's university had well and truly begun. We were told later that the pilot was a guy named Doc Watson. Where the "Doc" came from I have no idea but he was one hell of a nice guy. I attended his funeral a day or two later, and would find it hard to believe that as the firing party paid the Squadron's last respects there wasn't a tear or two shed like there was from my eyes. That I can tell you made quite an impact on my young life. And I still at times remember it as though it was yesterday.

While I was in Deversoir I ran into one of the English guys I had done my square bashing with. I remember him quite well for his good looks and good manners. We got talking and he said something I hope will stick forever in my memory of him. He said, "I always admired the way you and Sean would kneel down by your beds and pray, right in front of all us guys." He asked me if we'd felt self-conscious about it. I said "Yes we did, but you guys helped us to overcome that by not taking the mickey out of us", and I thanked him. He lost his life soon after we had that lovely conversation. He was fitting a rocket to one of the new Vampire fighter jets that had been allocated to our Squadron, when his partner in the cockpit who was an instrument technician accidentally set the rocket in motion.

He was standing right behind the rocket when it took off.

Now that's what I was told, I wasn't there. But it took its effect on each one of us in its own way and I can only speak for myself. Yes, I was deep in shock for a while after as you can guess. And maybe it would not have taken such an effect on me had we not had that conversation before his untimely death.

The dead airman's workmate was so devastated he had to be sent back home to England. I do know that they were very good mates. Both of them were doing their National Service.

The only duty most of us disliked was Guard Duty. It meant broken sleep and was also very boring. But having said that, we did appreciate how necessary it was to safeguard the aircraft, the ammunition and everything else that held our base together in a place where poverty was rife. The people around us were very poor indeed. I remember seeing small children dressed in rags, their faces covered in flies, a culture shock for me. I may have had to wear my father's cast-offs in my growing years, but at least I didn't have flies crawling over my face, or that sense of poverty that those children and their families had to live with.

There was a certain amount of petty theft around the base, but no aircraft were taken! Those we lost through mechanical failure or human error. The Tempest Doc Watson died in, I was told, had sprung a leak in the coolant radiator. Two more had to be written off from what I could gather. One of them unfortunately took the life of a lovely young Irishman from Bray with whom I had some very pleasant conversations. The story goes that a young pilot officer who'd just joined the Squadron made a bad landing approach. His wing tip caught the side of the narrow radar tower where the young Irishman was working and killed him. The pilot survived but the aircraft didn't. The loss of the last plane always brings a smile to my face when I think about it, because the only thing that got hurt was the taxpayer's purse and the pilot's pride. Another young pilot fresh out of training came in to land with the undercarriage up. His landing looked I'm told like the Fourth of July celebrations. That landing kept us laughing for some time I can tell you.

I too had a narrow escape from death's door but it had nothing to do with aircraft. It concerned my lack of faith to walk on water. A guy named Paddy from Dublin asked me if I would like to take a hired two-man canoe out with him on the lake. I jumped at the idea so off we went full of boyish excitement. We were gliding along happily through calm waters when I noticed my feet getting wet. Excitement quickly turned to panic as I shouted to Paddy 'we're taking on water fast.' We turned the canoe around with the crazy idea of getting as close to the boathouse as possible before the worst happened. Well, the worst happened very quickly and we had to part company with the canoe.

Paddy shouted from the water, swim left to the shore, it's nearer than the boathouse. Then he was off. Scared as hell I said to myself, 'you're on your own once more, what's new.'

I soon tired of swimming overarm. Real panic was taking me over and I saw my past appearing before me. I was about to surrender to it when the will to live rebounded. In a flash it came to me how easy it was to float. It had been from that position I'd learnt to swim on my stomach. I pulled myself together and went over on my back. Eventually very exhausted I reached dry land. It was wonderful to be alive I can tell you.

After Paddy and I had rested and talked over our experience we returned to the boathouse to tell the lady what had happened. Well I can tell you she had little sympathy for us poor young Irishman that had just survived a watery grave. That canoe cost a lot of money which will have to come out of your pockets. I looked at her in disbelief, but Paddy made for my dumbfounded silence in his rough Dublin vocabulary. He said 'Here we are lucky to be alive and all you are concerned about is a bloody piece of useless timber. In fact, worse than useless. It was a death trap.' The woman said, 'How dare you speak to me like that. I'll report you to your commanding officer.' So paddy said not to bother, 'we'll do it for you', and without further words we set off back to our billet to change.

The corporal in charge of us was preparing to go out as we came in. After hearing our story he put a piece of paper in front of us and told us to write down exactly what had happened. Then we were to both sign it and he'd take it to the adjutant to deal with. 'And for God's sake make some sense out of what you write or you'll have the price of that canoe coming out of your pocket.'

Believe it or not I had won a small dictionary as a part of my winnings in a poker game in Cyprus when one of the guys didn't have enough money to cover my hand containing four aces. So equipped with this dictionary, we managed to put a feasible story together that must have done the trick because we never heard any more about the incident. The outcome of this episode gave me a reasonable sense of satisfaction because it saved our commanding officer a few embarrassing discussions had one or both of us gone to a watery grave.

Not long before we were due to leave Egypt for the United Kingdom we were involved in another brush with disaster. A few guys from my billet had just returned from guard duty in the early hours of the morning and were settling down for a sleep when out of the stillness came this high-pitched voice yelling, followed by a rifle report. Then for what seemed to be several long minutes there was deathly silence then the yelling started again. Most of us were awake by this time with the hair standing up on our backs of our necks. We didn't have a gun between the whole bloody lot of us because we'd handed our rifles into the armoury when we came off duty. We could be classed as sitting ducks.

Our corporal acted quickly. He had us out of bed and down flat on the floor, but as there was no form of communication with the rest of the camp we were left guessing as to what was happening. We heard scuffling feet and the sound of jeeps approaching. Our corporal's courage and sense of curiosity soon got the better of him. He opened the door slowly and was greeted with a barrage of lights and confusion of Air Force Police running around armed to the teeth. However, he was soon spotted in the doorway and told in no uncertain terms to shut the door and stay behind it until the all clear was given.

Soon after daybreak, full of curiosity, we were informed that a few radical Egyptians had tried to enter one of the billets alongside ours. When they found their way blocked they fired a bullet through the door. As bad luck will have it the bullet shattered the buckle of the corporal in charge of the billet as he took the force of it. He like ourselves had been on guard duty and hadn't bothered to get undressed. I am still in the dark as to what brought this all about, but I did hear that this good natured corporal from Belfast had to undergo an emergency operation and would never be the same man again.

Well, with two and a half years of experience tucked under my belt it was nice to say farewell to all those people and places in the Middle East that had extended to me the hand of friendship.

Now my thoughts and emotions were focused on being united with my family once again, those who mattered most to me. Immediately I'd heard that I was due to return home I wrote to my mother giving her the dates but saying 'expect me when you see me' because there had been a number of cancellations due to one thing and another.

But Lady Luck was with our mob. We left on our appointed day. Standing on the deck of the ship as it was pulling out of Port Said my memory slipped back over the things I had done and seen, the experiences I had been catapulted into at such an early age. How would I see the changes in my family through these new eyes of mine, and how would they see me? What kind of emotions would pass through my father and me as we stood face to on equal terms of manhood? I knew I had no problem with him before I took off overseas, yet I still had uncertain feelings. You can't wipe away the past like you can with a cloth on a blackboard.

I had forgiven him, there was no doubt about that. But deep down scars take time to heal, and I believe in some way at that particular time it was more about my mother than me. All the suffering she had to endure at the hands of my father through bringing up the family and yet she never deserted her post. She may have slipped up a little from time to time but like Christ when we really needed her you can bet your bottom dollar she would be there for you. I don't believe anyone could give enough praise to a mother like ours. I'll leave that to your own hearts and imagination.

HOME LEAVE

The oceans were kind to us on our way back to the United Kingdom, the Bay of Biscay being on its best behaviour. The only event of any note was my being thrown out of my hammock on two occasions bruising my dignity more than my body. Our postings were read out as we lined up on the pier at Southampton. Sean and I were posted to Harper Hill in Buxton, and transport was waiting to take us there when we arrived at the station. After we had settled into our new quarters, we were taken up to the base camp for something to eat, then paraded to be welcomed by the commanding officer of R.A.F. Harper Hill.

Shortly after that we were paraded once more and informed that we were to be paid the next day, and granted twenty eight days leave. There was some other stuff I didn't bother to take in, because I was too focused on getting the hell out of there with four week's pay in my pocket, and being united with my family and all those things that had been out of my reach for such a long time like the ladies. Now here I want to make a sincere apology for a statement I made in my last book.

(I said not like the women who take your money up front as they do in places). In rewriting this book of mine I can see more clearly to remove the plank from my own eye before my poor judgment visualizes the speck in the eyes of others. I will just finish that with a note of thank you to those ladies who had to put up with me in the Middle East.

It wasn't till the evening of the next day that Sean and I arrived by train at Holyhead to board the ferry to Dublin. It was somewhere around summertime of 1949. To celebrate our homecoming we knocked back a few drinks and began reminiscing over the last two and a half years. We'd well and truly crossed the ocean of boyhood to manhood, and done it in a shorter space of time than those we'd left behind. It was as though we'd learned another language which only those who'd crossed those oceans would understand.

There was too much going through our heads in the early hours of that morning to sleep much. As we approached Dublin the sun was fighting to get its head through the clouds over the Dublin Mountains. It wasn't long before we were on a bus to take us to O'Connell St in the heart of the city. It had all been arranged for Sean to spend the night with us as he had already left his mark of popularity on his last visit. From O'Connell St we caught the bus to West Cabra. As we sat on the top of the double-decker bus I glanced across at the underground toilets that had given me shelter on those cold winter nights with a grin on my face, and gave God a silent prayer of thanks. In twenty minutes or so we were off the bus making our way to 82 Fassaugh Avenue.

Well before we reached the front gate my mother was there to greet us with tears and joy on her lovely face. She threw her arms around me, and I threw mine around her. She whispered in my ear, 'You'll never know how much I've prayed for this moment.' I was too choked up to reply at that moment, I just held her close.

At the front door my brothers and sister shared their warmth with me as they threw their arms around me with touching words of welcome. After that everyone gave Sean a big welcome. Then came the long-awaited moment that had been on my mind ever since I'd learnt that my tour of duty in the Middle East was over. I know I'd mentioned I had no problem with my father before I left for the Middle East, but yet there was a part of me that still lingered in the shadows of the past. So as we stood face to face he must have sensed what was going on in my mind for he quickly stepped towards me extending his arms and saying, 'Welcome back home son.' The next moment we were locked in each other's embrace and the past laid to rest where it belonged. He whispered 'Sorry old son.' I seemed to grow a foot taller that day.

To forgive those who really hurt you is one of the hardest things one has to do in one's lifetime. And I'm not talking so much about forgiving, but letting go. Leaving your mind free to take in things you really need for your growth.

After I'd received my welcomes Sean was brought more

into the family reunion. He'd made a good impression on his first visit so everyone was at ease with him. Sean didn't have to open his mouth to tell you that he was Irish. And he was well-versed in Irish history (in spite of a low-key education) with an answer for just about everything, right or wrong! In fact he was a master bluffer which made him such a good poker player. And when it came to whiskey drinking I don't think he would have been too far behind my father, but with a great sense of humour. God could he make me laugh when he was tanked up. My father seemed to sense these things, and they drew him to Sean.

After a wonderful evening my mother invited Sean to stay the night with us the day before we caught the boat back to Holyhead. Next morning I went into the city with him to see him off on the bus for Clare. Before he said goodbye he said, 'You really have a lovely family. It's hard to believe you all turned out so well with the rough time you all had with your father.' I kept no secrets from Sean. And he also said, 'I've got to say I found your father very intelligent and charming.' I said, 'To know me, is to come and live with me' with a big smile on my face.

Most of my leave was spent catching up with the past and present. I did go looking for my old friend John in the Boys' Home, but no one could give me any information on his whereabouts. The gap without any form of communication had been too long, but the memories had stayed alive. And I really believe it's memories that make it all worthwhile.

To me, my mother looked as beautiful as ever in spite of having a rough time with varicose veins. I could see little change in my father other than the decline in his drinking.

Gerald, three years my junior, had grown from the skinny and delicate kid I'd left behind into a humorous and wise young man for his years. My brother Ken had certainly grown. I could see now that my father was no longer king of the roost.

Several nights after I arrived Da came home fairly drunk and started to carry on in his old ways. Ken got him by the shoulders and gently pushed him down into his chair, telling him to watch his tongue. I was impressed I can tell you. Gerald, too, was well in charge of the situation. They took it in turns to gently keep my father in his place. Violence was no longer the order of the day. We were as near as you can get to being a normal family again. For the first time in all those dark years of the past hostilities had ceased. Now we could grow together helping each other as best we could to overcome the scars of the past.

My father did try and shape up to me one evening when Gerald and Ken were out. I pushed him down into his chair saying 'Don't tempt me, I'm not the gentleman my brothers are.' That was the last breath of bad air that passed between us, though I occasionally got some hard looks when he was drunk.

My sister Ann had shot up and looked well even though she had plenty to put up with being the only girl in the family. My heart went out to her at times, though I won't dwell on the reasons. That is her story not mine. Only three things I will say. Ann is a very special sister, a very special woman, and a very special mother.

Of my baby brother Tony and how he fitted into my homecoming I have few recollections. Sorry about that Tony but I believe we both have made up for that in the years that were to follow. And as I write this revised story of mine I am very much looking forward to meeting you in July when we go to Canada to meet our lovely sister Ann. What a lot of fun, laughter and reminiscing we have to do. I'm sure Canada will never be the same again. I know we won't!

Sean arrived during the afternoon of our last day in Dublin, and my father insisted on taking us out for a drink. What a turnabout from the past! Never could I have visualized the day that I would find myself standing beside my old man in a pub with a glass in my hand. There were a few thoughts running through my head that evening I can tell you, and I laughed to myself as I remember it. It's amazing the changes in our lives that time can bring about as long as we don't let the unnecessary things of the past tie us down. And even more amazing is the longing within us to reach that place we never thought we could, and continually grow from there no matter what anxiety or discomfort it may bring us. I will say it has taken me a long time to embrace that place within myself, but the time factor is not as important as the journey has been. And I really believe this can happen when your mind is free to wander into the future, and allows you to be you.

R.A.F. HARPER HILL

The following evening Sean and I were back in Buxton adjusting to the changes in our lifestyle. R.A.F. Harper Hill was as you will gather quite different from the land of pyramids with all its told and untold history. I could put my swimming trunks away and substitute them for whatever it took to keep the warmth in and the chill and wet out in this cold spot as winter began to show her feelings. The base camp I'm told was close to 1,000 feet above the town, built to house ammunition. Our task was to get everything ready to have it removed, where to I had no idea. The ammunition had been stored in a number of tunnels under the base camp, and a certain amount of it was found to be contaminated and had to be dumped. Our job was to repack all the wooden boxes that had started to rot because of the damp, or whatever other reason it could have been affected. As I was not expert in this field that's the best description I can give you.

The work wasn't hard, but the cold in winter didn't impress any of us. Mind you we weren't there to be impressed, but I thought I'd mention it anyway!

Apart from ammunition and parachutes, I can't remember what else was stored in the buildings around the camp. I was told things did go missing from time to time, but as they say, the time to take anything is anytime. Not that I agree with that, but even I too have my moments of weakness as you will see.

This wasn't so easy though, as we had to pass a checkout post before we made our way down to our living quarters after our daily tasks were done. After we passed through the checkout post we would make our way to the cookhouse for a very welcome meal. I never could figure out how far our living quarters were from the base camp, but I'd say it took us about fifteen to twenty minutes to walk down. We didn't have to walk down the road as we could take a shortcut down the hill walking through patches of grass and gorse. There were also trucks laid on to take us down to our living quarters, but I preferred to walk down when it wasn't raining. There was a sense of freedom brought about by opening your mouth and taking in to the clean fresh air, and turning your eyes to the scenery that lay before you. Mind you Sean and some of the others thought I was crazy. But I guess you have already realised that by now!

It was another kettle of fish though when the snow dropped its load in the winter. A gang of us would have to take shovels to keep the road open for trucks to service the camp. That could be very cold on the hands and feet but I don't remember it doing any of us any harm.

I must say I was very impressed with our living quarters. Each of us had a small private room and the conveniences were first class in my book after some of the dark holes I grew up in. Accommodation in the R.A.

F. I certainly have no real complaints about. And when I wrote one of my infrequent letters I could do so in privacy with no one looking over my shoulders ribbing me over having to use my dictionary. My lack of education I let haunt me for the greater part of my life, so I loved my little room where I could read, write, and dream in peace. This along with the sense of dignity that was allowed to me, is something I shall always thank the R.A.F. for.

Apart from Sean, I made one other good friend during my stay at Harper Hill. Fraser Duff, Jock to his friends, worse to those who got on the wrong side of him. Jock was a very talented soccer player, and very much in demand with some of the local clubs. I know he represented Buxton on a number of occasions. He had been conscripted into the R.A F. to do his two years military service. Mind you he wasn't impressed like many of the others who had been called up to do their term of service, so I just let him rave on about it.

Jock stood a little taller than me with good looks to match his excellent physique. And apart from the occasional temper flare-up, he was one of the most likeable characters I have ever met. In particular I admired his honesty and fearlessness. You knew where you stood with Jock.

I really enjoyed Jock's company and the things we shared together over that short period of six to eight months when his term of service was due to expire. After he left there was a low period in my life for a while. I guess this is something that happens to most of us when we've been close to someone who can sense our needs, and we theirs, and then fill them in some way. The moments when Jock and I would give each other a hard time would melt away as quickly as they came. We were like children at heart, untouched by society's cynicism and greed, unspoiled in our attitudes.

With a year left to serve I more or less said to myself let's put what I can into this year that I won't forget for a while, to see what I can bring up from both my conscious and unconscious mind. From there come many joys, or many sorrows.

As a way of filling my social needs I took myself up to Manchester when a 48 hour pass was available to me, to watch the famous Manchester United team give so much pleasure to their supporters at their home ground Old Trafford. I was never on my own as I would meet up with some of the guys from the camp somewhere along the way, and if not, I would make new friends. In those days people seemed a lot friendlier. They didn't have much but they were more than willing to share it. Though I can't say that I liked the weather in Manchester, I found the people second to none. Some of the best sing-along pubs I ever set foot in were in Manchester, and my memories of those days still bring me laughter and a few tears.

Like many others, my emotions turned to tears the day of the Munich air disaster, the day the cream of British football was taken away from us. But their memory still lives for me because I was privileged to see them play on a number of occasions before fate intervened. And that I believe is what life is so much about, memories. The bad ones I let go and in that way the good ones support me in my journey into the future, the unseen.

I did have an interesting experience in Manchester. It happened at the tail-end of the day. Along with around eight of my colleagues, I missed the last train to Buxton. We were all very much under the charms of alcohol. We began looking around for some form of transport to get us back to camp, but all we could find was a bus which went only half way, leaving us with about twelve miles, and that steep hill from Buxton to reach our camp.

The earlier euphoria when we got the bad news we'd missed the train was soon replaced with some bad language as the blame was passed from one to the other like a rugby ball. I said, 'If one's to blame we're all to blame and if we keep pulling the oars of this situation we're in, were never going to reach the parade ground by eight in the morning, and you all know what that means.' No one attacked me either physically or verbally. Sometimes it's amazing what alcohol can do for your personality. Maybe I wasn't my father's son after all and Ma hadn't told me about the milkman!

When the bus dropped us at its last stop we staggered off preoccupied with thoughts of the long footslog to camp. With so many of us there was little chance of getting a lift, especially just around midnight. In fact, it seemed that passing vehicles increased their speed when they saw us trying to hitch a ride, and who could blame them. We must have looked like escapees from a chain gang with some of us in civvies, and some in uniform all looking the worse for wear.

We did manage to make it to our living quarters just in time to clean ourselves up and catch one of the trucks to take us to the cookhouse for a much needed breakfast. After morning parade I reported to my sergeant for duty. He took one look at me and said, 'You look like you've been on your feet for a whole week.' I said 'I feel like it too,' and I told him the whole story. He said, 'Take yourself off to that little hut over there for a few hours shuteye, and I'll call you when I need you.'

That was the wonderful kind man he was. So human from his head down to his toes, but strict when it came to discipline, letting us know who held the reins. Sean and I knew him somewhat better than the others under his wing though he had no favourites when it came to getting the job done. But he knew that he could count on Sean and me when it came to getting the job done. He could count on us to go that extra mile if the necessity arose, as it did from time to time.

One day our sergeant invited Sean and me to his married quarters for a meal, and to meet his family. I immediately fell in love with his daughter. She was lovely to look at and had a personality to match. His wife was a charming women who couldn't do enough for us. After dinner our sergeant asked us if we'd like to go down into the town for a drink, and a game of darts. We jumped at the suggestion and his wife said, off you go, and I'll have some supper ready when you get back. I was really delighted when his daughter said she'd join us and you can guess my mind and body went into overdrive. Once in the pub and playing darts, however, both Sean and I were put to shame by the skill of both our host and his lovely daughter. So much for a young fool trying to make a good impression on a young lady.

This young woman was very different from my very short and varied experiences with the opposite sex as you'll have already gathered by now! I did have a few mild flirtations in Buxton, and when I was home on leave, but this young lady had to be the cream of them all in my romantic mind of mine. So beautiful and natural in her movements, and in the way she related to us all.

I could see a lot of my mother in her.

But my poor hopeful heart took a bad knock when after a delicious supper we found ourselves free to talk, her mother having retired and Sean and her father being deep in conversation. I'm sure she sensed my strong attraction towards her, my boyish openness would have been a dead giveaway. But being a high principle girl she was, she told me that she was engaged to be married to a corporal in Malta. But even after that shock to my romantic system I felt a certain chemistry going on between us. Inexperienced as I was in the field of romance I knew she liked me, felt comfortable in my presence.

I could read it in her beautiful eyes and feel it in her reactions to things I said about myself. However, there was that high wall between us. So a little later with my head swimming around in all directions Sean and I took our farewell and rambled back to our quarters.

It took a while for me to get to sleep that night as that song the Impossible Dream kept haunting my poor almost broken heart.

Then to add to this I was taking an evening stroll up the main road when she called out to me from behind. Like me she liked to walk a few evenings each week. Well all I'm going to say about that evening without going into details, what kept us within our self-enforced boundaries that night is something I ask myself when I'm tiptoeing down memory lane.

Perhaps learning how she really felt about me gave me the strength not to climb that forbidden wall, yet gave me something to cling to later when the going was really tough.

About eight months before my term of service was due to cease, Sean and I were sent to work in the parachute store. Our job was to pack the parachutes into cardboard boxes to be dumped as their useful days were over. Well that's what I was told. I couldn't believe my eyes when I saw them all lying on the floor of a large room looking as if a regiment from the Airborne Division had just landed. We were given our instructions and left to pack the parachutes on our own.

I later commented to Sean that it was a shame for all those parachutes to come to such an ignominious end and that maybe I could save one. He gave me a strange look and asked what the hell had I in mind. I said, 'I'm going to take one of these and carry it home next week when I go on leave.' He said 'you crazy bastard, you'll never get past the checkout point with one under your arm. They'll send you over the wall, and throw away the key. Don't be such an idiot.' I said, 'I'm going to wrap it around my body under my uniform.' 'You're fecking crazy' he said, 'You'll look like a barrel. They'll spot you a mile away. And anyway, what are you going to do with it when you get home?' I told him I'd find a better fate for it than the one awaiting it from here.

I deliberated on my plan for several days before finally putting it into action. The dark wet winter evening was my trump card. On this particular evening I removed all my clothes, and with Sean's help wound the parachute around me. Then I got my clothes minus my jumper and vest back on without too much trouble, but getting my trousers and jacket on was a marathon in itself. What a dead giveaway! We laughed till the pain got too much for me and I collapsed onto one of the boxes, but even that was mighty uncomfortable.

I told Sean to go ahead of me and hand the key to the parachute store in at the checkout point. No way did I want him to become part of my crime. I'd even worked out a hopeful alibi for him should I get caught. And he wasn't too worried because I'd got him out of a few scrapes in the past. Then just before we were due to finish another piece of good fortune presented itself to my aid. It started to rain. Now I could put my cape on which would cover this baggy figure of mine. So sweating like the pig I resembled I set off to the checkout point with all the guilt-ridden courage I could muster. As I was about to pass through a voice called out, 'Airman, I want to see you!' Well, I just about soiled my pants as I turned to face the voice. 'No, not you' he said, 'the fellow behind you.' I quickly turned my face away so it wouldn't betray me completely, and then struggled to get my feet working again. Then, with one sudden spurt I cleared the danger zone and headed down the hill and didn't stop till I reached the door of my room. I missed my evening meal but I'm quite sure it wouldn't have got past the knots I had in my stomach.

When Sean called to see me later he said, 'you've got more guts than I gave you credit for. I've had my fingers in a few pies but that escapade of yours puts you a few streets ahead of me.'

A few days later I was off with my parachute stuffed in my kit bag to spend ten days with my family. After the greetings were over I unpacked the beautiful white parachute and asked my mother if she could use it for anything. She said we've just been allocated a new Housing Corporation house in Raheny, I'll find a use for it there.

And she did. Most of the curtains for that house were made from that parachute. Maybe the devil isn't all bad. Not as bad as the church has made him out to be. Maybe it's the teachers we have to be wary of. The Pharisees in the society we live in.

DUBLIN AND THE HAMMOND LANE FOUNDRY

Once again faith was to intervene in my life, and dictate its terms in no uncertain fashion. After another few months in Buxton I was no longer under the security blanket of the R.A.F. and the things that had helped me sustain me over the previous six years. That place where I had somewhere to sleep, something to eat, something to clothe my body, something to rattle in my pocket, and very little to worry about.

You could ask yourself why I didn't stay in the Royal Air Force until I received a pension. With my background of non-education it would have seemed the sensible thing to do. They'd asked me to sign on and even promised to teach me a trade. You could call that a golden opportunity if ever there was one. But something deep down inside me was saying there is more to life than security. Comfortable courage, my inner instinct was telling me, is not the place to get stuck in.

Well it wasn't long till the money I received from the Royal Air Force ran out including the six weeks social welfare card they gave me. And having no skills of value in the city of Dublin at that particular time, early 1950, was not something to boast about.

However I didn't give it too much thought as my brothers were working for the motor trade and Da was still pulling in a few quid. And I had somewhere to sleep and something to eat.

Da had an old Morris car. I can't remember if it was a six or four cylinder one. It didn't break any speed records, but then we Irish are never in a hurry to get anywhere in case we might miss something. A good time, for example! With the help of my two brothers, Da was slowly paying the car off. I say slowly because in those days that was the only way you could get something like a car, and if they tried to get it back off you, if you couldn't keep up the repayments, they were lucky to get it back in one piece.

As Da didn't like driving around I took on the job of chauffeur, purely on a voluntary basis, as Da still needed his drinking money after he'd contributed towards the housekeeping. He could no longer hold on to it like he used to - my brothers saw to that. So I quite enjoyed driving him around. I had actually passed a driving test in England before I left the R.A. F. They very kindly paid for it. I passed the test without any bother. But I did feel sorry for a woman that was about to take her tenth test. I could see how nervous she was. As she took off with the instructor I partly guessed the red light was already against her. Yes, she failed.

Da no longer travelled any great distance because of ill health. Drinking, smoking and two doses of pneumonia had left him with a very dicky ticker. How he ever reached the age of sixty-three is amazing in my book. On two occasions he was at death's door but no-one was there to open it for him. He had been in two car crashes, but he'd just walked away from them looking a lot better than the cars did.

The amazing thing about driving Da around was the fact that I started having a few drinks with him when we were heading home in the evening. I never thought I'd see the day when I'd be drinking with him, and he paying for it. There is justice after all, but only if you are prepared to wait for it longer than usual.

As we didn't have far to drive home from the pub, there was very little chance of me being pulled up over the limit unless I ran into something. Mind you, you could get away with almost anything in those days. Anyway the thought never entered my mind, and I'm sure, even less my father's mind. He may have been pulled over for driving under the influence but I can never remember him going to court over it. He could talk his way out of just about any situation and create an entirely new one, just like any politician or lawyer could.

As I mentioned before, Da could still get a bit out of sorts after a few drinks, but none of us took any notice of him. We were no longer looking down the barrel of a shotgun. It was now the reverse, and lucky for him we were a lot more forgiving than he had been. As a youngster I never thought I'd see the day, and I must admit that I felt a smug sense of satisfaction creeping through the corridors of my being.

At the same time I don't believe in an eye for an eye. If we don't learn to rise above revenge we will always remain its victim. Man's sense of justice has a very limited range because he seldom rises above it.

About three months after I arrived home Da came home one evening and asked me if I'd be interested in serving an apprenticeship to become a motor mechanic. Well, by this time I was ready to tackle anything. I only drove him around when he had to go outside the city, otherwise he would use the bus, or get a lift off one of his friends. So without the bat of an eye lid I said yes I would. Having too much time on your hands is neither good for your pocket, nor your morale.

I had already spent around a year in my Uncle Harry's garage before he passed away so I had a little knowledge under my belt, and being able to drive was also another asset. A few days later I drove Da around town to a few places he needed to attend for his business, then later we stopped outside this very large building called The Hammond Lane Foundry in a place called Ringsend. Then Da took me into a small office just inside the main gate, and I was introduced to a man called Mr O'Brien and another man called Mr McKnight. Mr O'Brien was the garage manager, and Mr McKnight the transport manager. Then Da took off and said he would come back in about an hour as he had a few things to do.

I knew he'd have had a few drinks ahead of me by that time, but I wouldn't begrudge him that. It was his money, not mine.

Mr O'Brien gave me the once over and then took me to meet the garage staff. I was first introduced to Old Jim.

That was the title that had been bestowed on him. Next was Charlie, then Willie McKay. I took to Charlie and Willie straight away, but had some reservations about Old Jim, which proved to be right in the years to come.

After Mr O'Brien had gone through the do's and don'ts he wanted to test my driving skills, so off we went in a little Standard 10 used for garage work and for driving him around. Well, after a short drive I got one of those rare compliments I ever got from him. He said 'if you work as well as you drive, we'll get on fine.'

A week later I started to serve my cut short apprenticeship that I once started with my Uncle Harry. I thought that was quite ironic in a way. Second time around Terry was something that was now becoming a part of my life. And I didn't realise it till I started to rewrite my story. Makes me wonder what changes and so forth other authors might find if they had rewritten their stories. Might get some feedback on the comment that could prove interesting!

Shortly after I started my apprenticeship I bought myself a bike on the usual hire purchase system. Cycling was second nature to me as I have already described. Not only was it a necessity for my job, but also for my fitness.

The Hammond Lane Foundry was owned by a Mr David Frame, at least he was the Managing Director. How the financial running of the business stood I have no idea. I had heard that his father, a Scotsman, had started the firm by going around collecting scrap metal. There were quite a few different departments in the foundry which specialised in creating things like stoves and boilers and other items for the domestic market. I wasn't allowed to wander around the other departments unless I was sent there for some reason so that's the best description I can give you.

The garage was situated on the left hand side as you came into the main gates and was capable of accommodating three trucks with not much room to spare. There was a pit for working on trucks at the top left hand side of the garage and a hoist for working on cars at the front left hand side. Half way up the garage on the left was a storeroom which also served as an office for Mr O'Brien. That's where he kept his finger on the pulse of the mechanical side of things, but for me the most important room in the building was the room at the very rear where we had our morning tea, lunch and afternoon break, and kept warm on a cold winter's day. We did all our bench work there and anything else we could drag in to work on. The two main reasons for that being the pot-bellied stove in the centre of the room, and our desire to keep out of the range of the sharp eyes of Mr O'Brien and Mr McKnight. The transport office of Mr McKnight had two large windows that looked straight into the garage where those two pairs of sharp eyes were kept focused on us. In the winter time more so as they would be keeping their backsides warm with the coal fire behind them as they chatted and kept us in focus.

We didn't get away with much, but by God we tried.

Now you may be wondering about the other side of my life. The romantic side, as most of us has had one in some form or another. Well, as you can already see to date it hasn't been anything to boast about. Quite the opposite would be a better description.

What I omitted to tell you was that when I was in the R.A.F. I came home on one of our ten day holidays, and went up to see my old friend Tommy Hendrick in Inchicore. When I arrived I was introduced to a lovely looking young woman called Sybil Quick and her sister Eileen. As soon as my eyes fastened on Sybil I liked what saw. I did read somewhere that the eyes are the most inconsistent organ in your body, and that could very well be true. Maybe more so in my case! I guess when you're young and vulnerable with an imagination like mine anything can happen. And eventually it did.

She didn't say much at our first meeting, so I more or less left it at that. A few days later I rang Tommy and asked him about her. I told him I liked what I saw, and then asked him if she was going with anyone. He said as far as he knew she wasn't. He said that she worked at Nicholls Coal Merchants in Westmoreland Street.

After getting some of my boyish courage up I rang her. I could sense straight away I had taken her by surprise but after a short conversation she agreed to go and see a movie with me.

A few evenings later we had our first date and we seemed to get on well together. I can't remember what the picture was about, probably because my romantic mind more or less blocked it out.

After it was over I believe I asked her if she would like something to eat before she caught the train home. So she suggested going to an Italian ice cream restaurant called Capoli's. It was the first time I'd been there but it was to become a stamping ground for us in the years to come.

We both smoked at this time so we had that in common. I arranged to meet her a few days later before I was due to go back off leave and we went to see another movie. Then the day before I left, Sybil invited me meet her father and mother. That, as most of you know, can tend to become the more serious time in a relationship. You're getting the once over for whatever's in store for you. Her parents lived in Sutton right beside the railway station. Her father was a railway clerk who worked at Amiens Street Station. The visit went down alright with the family and myself as far as I can remember, then a while later I took my leave and told Sybil that I would write to her. Off I went with a new prospect in my life that could lead to a more flexible kind of romance than the shady hit and miss ones I had allowed myself to be drawn into.

When I arrived back in Harper Hill I told my good friend Fraser all about Sybil. I wrote to her, and she wrote back to me. Eventually it was time to go home on leave once again. This time I was quite looking forward to it as you may well understand.

We met a couple of days after I arrived and had dinner in

town. But I sensed a change in her. She had all of a sudden got this craze for ballroom dancing, and kept telling me how much she loved it.

Then she started raving over this guy that was teaching her. Well I've got to say with very mixed feelings that any chance of a blossoming romance had been dealt a severe blow. I at that time had two left feet, so dancing was not something I was going to impress any woman with. So the shadow of doubt started to linger in my mind. I hadn't reached that love sick state where a guy or maybe a woman finds themselves in that place where they will do almost anything to keep the impossible burning for the inevitable to take its toll.

I did go out with her once before I left, but saw fit to leave it at that without telling her. She did write to me but I didn't feel good about it. Something told me that for my part of it the romance wasn't going anywhere. I never replied.

Well lo and behold, about a month after I'd begun work my father came home one evening and told me Sybil had rung looking for me. I had a lot of mixed feelings because I was on my own and feeling vulnerable so I decided to meet her.

We had something to eat, and from that moment the romance was back on again. You never know what's around the corner till you get there.

I certainly became very involved in this on, and off, and on again romantic adventure that faith had had propelled me into. I'd go home to have my dinner after work, then clean up and cycle somewhere around five to six miles to be with the woman who had more control over me than I had over myself. And I find that an interesting comment as I now look back over my life. I cast no blame on Sybil for allowing myself to be placed in this vulnerable garden of thorns and roses. I say thorns and roses because that's the bed most of us have to lie in, in any kind of relationship, and you will see this more clearly as I take you with me through my life.

So as mentioned the romance was in full swing. On the very wet evenings I would throw my bike in the luggage compartment of the train, then cycle from Amiens Street Station to West Cabra. I could get pretty wet at times, but when you're young and fit love can just about override all obstacles. And it can be classed as a fire burning within you, and you never really knowing whether to feed it or deny it.

Eventually Sybil's parents didn't mind my staying there at the weekends. So I bought a wooden folding bed, and a small thin mattress to go with it. That saved me cycling home on a Friday and Saturday. So this became my new romantic venture until the time we got married. We decided to save for two years before that event. We'd go to the movies once a week, and save what money we could.

During the summer we cycled quite a bit and went swimming down at Sutton Beach The Hill of Howth was our favourite place. It was a lover's playground and that's what we used it for, as well as for exercise and walking. Sybil's mother and father were a nice couple, but mind you the mother tended to fight a lot with Sybil and her sister Eileen. The mother did all the cooking as the girls were not allowed near the stove. The real reason behind that I won't try to guess. All I will say it makes life that much harder on young women when they get married.

I always found Sybil's father to be a very jovial man. I'm not sure what religion he was, but he was not a Catholic as his wife was. The Catholic faith didn't bother him like it did my father. I know he wasn't wrapped in it, just let it be as it is. Along with the mother and the two girls we'd go to Mass on a Sunday, and when we got back their father would have a beautiful breakfast ready of bacon, fried eggs and fried bread waiting for us. I can't tell you in so many words just how much I enjoyed those breakfasts. They were cooked to perfection. His main hobbies were listening to music, especially opera, and walking.

Eventually the time came for us to marry. We booked a place in Torquay for a week for our honeymoon. We were married on a Friday at Baldoyle Church in 1955. Being Catholic we weren't allowed to eat meat on a Friday so it wasn't a very appetizing wedding breakfast. A few people commented on that, but it was what we had to do so we could take the ferry to Liverpool early in the afternoon.

I must say everything went well, and both our families

and friends gave us lots of loving support.

Then later in the early afternoon we caught the ferry to Liverpool to catch a train to London, and then on to Torquay. When we arrived at Anseys Manor we were very impressed with both the reception we got, and the place itself. What took our fancy most was the fact we could go swimming any time we liked. All you had to do was make your way down the beautiful garden through a gate at the bottom, and hey presto, you were on a lovely stony beach. We swam every morning before breakfast, and whenever the fancy took us. We also took a number of bus trips around that beautiful area. That was one place that will always linger in my memory.

What I forgot to mention was that we had put in an application for a corporation house in a place called St Anne's Estate in Raheny and our application had been accepted. We had been allocated a house in Fassaugh Ave, no 23. So the idea was to come back and stay with Sybil's parents who had now been allocated a house there themselves. Then we would buy some furniture and move in.

When we got back we were hit with a bomb shell. We found a letter waiting for us from the Dublin Corporation of Housing informing us that we were not entitled to a house. Well as you can imagine we were just about floored with anger and disappointment. So we wrote and told them that they had approved our application and had granted us a house, why the turnabout? Well I won't go into the details, for I'm sure by now that most of you know what kind of hypocritical excuses government departments like to evade the truth with. But when something, or someone throws stumbling blocks in the path of your future I believe from my past and present experiences that your mind is telling you 'Stay where you are and get swallowed up by it, or do something about it.' Well that's exactly what I did. My wife and her parents thought I was crazy. But I'm sure you are well aware of that by now. Anyway I went to see the Parish priest and put my case before him, along with the approved application I had received, and the letter that reversed it. About ten days later we received a letter to say we had been granted a house at 23 Fassaugh Avenue, Raheny. Well I can tell you we were over the moon, and back again. And besides getting the house, we were very glad to get away from Sybil's mother. I saw a side to her that had not shown itself before, or maybe, trying to be the peaceful guy I try to be, I didn't want to recognize it. I often wonder how many of us have been dropped into that experience, and failed to deal with it until it had done untold damage in some way or another.

So we bought a bedroom suite, a breakfast table and chairs, and a stove. That was all we could afford.

Then about three or four months later Sybil came home and informed me she'd had a row with her boss and had thrown her job in. I said, sympathizing with her, 'that's ok you'll easily get another one.' She was a very good shorthand typist. And to tell you the truth, I was just about fed up with her coming home and telling me all the problems she was having at work.

So our married life went on, but this time living on my wages of four pounds a week. It was a tight budget but I thought it would get better when she got a job. But that never happened. And I can say that is something that has always puzzled me to this day. She told me that she had never really got on with her mother, and I could understand that. But she was never open to mixing with other people like her sister Eileen. There seemed to be some kind of a dark shadow that was following her from her past. I remember quite clearly from one of our first meetings as we were walking along O'Connell Street when a guy drunk as a skunk nearly bumped into us, she gave a little scream and made me cross over to the other side of the road. She was petrified. She did tell me later in a roundabout way that her uncle who was a police sergeant, was not a man to be around when he was drunk.

After that I'll leave it to you. I never heard much about her side of the family. And after that episode I made sure she never came across my father when he was under the influence. And I'm sure you can gather from all this that my drinking days were now over.

My wife's father was a great friend of a Mr McHugh who owned a shop in Talbot St in the city. I don't remember his Christian name. At that stage in my life the seniors or the so called nobility were classified as Mr, Sir, or in certain circumstances, a pain in the neck. The social ladder is seldom gracefully climbed. Only

One Man has ever accomplished that, and He ended up on a Cross.

Mr McHugh's shop consisted of a variety of items tempting to both rich and poor alike. He sold washing machines, fridges, bicycles, mechanical scooters, toys and so on. Anyway the story goes like this. My father-in-law invited Mr McHugh, his wife, and their son and his wife to dinner one evening. Naturally we too were invited, and that was to seal a great friendship between Mr McHugh's son Ronnie, his daughter-in-law Emily, Sybil and me that was to last until we left Ireland. One Saturday they'd come to our place for dinner and the following week we'd go to their place. After dinner we'd play all kinds of card games and laugh and joke until around midnight. This went on until our children arrived. We also went to the movies, cycled and swam together. I remember that day so well when we all cycled to Portmarnock to go swimming on one of those really hot days that don't happen too often on Irish shores. We'd all enjoyed a good swim then gone back to lie on the beach to work up a bit of a tan before revisiting the water to cool down. About an hour later Ronnie started to complain that he wasn't feeling too well and one look at him told us why. Ronnie had very fair hair and skin that didn't take kindly to the sun.

We all got dressed quickly and after what seemed a never ending cycle ride for Ronnie we managed to get him home to our house, and put him in a cold bath to cool off. He was sick and sore for a few days after, but made a recovery thanks I believe to that bath the Good

Lord provided him with.

One of the highlights of our years together came about at Lent. Being of the Catholic persuasion, from Ash Wednesday to Easter Saturday we'd give up something we enjoyed, then on Easter Saturday make pigs of ourselves with whatever delicious food we could afford. Boy, did we enjoy those meals.

Through Ronnie, who worked in his father's shop, I got myself a scooter. I already had a James 150cc motorbike that I'd bought for seven pounds. There was no room for a pillion seat for my wife, so that influenced me to buy a scooter. Mind you, it didn't take much encouragement in those days to get me into debt. Once they brought out hire purchase in Ireland most of us became guinea pigs. I managed to keep up with my repayments on the scooter for about a year and a half even if I was late with the payments, but eventually, they became too much for me.

Without any fuss Mr McHugh said he'd sell it for me and we'd work out the difference. And he never he never asked me for another penny even though a little bird whispered in my ear that he'd lost out on the deal. He was a lot like my Uncle Harry in many ways.

My wife had a lot of fun on that scooter. Especially in the summertime when it didn't get dark until around ten thirty. We'd go off into the hills around Dublin picking blackberries. I'd never picked and eaten so many blackberries in all my life as I did in those days. And Sybil's parents and mine had their fair share. Let's say my venture into debt brought not only its worrying experiences but also some very memorable ones, including a few falls on the icy roads during winter.

My next little venture was an Austin A30. It was burning oil and the interior looked like a dozen cats had been trying to sharpen their claws on the upholstery and roof cloth, but for ten pounds beggars like me couldn't afford to be fussy. My wife said I was mad, but she didn't know me as well as I did. Anyway I patched up the upholstery and whipped a set of rings on it. It didn't completely cure the oil burning problem, but certainly improved it.

Now I had four wheels under me instead of two and no repayments to make. I was now able to take my wife's parents and my mother out for a few little outings. My father was quite happy to stay at home. Around this time our first baby had arrived. Peter was quite an amazing son. Quiet as a mouse. You wouldn't think there was a child in the house. I remember on one occasion he fell out of his cot, and not a tear he cried. Over three years later our daughter Alex arrived, then just over a year later Rachel was born.

By now the old A30 was on its last legs. So once again temptation raised its head in my direction. One of the guys in the office at Hammond Lane Foundry informed me that he was selling his Morris 1000. He wanted £60 for it. I took it for a test drive and fell in love with it. On that particular day I believe I was more in love with the car than with my wife. Maybe it was because it would do what I intended it to do, and would never ask how, where or why.

So once again I went back into debt, which for me was always only a matter of time. This car was a lot more reliable and luxurious than the old A30. It was a real pleasure to drive, and take my family out in.

Then came the first sad moment that most families must experience at some time or another, the death of one of them. I was well and truly in dreamland in the early hours of this particular morning when the sound of pebbles striking our bedroom window awoke me from my slumber. When I went to the half-open window I could see my brother Gerald who was calling me softly not to wake the neighbours. 'Terry could you come down to the house, Dad's dying.' My wife heard nothing, she could sleep through an earthquake. As she didn't breast feed, I got the job of bottle feeding our kids if they woke up in the early hours.

So I got up as quickly as I could telling my wife to stay and look after the kids. But when we arrived at Da's house he had passed away. When I went into the bedroom where he was lying I must say he looked very much at peace, but lacked that beautiful smile I still remember on his brother Harry's face as he lay in his coffin, which I have already mentioned. I'm not sure how long I stayed in that room with Da allowing the memories of the past to flow through my mind. I felt no real sense of sadness, but did feel a great sense of peace. I had to question myself on this. Could it have been that deep inside me I'd not fully forgiven him for what he'd done to the family and myself, and now with his passing from us he alone would have to make his peace with God. But there and then I made my final peace by kissing him on his forehead and quietly left the room to join the rest of the family. Though I felt much moved inside, I didn't shed a tear until about six months later. I was bending over the mantelpiece above the lounge fire when all of a sudden the memories flooded back and the tears ran down my cheeks like rain.

About four to five months before my daughter Rachel was due to come into the world I was informed that my firm would be moving premises to a suburb called Bluebell in the near future, which was going to be quite a distance for me to travel. And at the same time because of this and other factors, I was feeling very unsure as to what the future held for my family and myself.

Unknown to me the winds of destiny were about to steer me on a course that would bring great changes for both me, and my family. I had already conquered the first of the challenges I believe fate had in store for me, but now I was about to embark on that one that would eventually teach me what it's like to be a real human being.

Shortly after I got the news that my firm would be moving I took one of my infrequent strolls alone through the woods of Saint Ann's Estate on this particular Saturday morning after breakfast. My wife didn't like going off on my own so that's why I said infrequent. Anyway, as was on my stroll I got talking to this man who had just come back from New Zealand. He told me his mother was in poor health so he had to come back and look after her. What I call a really nice man. We got talking in depth about what life held for both of us. He would be my senior by twenty years or so, and was well travelled and seasoned in life so I listened to what he had to say. I told him of my situation and out of the blue he suggested to me that New Zealand would be a great place for me and my family. He'd lived there for quite a few years and was slowly filling my imagination of what a wonderful place it was. So from that moment on, though I didn't know its full implications, the seed was sown in my mind, and nothing was going to interfere with its growth.

A few days later we arranged to meet so he could give me some literature on New Zealand. He also gave me the address of New Zealand House in England where I could write to. 'They'll send you a list of job prospects' he informed me. So that's where I started from.

When I got home I told my wife and of course she said 'You're crazy.' And I said, 'Yes I'm well aware of that but nothing is going to stop me from giving this chance my best shot for the sake of my family and myself.' It took quite some time to convince her how serious I was, but in the meantime I started to get the ball rolling.

A while later I wrote to New Zealand House in England and informed them of my intentions. They wrote back saying they'd have one of their representatives visiting Dublin on a certain date to interview people who wanted to emigrate there to see me. Boy, did that push a few buttons in the uplifting department for me. The very thought of experiencing another adventure in my life filled me with those same prospects I had when I escaped the clutches of my father and joined the R.A.F. It was as though fate was repeating itself, but this time I was no longer a free agent. I now had a family to support with no idea of what the future held for us. I must admit that all sorts of chills were running through my mind as I tried to envisage the prospects that lay ahead. We'd have very little in the way of money when we arrived in this new country, but deep down inside in my gut I knew this had to be the right choice.

In the meantime another bundle of joy arrived to join our family.

Rachel made us a family of five. Now I could start planning for the next big move if all went according to plan. About a month later I got a letter from New Zealand House that I was to be interviewed in Jury's Hotel on a certain date. The day arrived for my interview and with my heart in my mouth, something like that time when I was interviewed for the R.A.F. But this time the circumstances were far more involved because of those who depended on me. I placed my cards on the table once again, and bingo I hit the jackpot for the second time. The gentleman who interviewed me was a real nice guy. He must have seen the green sense of apprehension written all over my face, and my eagerness to take this big step in my life. So my interviewer filled in a form with all my details and some references a few friends had given me. Later I received a letter from New Zealand House informing me that my family and I were eligible to emigrate there, so all systems were go as soon as I found a sponsor. Alternatively we could pay our own way there. The gentleman who interviewed me gave me a list of firms that I could write to that might be willing to sponsor us. I wrote to three of them enclosing a reference from my boss Mr O'Brien, and the first to come up with the goods was South Auckland Motors in Otahuhu. They said they would be willing to fly us out on a certain date, meet us at the airport in Whenuapai and take us to a motel in a place called Papatoetoe. They'd pay two weeks rent in advance which would allow us time to find somewhere to live. There was one stipulation with this package. I would have to stay with the firm for two years. Well that I thought wasn't a problem for what was on offer, so I promptly wrote back accepting their offer. We put our house on the market for £2,500 and left the rest to providence. In the back of my mind that old saying came up 'Do it not because you must, but because it gives birth to a new creation.'

I had kept my mother informed of our intentions. She being the mother was right behind me. She said I will miss you and the children, but I admire you for taking such a big step as this. May God go with you.

With no disrespect to my wife the relationship between her and my family was a very low frequency. I will go into that a little later.

Rachel was only a few weeks old now, so you can

imagine my state of mind as I waited with a great sense of anxiety for the confirmation date to fly out to New Zealand, and for the sale of the house. Being an impetuous individual, once my mind is set on doing something I am inclined to throw caution to the wind and hope it doesn't blow back in my face. Speaking for myself which is all any of us can do, committed to constant change without too much deliberation, I believe I am fulfilling God's purpose for me, but what God has to say about that I'll have to wait to find out.

About six weeks later I received a letter from South Auckland Motors confirming the date they would fly us out to New Zealand.

Shortly after that I found someone to take the house off our hands. Even though we didn't get the full asking price, everything seemed to be falling into place very nicely. I then arranged to have our little Morris Minor shipped out six weeks before we were due to leave because my friend who had put the idea into my mind about emigrating there told me that it was very necessary to have a car there. And more so with a family.

Three weeks before we were due to fly out, I got another letter from South Auckland Motors to say they couldn't fly us out for at least another three months. They were very apologetic about it.

Well that was a kick in the arse if ever there was one. We were committed to moving out of the house on the date we were due to fly out, now we would have to find somewhere furnished to live until our new flight was confirmed. We had already pre-sold our furniture, and whatever else wasn't feasible to take with us.

I wouldn't dream of putting any pressure on my mother, or any of my brothers to put us up till we were due to fly out. So I said to my wife there is only one course of action open to us, we must pay our own way out. She said that will not leave us with enough money for a deposit on a house. I said then we'll just have to take pot luck. This didn't all come about for nothing. And when you reach the point of no return, what future is there in turning back.

So she agreed, and I really believe that was what faith had already planned to give us a deeper sense of freedom, and at the same time, test our ability to cope with having less in our pocket.

Undiscovered character is manifested in moments such as these, or lost in them, and whatever I owe to my predecessors and those who suffer through no fault of their own, then I hope in some way this is my way of saying thanks to them, and to God.

So off we went to the travel agent and they came up with a figure of £1,350. My wife drew me aside and said again that won't leave us with enough for a deposit on a house. I said again we'll just have to take pot luck. I won't tell you what she said, but she did agree in the end. So I told the travel agent that I would have to write to South Auckland Motors and give them a date when we could fly out to make sure that suited them. I received there reply over a week later and that was fine. Just get the travel agent to let them know what time our flight would arrive, and they would have someone to meet us.

Now it was only a matter of time before we were on our way to be challenged to a new way of life. But I also knew in my heart and soul that whatever changes this new lifestyle would bring, a part of me would remain in this land of Saints and Scholars. The combination of generosity, music, humour and its timeless sense of myth and spiritual values are great gifts that my country has given to the rest of the world. Somewhere in the back of my mind I felt I would come back one day and revisit that part of my soul that I was leaving behind. And how right that turned out to be as you will see for yourself as you read on.

My great sense of sadness at that particular time was having to leave my lovely mother and brothers behind. My sister Ann had already emigrated to Canada. I loved my mother dearly. No son I felt had a better one. But she was right behind me in my decision because that was the type of person she was.

My wife's father had passed away about a year before we left.

They had moved into a Corporation house like ours, just a few streets away shortly after we were married, but her mother could not afford to keep up the repayments. We invited her to live with us.

Unfortunately she was not an easy women to get on with. I came home from work one day to find my wife very upset and in tears because of her. I tried to smooth things out, but it got out of control and I had to say to her 'If you can't accept our hospitality without causing trouble, I must ask you to leave.' She said 'I don't have to stay with you, I'll go and live with my daughter Eileen.' Eileen and her husband Hugh had a house not far from us in Saint Ann's Estate. Next day she moved in with them, much to my delight I have to say. Mind you that didn't last all that long which didn't surprise me. They moved to England. I often thought to myself what a wonderful favour she did for them. They did very well for themselves in England. They're both dead now, but I visited them on several occasions and we would have some laughs over it. After they left the mother moved in with her sister.

When the day came for the first stage of our big adventure all my family came to see us off, and after a lot of hugging, laughter and tears we boarded the flight to Heathrow to connect with our flight to New Zealand. After a six hour delay we were on our way. I can't remember much about the flight because we were busy looking after the children's needs and trying to get some sleep. I hardly slept the night before because of the build-up of emotions that kept running through my mind. But I do remember how good the children were during the whole trip, and how we were all cared for. When we stopped at Darwin to refuel we were checked over by the medical people there and they found that my wife's vaccination for smallpox hadn't taken properly, so she had to be vaccinated again. That was a bit upsetting as you can gather, but like anything else of that nature it got sorted out. The flight from Darwin to Sydney was quite amazing for me. We had complete darkness on one side of the plane, and a lovely sprinkling of sunshine on the other. I kept going from one side to the other and chatting to other people about it.

Our next stop was Sydney, then on to Whenuapai Airport where we were met by a representative from South Auckland Motors. The representative welcomed us, and took us to a motel in Papatoetoe which was to be our starting point in New Zealand. He told us that his company had paid two weeks' rent in advance which would hopefully give us enough time to find somewhere to live. We'd only been there for five days when we learned that our car had arrived so I very quickly collected it after it had been inspected, and the battery charged. I was then told I'd have to obtain a New Zealand driver's licence. I promptly arranged to be tested and passed without any bother.

Now that we had the car we started to evaluate the rental accommodation situation. We thought the South side of Auckland was nice enough in its own way, but felt something was missing. We were used to growing up by the sea, so after searching through the map of Auckland, hey presto the North Shore beckoned to us like a lake would to a flock of ducks. Straight away, before we'd even crossed the Harbour Bridge we were hooked. It was the ocean with its lovely beaches that drew us to its bosom. We drove over and cruised around the fabulous beaches which confirmed the picture of where we wanted to live. I popped into one of the dairies and asked where I could get a paper that listed houses or flats to rent, so they provided me with the local rag. We found a two bedroom flat to let for seven pounds a week on Seaview Road in Milford and off we went to Barfoot and Thompson's to state our case. Being new in the country we didn't have any references, and even tougher than that, we had three young children. But they were very decent and offered us a two bedroomed flat on a trial basis. We must have well and truly passed the test for we were there for three years.

I had now started working at South Auckland Motors and was not impressed with having to drive backwards and forwards over the bridge five days a week. Then out of the blue I spotted an advertisement in the local rag from a firm calling themselves Lyon Ford in Hurstmere Road looking for a motor mechanic. I gave them a ring from a call box as we couldn't afford a phone.

A couple of days later, around seven in the evening, a man called Hal Burt from Lyon Ford called around to see me. He was the Manager there. After exchanging a few pleasantries I showed him my references from my firm in Dublin. He offered me the job right on the spot. There was something about him I took to the moment I met him. I can't say in all fairness that I meet too many people that I find really genuine, but he was one of them.

I told him that I would have to give two weeks' notice to the firm I was working with, but that was no problem because we had paid our own way out. I was over the moon about getting this job so near where we were living, plus the fact I wasn't happy working at South Auckland Motors. It had nothing to do with the conditions or any sense of unfriendliness. I just got this feeling that I didn't fit in there. The wonderful thing about all this was being free to go wherever I wanted. By making the sacrifice of paying our own way to New Zealand we were tied to nothing and no-one.

When I handed in my notice the boss was not too pleased. He told me I'd have to pay back the money for the motel he had paid for us when we arrived, which I thought was fair so I said I would do it over a number of weeks. What little money we had left had been spent on necessities to furnish our two bedroom flat and other bits and pieces.

GLENFIELD

Step by step we started to adjust to our new surroundings with both excitement and bewilderment. Exciting because Milford Beach was just down the road from where we were living, and in less than a week after we moved in at the weekends we were swimming, bewildering because we were the only ones in the water. I got the impression the locals on the beach thought we were something in the line of freaks. It was now late October 1965. Mind you I could well understand that when we became acclimatised, but at that time we were still very much greenhorns. Rachel was in a bassinet and well protected from the sun. Alex had a pair of frilly togs, and Peter, my wife and I wore our swimming gear. I'm sure the locals were saying to themselves 'Bloody mad immigrants,' but boy did we enjoy that first swim and all the others to follow. I didn't have to teach my children to swim. They taught themselves believe it or not

As we didn't have any real home maintenance to obstruct our leisure time, most weekends in the summer we'd take off for the day to explore some part of the countryside. I'd say we covered quite a bit of the North Island in the first three years that we lived in our flat in Milford. Our little car was a real blessing. If I have done one thing worthwhile in my life, then it had to be taking that car to New Zealand.

Things settled down very well for me working at Lyon Ford. Our boss Jerry Lyon was a real gentleman. I remember on one occasion I removed the engine from his V8 to put a set of rings on the pistons. I laid the pistons so as they would go back in the same order that they came out in, then fitted the rings and replaced them back in the same order. Then I took the engine block outside and washed it, then brought it back and re-fitted the pistons. When I started the motor up after I had assembled everything I heard this strange sound. That was a very worried moment I can tell you. Then all of a sudden with the help of a keen ear it was suggested to me that I had not put the pistons back in their right order. Then all of a sudden I realised I must have put the engine block the other way round after I had washed it. So as fast as I could I reversed the whole procedure and every turned out fine. Everyone as you can well guess had a good laugh at my expense, but nothing else came of it. But it bothered me to the extent that a few days after I went and knocked on Mr Lyon's door, went in and apologised for what had happened. He said 'Terry, sit down and have a coffee with me.' Then he asked me how things were going for me and my family. Then he completely let me off the hook by saying, 'The man who never made a mistake never made anything.' I thanked him and left his office in a lighter frame of mind than before I went in.

With only two months until the time when we would be eligible to use the children's allowance to purchase a section and build a house I contacted a representative from Beasley Homes. He put together a plan for a three bedroom boomerang shaped house to be built on an almost quarter acre section in James Street, Glenfield. It was a right-of-way section and very steep, but with a bank account like ours we couldn't afford to be choosy. But believe you me, I was very grateful that the good Lord had seen it fit to provide us with another house. And also what I didn't realise was that this time He was going to make me suffer for my past sins, then lead me to that road that would change my life forever should I choose to follow it.

My wife was not very happy about moving from Milford. Nor was she convinced this was the right move. That took a bit of working on but I feel God put in His tuppence worth that paid for the candles I'd lit in the church to change her mind!

While we were waiting for the house to be completed we would drive up there every so often to see how things were progressing.

I found that very exciting. And the thought of having a place of our own even more exciting.

But I will say I did enjoy the experience of living in Milford. There was a lovely couple who lived in the end flat who had become very attached to our children. And I must say Peter, Alex and Rachel never gave us a moment's trouble, keeping to the area of the garden we lived in. I will always be grateful to them for that among other things. I well remember one Christmas we bought a double swing for them and they used to have so much fun on it.

Well the time had arrived to move into our new home. So I fitted an old tow bar to the car, hired a trailer and after a lot of forwards and backwards we moved into our new house in early November of 1968, with a great sense of enthusiasm and speculation as to what the future might hold for us. I try to tread as carefully as I can when I involve my family's feelings, or any others for that matter, as I walk and stumble my way to meet my Maker.

We were given two options regarding stretching the money to build the house. We could have ranchslider doors fitted in the lounge, or a one car garage underneath the house. We decided on the garage — that turned out to be a very sensible choice even when it flooded during our first heavy downpour. I won't go into the complaining department by saying what should have been done to avoid this. The fact was we were very green Irish goslings when it came to being taken advantage of. We couldn't afford a drainlayer to stop the water coming into the garage, but I'm not going to tell you how I fixed the problem. We Irish have gotten into so much trouble giving our secrets away for nothing and look where it's got us! And to be honest there is another reason, I might get hung for it.

If you'd like to hear more about the crazy rough and wonderful years we spent in Glenfield with the kids growing up, I will let them tell you. I need to get this rewritten story of mine finished before I go to Canada with my daughter Rachel to visit my sister Ann on the 2nd of July (in 2014).

Now I am going to skip forward to 1985. I was now fifty five years of age. Not fifty three which I mentioned in my last book because of mixed up communication with those who tried to help me. Not their fault, but mine. This time what you read is straight from the steering wheel in my hand apart from it being proofread.

Even though I didn't know it at the time, the turning point of my life started with my breakdown in 1985. I woke up on this particular morning feeling as though my body had completely given up on me. It was the most horrible feeling of hopelessness to ever touch my being. I could hardly move my limbs, and my body felt as if all the blood had been drawn from it. I asked my wife to send for the doctor. In those days the doctor would pay you a visit without too much bother. Anyway the doctor came and checked me out. He gave me an injection and told me to come and see him if things were not improving. Well, about half an hour after the injection I felt worse. It was now coming up to Christmas and the weather was quite warm. Later I dragged myself out to the back door steps and sat in a chair completely demoralized. I felt as if I was living in a void. In my shattered state of mind I found it hard to relate to anything except anxiety.

Being the only breadwinner of the family sent all sorts of questions flooding into my head, though that didn't come into focus that day. But as time went on and I felt no improvement I managed to drive myself down to see my doctor and ask him if I should see a psychiatrist. He didn't think that was necessary and prescribed some tablets for me to take. Well with no disrespect to him they turned out to be no better than a lollipop for a toothache. My wife had rung my workplace to let them know I was unwell and could be off work for a while. They very kindly said that they would keep my wages on, and hoped I'd soon be well. I knew I had two weeks' holidays to come, and two weeks' sick pay so that would give me some breathing space.

Four days later feeling no better I arranged to see a psychiatrist. After the first consultation he put me on tablets called Atavan which I eventually became hooked on for close to five years. Yes, they helped me back to a certain stage in my life so that I could go back to work again, but at the same time left me with a false sense of security. When I went back to work a month later I could no longer concentrate on the mechanical side of things. My confidence in that department was completely shattered. So they very kindly gave me other tasks to do. I had no problem with driving, so I became a run-around driver collecting parts, taking customers home who left their cars to be serviced, and also being dropped off in certain places to collect used cars to be serviced and cleaned up for sale on our used car yard. I must say that I enjoyed going down the Island and driving these cars back to our firm. I guess the main reason for that was I had no real responsibility on my shoulders. Dealing with the aftermath of my breakdown had left me very vulnerable to responsibility, other than the lighter side of things I had to deal with.

About two years later my teeth started to crumble. I had to have them all taken out. Looking forward to having a set of dentures to solve my problem, there was another nasty shock in store for me. I just couldn't tolerate them in my mouth! I had another pair made up for me about six months later with the same result. So for appearance's sake I had to tolerate them when I was working, but I must say with great difficulty. As soon as I left work they were out. My wife wasn't impressed either. Mind you our relationship had been showing signs of deterioration ever since my breakdown. She found that hard to deal with, and I can understand that to a certain degree. But at the same time my wife was not an easy woman to live with. I feel it had a lot to do with her childhood. She felt insecure when it came to dealing with people, and because of that we became a very isolated family in regards to the children or myself having friends to come and visit us, or we them.

Then at the age of fifty-eight I could barely pass any urine. I was sent to see a specialist who recommended that I have an operation to solve the problem. I said to myself 'this getting old can be a real bitch at times. I wonder what's next on the list.'

Please bear with me as I pass all this doom and gloom onto you about my life but it is necessary for you to understand the depths I had to go to bounce back to where I needed to be. Sometimes you have to go to within a hair's breadth of hell just to find out it's not where you want, or need to be.

Anyway, I was now getting to the bottom of the tunnel with just a little way to go: 'little by little faith comes to us with its own lessons.'

I had my operation and came home a few days later with my pipe unclogged. I was told to drink plenty of water. About six hours later my water works closed down completely and I had to be rushed into Auckland Hospital almost screaming like a stuffed pig. Mind you I have never heard a stuffed pig screaming but the terminology seems to fit the picture. I can't remember too much about the time lapse between my getting out of the ambulance and have the catheter inserted into my bladder, but boy, the relief. My gratitude goes out to the ambulance driver and the person who inserted the catheter, and all I can say is God bless you both.

About five hours later I started to get terrible pains in my stomach, and I mean terrible pains. They took me for an x-ray and gave me all sorts of tests and pain relief tablets but nothing would take the pain away. Around five o'clock in the morning I started to feel a strong tingling sensation running down both arms. All of a sudden it dawned on me, I was experiencing withdrawal symptoms as it was about sixteen hours since I'd last taken the medication my psychiatrist had prescribed for me, and I was on quite a high dosage. I called for a nurse and told her what I believed was my problem. I asked her to ring my wife and have her bring the tablets in as soon as possible.

They duly arrived, I took one, and everything seemed to settle down again. However it was from that moment on that the full implication of my addiction dawned on me. And that realisation painted a very scary picture for me. I knew there and then it was not going to get any better, only worse as the years crept by.

So that became the turning point in my life. The will to survive had once again thrown down the gauntlet, but this time it brought a big wake-up call. The fog that had clouded my brain for so long was slowly starting to lift even though I wasn't yet fully aware of it. I now sensed a new me evolving and realised that I couldn't rely on anyone else to get me out of the hole I had reluctantly put myself in. With God's help and my own perseverance I could claw my way back to becoming a real human being again. I knew it was not going to be easy, but at the same time where else is there to go when you hit rock bottom. You're left with only two choices. Either you stay there and slowly die, or you climb back up and get on with the reason why you were born.

And that, I now fully believe, is to live life to its greatest potential.

Happiness can be now, later or never. It's just a question that is answered or remains unanswered.

Shortly after my operation I was made redundant at my work place. I was in a union at the time and was informed that I would get some kind of redundancy package. That fell by the wayside and I wasn't mentally strong enough to pursue the matter at that time. But God never closes one door without opening another. I found myself a job as a vehicle tester in a testing station in Sunnybrae Road. I had only fifteen months to go till my sixtieth birthday and had my sights set on retirement. The government superannuation would be available to me then. I was slowly weaning myself off my drug addiction. I was that determined to get off them that I read for hours and listened to music in the lounge, rather than take what would give me an easy night's sleep. My wife was not behind me in this, but she did not understand my need to become more like a human being again. And the very thought of this was giving me the strength to do it. I also knew that a lower income would mean cutbacks in our ordinary day-to-day living, but we did now own the house so I wasn't in the least worried about it. Peace of mind should never have a price tag on it. What makes us human is our willingness to be challenged for what we believe in.

I won't go into detail about the fifteen months I spent at the Testing Station but it was a hard old slog because of the long hours and the abuse I got from some people when I failed to pass a car for its Warrant of Fitness. In those days we didn't have the same privacy to carry out our task that they have today. The owners' watchful eyes told you they were holding their breath as you inspected their vehicles. But in all fairness to the job, and to the people I had to deal with, I had no real problems other than a number of ear bashings.

I didn't tell my wife of my intention to fully retire when I was sixty as I knew it would not go down very well with her. And I could see that the gap in our marriage was slowly widening. I well remember those times I used to spend hours in the garage dreaming for the need of someone who could accept me for what I was, instead telling me what I should be.

Then a stroke of good fortune fell our way. Mind you my wife didn't think so. I met a friend of a guy I used to work with in Lyon Ford and mentioned to him that I had quite a big section on our property. Jim had dropped in a few times to see me. Anyway this guy was looking to build a house on a section that wasn't going to cost him too much. Nothing new about that. So he came up to see me and had a look at the section. Then about a month later he offered me eighteen thousand dollars for half the section. He had seen the plans and checked it all out. Well to a poor old guy like myself it was like winning a prize in the lotto. I said 'I'll talk to my wife and get back to you.' So I told her and the response was not good at all. But I had been through all this before as I'm sure you're well aware of by now. So she finally agreed, and not too long after we got a cheque for nine thousand dollars each. I bought another car, and she bought one. Now I was free to do my own thing.

It wasn't till until the week before I was sixty that I informed my wife of my decision to retire. She said 'how are we going to manage?' I said 'well maybe you could find a job, I can't handle it any more.' And I meant that in all sincerity. I was really worn out. Trying to keep the house and section maintained, as well as working was slowly driving me into the ground.

Anyway she found herself a job so that I thought would be good for her. It didn't turn out that way, but I won't say why.

My big day came on the 21st of October 1998, and unknown to my wife I celebrated it with a can of Lion Red beer with a mischievous smile on my face. The very thought of not taking orders from someone else, and doing near enough to what I wanted to do was slowly bringing back a lot of strength into my life. Mind you I was still married so I couldn't do exactly what I wanted to do, but for the moment half a loaf was better than no bread at all.

My son Bernard was the only one living with us now, and he was working so there was no concern for me in that department. I must tell you what he did for me about six months before, for which I will always be grateful. I had come in one evening after cutting the grass, made myself a cup of tea, and sat down to relish it along with a cigarette. Bernard was sitting at the other end of the table. Then I noticed him trying to brush away the fog of smoke that was heading towards him. That was enough to get the message across to me. I'd never given any thought to my children as I'd smoked in their presence over all those years. It hit me like a rocket out of the blue. What a selfish bastard I'd been. None of my children smoked and that was all the evidence I needed. I stopped smoking that very day and not one cigarette has touched my lips since.

When I thought back over the years about my children having to endure the smoke from both my wife's and my own cigarettes I can tell you in no uncertain terms how guilty I felt about it. My wife didn't come to the same conclusion, but that's another story best left unwritten.

So I was retired — what do you do with time on your hands? I had the usual work to do around the place but was in no hurry to do that. I needed both an inside and outside challenge and an inside challenge in my life. I needed to be involved with people, doing something worthwhile. So I took myself off to the North Shore Hospital to see the Chaplain and asked him if I could be of service there. I gave him a rundown on my background, and he suggested I could start by visiting some of the elderly people who were recovering from one thing or another, and then after a while report to him on how I was coping. He said 'I'll put you in touch with those who need a kind ear to listen to whatever they might have to say, but don't get too involved or you'll do no good to them or yourself.' Enthusiasm is one thing, but how you go about it is another.

I was only there about a month when one of the men I visited told me that he was afraid of dying. I didn't pursue it, just tried to comfort him. But a little later he told me why. He said 'Terry, I've never done anything I consider worthwhile with my life. It's been far too sheltered.' I can't remember how well or otherwise I responded to that with the little experience I had so far accumulated, but I will say for my benefit, it was another wake up call. It was as if those words of his had been directed at me. I never saw this man again but promised myself that I was going to do something with the remaining years of my life, and to date I believe in some way I have kept that promise to myself.

About a week later I was taking one of the elderly patients to the chaplain's Sunday service when I noticed a number of other people being wheeled in. What caught my eye was how handicapped they were, and my sense of compassion strayed immediately in their direction. It was as if God was again opening another door for me. The next morning I talked to the Chaplain about the direction my feelings were pointing me in, and he said, 'Terry, I believe God has a few plans in store for you. All you have to do is let yourself flow along with them.' At that particular time I had no idea of the deeper meaning behind those words because I was only on the fringe of leaving the prison I had unintentionally built for myself.

Around four days later I approached the person in charge of Ward 11 as it was called at that time, and asked if I could be of some use in this department. After a little run down on where I was coming from, I was told that they would give me a trial run to see if I could cope with helping out in some way. Well I must admit I was all at sea at first, along with all my enthusiasm. But as time went on things started to fall into place as the weeks went by. I became very involved with a man called Graham Grace whose photograph will give you a better picture of him that my description could. I never met his family, but obtained permission from them to take a photo of him.

Graham was the first of all those lovely people who helped put me back on my feet. My life would have been so much less without him in it. He couldn't talk, but he didn't need to. Just the way Graham looked at you and smiled was a sheer joy in itself. I'd feed him at lunch time, and sometimes we'd have a few upsets, but that was all part of the experience. Sometimes I'd do a few wheelies round the ward and he loved that. Mind you I did get told off once for a close call so I was more careful after that. I fed some of the others, but in the two years I spent there Graham was the one I spent most of my time with. As for the nurses, no words in the whole of the dictionary could express their devotion to those beautiful people in ward 11.

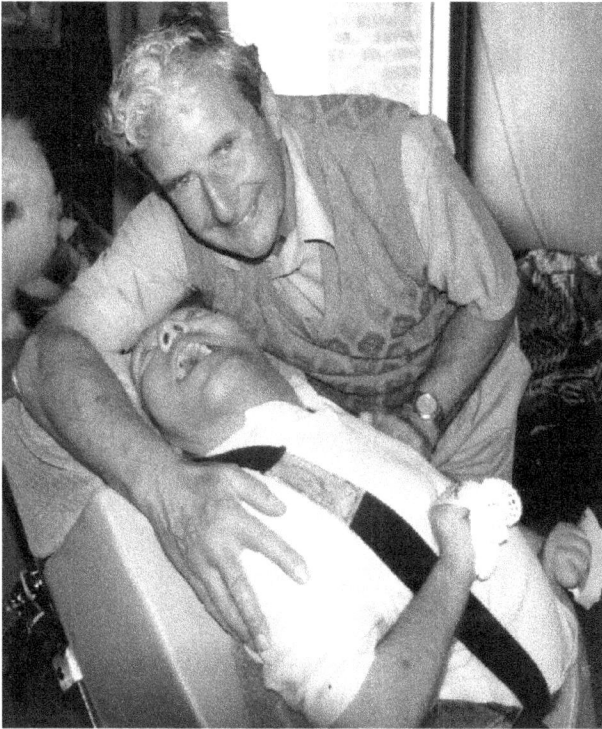

Graham, my laughing mate

DUBLIN

In May 1989 I received a letter from my brother Ken asking me if I would come home to visit my remaining family in Dublin. He said 'you'll have somewhere to stay, and we'll give you some spending money.' My brother Gerald had a three bedroomed house with only himself living there. It had been the family house, so Gerald could be classed as the last of the Mohicans. I could have said the Robinsons to reign there, but that sounded a bit dull. This house has to be one for the books. It was the only house we didn't get kicked out of because my father was actually in the process of buying it when he died. That's a little bit of history the Robinsons will always relish.

And I have to tell you how this letter from Ken had it its beginning. About four months earlier my sister Ann, by now living in Canada, came to see us for a quick visit. She and her husband Tom were on their way to a wedding in Australia so they decided to pay us a visit. It was wonderful after all those years to see my sister again. We never had any kind of a real family life with my father's drinking, so this was something special. And Tom her husband was a real nice guy. Anyway Ann being a very astute woman spotted the weakness in my character, and sensed that all was not well with my marriage. So when she got back to Canada she passed her feelings onto my family in Dublin. And that in turn brought about this letter from my brother Ken which helped to turn my whole life around as you will see.

I talked to my daughter Rachel about Ken's offer and she arranged for her husband-to-be to lend me the money for a one way airfare to Dublin. She said, Dad, this is just what you need. Rachel herself hadn't long been home from visiting my family in Dublin, and she had the time of her life there. The family had fallen in love with her the moment she arrived for she is a true Irish Colleen with all the trimmings to go with it.

When I told my wife about Ken's offer, she said 'I won't be going.' I said to myself 'how right you are!' The only member of my family my wife had taken to was my mother, and even that was low key. Whenever I slipped down after work to have one of those lovely mother and son moments, and give her a few bob when I had it, I'd have to tell a few lies when I got home to explain why I was late.

I was now starting to get within reach of ending my drug addiction and was starting to feel quite proud of myself knowing I'd soon be completely in charge of my mind and body, to a degree I had never really been before.

Now the timing was just about as perfect as one could get it. I'd given up trying to wear my dentures but didn't even give it a second thought. I don't need them to tell you who I really am. If people have to put on an appearance to please others then I feel very sorry for them. In many circumstances we really only suffer because of the picture in our minds. So with the bit between my gums I flew back to the land I was born in.

On the first stage of my flight I fell into conversation with the two women beside me, I said, don't expect a big smile from me. Then I related a little of my bad experience with dentures. They both said they'd never have noticed it if I hadn't mentioned it. That was a boost for my morale. Very discretely in the course of our conversation they asked me to share something of myself. I guess my new found sense of enthusiasm must have aroused their curiosity. I gave them an honest run down of where I was coming from, and all the excitement that was building up within me at the thought of seeing my Irish family in Dublin again. I can't remember where they were bound for.

As we flew over the mainland of England memories of the days I spent in the R.A.F. began to circle through my mind. It was as though I was revisiting the past. What pleasant memories they were. It was a long time since I felt as happy as I did at that moment. And what made it so worthwhile was the fact I was no longer under orders from anyone. I was now a free agent only responsible to God and myself. Nothing but death or some kind of immobilization could stop me now. Jesus had already paid the price for my freedom. All I had to do was gather it in and lay the results at His Feet.

After passing through customs at Heathrow I boarded a plane for Dublin. I was quickly into conversation with one of my countrymen sitting beside me, but can't remember what we talked about other than my telling him how excited I was about my homecoming. As we approached Dublin Airport I was really choked up with indescribable emotions as you can well imagine. I was about to land in a country that not only gave my mother the labour pains of my birth, but gave me the pain I had to go through from childhood to manhood. That was only a momentary recollection however. Things were becoming less and less clouded in my mind's eye as the new days of my life unfolded before me. A great sense of adventure was taking place inside of me as I was beginning to realise that I had many possibilities to build on. But, mind you, that also brought its own scary moments of doubt with it. At the age of sixty there was no way I could be classed as a knight in shining armour. No teeth to give you that amorous smile, no great gift of self-confidence, and a mind and body pretty scarred because of my incompleteness. Now, however, I had a chance to try to redeem myself, and as you read on I think you'll see I gave it my best shot.

As the big emotional moment arrived, and with moist eyes, I walked out to the arrival to be greeted by my three fabulous brothers Gerald, Ken and Tony. As we stood locked in each other's arms I knew the only thing that had changed for us was the years, and not our love for one another. For me this reunion went far deeper than I am capable of putting into words, or expressing in any other way. It was as if I'd had to go through hell to reach Heaven.

We all went back to Gerald's house in Saint Anns Avenue Raheny, and reminisced over a cup tea, the life-saving drink that I believe God in His wisdom bestowed upon the Irish. We could go to confession and have our souls saved, but without a cup of tea we would not have a soul to save.

A little later Ken and Tony went off to work, so Gerald and I carried on from there. Gerald never married so we just had each other to amuse and we certainly did just that.

Tony dropped in the next day after work and gave me a cheque for fifteen hundred pounds. That nearly blew me away. I'd never had so much wealth to myself in all my born days. There was five hundred from Tony, five from Ken, and five from my sister in Canada. That was another very emotional time for me because of all the love it brought with it. Not just the money, but the great thoughtfulness it expressed.

With Tony – Brothers Forever

In no time at all I was given a taste of something I'd long forgotten about - Irish entertainment. My brothers and their wives took Gerald and myself to a show in Clontarf Castle, and what an evening it was. This had been a long time coming, I thought to myself, but it was well worth the waiting for. That evening I felt a great weight being lifted from my shoulders. Those years, hours, and moments that had been such a drag on my whole system were fast disappearing and I vowed there and then that I would never let them back in my life again. I'd been living in a fool's paradise, letting life pass me by. Well it was all go after that. Terry was still very much alive and well, that was just the incentive I needed.

SAINT ANN'S PITCH AND PUTT

About two weeks later, with my adrenalin perched at the top of the scale, I wrote to my wife to tell her, as tactfully as I could, that our marriage was over. I must admit that there was a certain amount of Dutch courage involved here because I was so far away from the lady whom I had let rule the roost for quite some time. I now had become aware with each passing day that I was becoming more capable of dealing with anything that stood in the way of my new found freedom. And I offer no excuse for allowing myself to be dragged down to such a low level of life, nor do I blame my wife. I was a victim only because I allowed myself to become one. If you live with someone who puts you down in one way or another, are you not a participant? If two people can't grow together in some way, they shouldn't be together.

On two occasions my brother Ken took me to Bray Golf Club where he used to be a member. The first time I walked around as his caddy to watch him play I was very impressed indeed. If I remember correctly he was playing on a five handicap. Golf was a big part of his life, and though I didn't know it at the time, I too was about to be bitten by the golf bug. It was slowly working its way into my bloodstream just watching him play. Ken must have sensed it because a week later he took me out to a pitch and putt course. I was well reimbursed that day for caddying for him. And not only did he treat me to a lovely meal the day I caddied for him, but he also introduced me to a very palatable drink called Bushmills and Red Lemonade which I really enjoyed after living all those years in a house with no beer just to please my wife.

What put the crowning glory on all this was not having to drive. I just about always finished up three drinks or more ahead of Ken. I was now starting to live the life of Reilly. I have never found out just who Reilly was, but I've been led to believe he enjoyed what he did, and that's good enough for me.

The second time I was about to caddy for Ken the rain made its presence felt, so discretion being the better part of valour, I settled for a nice cosy armchair in the clubhouse, topped up with something to eat and drink. And being in Ireland I knew I'd always find someone to talk to.

Ken was playing with a good friend who'd brought his new lady friend with him. The scene was set for a new learning experience for this lady and me while the others pursued their game. Our conversation got off to a flying start because of our eagerness to be open and honest with each other. I'd now reached that place in my life where I could unreservedly expose my strengths and weaknesses without being afraid of how other people would accept them. Looking back, I realise I'd come to terms with the fact that I had a message to leave behind when my time came to depart this life.

This lady had been through her own hell and had just recently met this new man in her life. A lovely tender relationship was developing because life and living had taught them both that sex without understanding each other's need for space and respect would only take them back down into that dark alleyway from whence they'd come. The ocean of passion has drawn many a soul to its own hell. The lady said they were taking plenty of time to really try to get to know and understand each other. With enough space for each of us to be what we need to be, and with the recognition of who and what we are, there is every chance that we can grow together. Otherwise stagnation can rear its ugly head.

We talked in depth with no holds barred about what affects both men and women in relationships. That was the most refreshing and enlightening conversation I've ever had with someone of the opposite sex. I have no idea of the outcome of that relationship, but at the very least it had to be off to a good start.

A week later Ken took me to a Pitch and Putt golf course for my first lesson. He lent me three clubs from his back-up golf set. That evening the die was cast for a new addiction in my life, and though I was to find it frustrating at first it was a lot healthier for my system than those tablets I'd been taking for so many years.

When I got back to Gerald's house I told him I'd found a new love in my life. He said, 'Well she's not staying here in my house.' Gerald had been jilted when he was about twenty and never let a woman get even close to his trousers after that. I told him what my new love was and he said, 'You've fallen on your feet. There's a pitch and putt course right here in Saint Ann's Estate so you will be able to play to your heart's content. Even better there are four old clubs in that cubby hole under the stairs. You could be on your way to stardom, but somehow I think you might have left it a bit late.'

For the next nine weeks, except for wet days, you'd find me doing battle with the pitch and putt course, sometimes even twice a day. For the first time which seemed like an eternity I was having the time of my life, and there was nearly always someone to play with which made it twice as entertaining along with the tips they gave me.

I can't remember one dull or boring day during the eleven weeks I spent with my family in Dublin — parties, family outings and all those trips Gerald took me down memory lane revisiting places we grew up in, rough as they may have been. All this, thanks to my brothers and sister who not only showed me a door I never thought was there, but also opened it for me. My cup had been filled to the brim and I'd tasted a wealth of experience and joy from every sip I took, for now I was in control of my life.

It was as though God was saying to me, 'Now that you're prepared to do something with your life you might just make the grade and be of some use to humanity. I know you're a bit of a fool but I suffer fools to come unto me.'

It was getting close to departure time so I decided I would fly to Canada to visit my sister and her family in

Toronto and spend three weeks there with them. I had enough money to cover the flights that would take me back to New Zealand, and some spending money for my latest enjoyable extra, a drop of the old dram. So on the evening of the day before I was due to fly out, Gerald and I took ourselves off to a pub in Raheny for a farewell toast. Boy, what a night it was. The liquor got to Gerald's brain quicker than it reached mine. He was always two or three drinks ahead of me. He had a lot more experience in that department than I had. But the one thing that stood out for me on that memorable evening, and still does to this very day, was Gerald sitting on a high bar stool giving me a lecture on how I'd let my wife control my life, and me very meekly saying with, 'You're so right Gerald, you're so right,' while all the time trying to keep a straight face as he stumbled through his somewhat incoherent speech, and all the strange faces he was making. Every time those special moments come back to me I just burst out laughing. As someone once said, we don't remember days, we remember moments.

When closing time came we both staggered the twenty minute walk back to Gerald's house. This would normally take us ten minutes, but I had to allow for the zigzagging and the times we stopped to discuss something that I'm sure wouldn't have made sense to anyone except the Good Lord Himself.

I bet He was saying to Himself, 'I've certainly got a couple of prize cuckoos down here.' Then again, even wise folk have to have their moments of foolishness otherwise how could they have become wise? God knows we Irish love making loopholes to escape from, and I've got a strong feeling that the English gentry were some of our best teachers.

It must have been close to midnight when we got home. After a cup of tea and a few cheese sandwiches the party really got started. Gerald got out all the old 78 records that he'd collected over the years and we sang and danced our way into the early hours of the morning, with a bottle of whisky to keep the show on the road.

I can't remember falling into bed, but that's where I was when Gerald woke me up around seven in the morning and he looking like something like the cat had reluctantly brought home and didn't know what to do with it. He said 'You've got one hour to get ready before Tony arrives to take you to the airport.' When he asked me how I was feeling, surprisingly enough I just felt a bit hazy I said, but was ready for my next adventure. The he said 'You must have inherited some of Dad's genes, so watch it or you may become the next drunk of the family. And for God's sake don't mention last night or I'll be in hot water.' That I thought was the last thing he need right now looking at him, but a cold shower might help.

Tony arrived and took us to the airport where we were joined by the rest of my family. After fond farewells, I flew out of Dublin to Heathrow to catch my flight to Toronto.

TORONTO, CANADA

As I settled into my favourite window seat on the plane and we flew out over the rooftops of London I felt on top of the world about the changes that were taking place in my life. The mere thought of it brought tears to my eyes. They talk about being a born-again Christian, well I'd never experienced that as far as I can remember, but I could definitely go along with being a born-again Irishman. I don't think you could class the Irish so much as Christians, but more as all-rounders for Christ and humanity. Daniel O'Connell puts a colourful touch to this with his words. 'Irishmen I call on you to join in crushing slavery and in giving liberty to every man of every caste, creed and colour.' And I will throw in another slant with a quote of my own. 'You can't go beyond yourself without a cause greater than yourself.'

My flight to Toronto was very relaxing and pleasurable with its second-to-none cabin service. I was flying Air Canada. There was one little moment I relished. I had to get past a hostess to get to the toilet. She was attending someone and there was very little room to get past her, so I put both my hands on her waist to guide myself past with an excuse me, and got a lovely smile off her. I well remember when I told my sister's husband Tom about it, he said they could put you in prison for that kind of thing these days. I said to him, until such time as my luck runs out, I will take my chances with little playful actions such as this. And if I wind up in prison, I will always remember that you once warned me.

As I gazed down on the floating icebergs I thought how sensible I was to be up in the air and not down there. You can take what you like out of that. As we touched down in Toronto the fever of excitement was once again climbing the scales. I asked myself, is this really happening to me? Will I wake up only to find I am dreaming? Am I still one of the many of those lost sheep? But no, thank God, it was all happening and there was no need to pinch myself. I'd been bruised enough already.

Once more I was welcomed into the arms of my sister and her husband Tom. Soon after that I was whisked back to their house in Mason Road. Over the first week I met the rest of their lovely family. Before I'd left New Zealand Ann's daughter had written to me. I can't remember everything she had written, but the punch line was full of kind words of concern for my well-being. It was obvious that my sister had told her I wasn't a happy chappy. And, looking back now, I really believe that was just what I needed to give me that extra push. I will always be grateful to Betty for that...

Besides wanting to see my sister again, there was another reason for going to Canada. I wanted to thank Ann personally, and to spend a little time with her explaining in more depth the kind of person I am now, instead of the control freak I had allowed myself to become.

A few days after my arrival Betty took me and her two lovely young daughters for a drive down to Lake

Ontario. It was a beautiful day as I remember it, and after walking for a while one of the girls started to feel weary. I put her on my shoulders and away we went. That brought back wonderful memories when I used to carry my own two daughters on my shoulders when we tramped in the Waitakere Ranges. Being the smallest Rachel spent more time on them than Alex did. But there was one time I still remember that sends a shudder down my spine. I was wearing jandals that day and I had Alex on my shoulders. When I started on a very dry downhill path I suddenly lost my footing and poor Alex came crashing down onto the ground hitting the back of her head. She was in shock and quite a lot of pain. And when I saw a trickle of blood come from one of her ears I nearly had a heart attack. All sorts of hellish thoughts were going through my mind. As quickly as I could I got her back to the car and we all headed for the hospital where they examined her on for an on and off period of about five or six hours. Shortly after that we were allowed to take her home, but were told to keep a close eye on her. I can't remember how many times I got out of bed that night to check her on her. I got very little sleep I can tell you, but thank God there were no further complications. Boy was that another wake up call for me.

I enjoyed my three weeks' stay in Toronto taking in the sights and talking to all sorts of people as I walked the streets around my sister's home. Both Betty and her husband Tom worked during the week, so I kept myself amused and fit that way.

About two weeks or so later I received a phone call from my brother Ken's daughter Ann who was living in a place called Hamilton with her boyfriend. She asked me if I'd like to come down to visit them for a couple of days. Without the slightest hesitation I asked her how to get there. I was fast leaving that old world that had held me in its grip by trying to reason everything out before daring to take the next step. Always keep your options open and never take life too seriously, that way you'll succeed where millions have failed.

I learned the quickest way to get to Hamilton was by train which would avoid any inconvenience to my family. Two days later I was drinking in the countryside scenery as the train headed for Hamilton, where unknown to me at the time I was about to experience another colourful chapter in my life.

My niece Ann was there to meet me, and we threw our arms around each other to gather in another wonderful family reunion. Then she drove me to where she lived with her boyfriend whose name like so many others has gone up in smoke.

Our meeting was a touching moment for both of us. I'd never had the chance to get to know her as a child for two reasons. The first I won't go into because it would mean pointing the finger at someone else. The other reason was our moving to New Zealand.

After catching up with the past over something to eat Ann took me on a sightseeing tour around Hamilton until her boyfriend was due home from work. After being introduced to this pleasant young man the pair said they had a little surprise package set up for me. Off we went to a pub-cum-restaurant for a meal and a few drinks. I must say that I was very impressed with the layout of the place. It had the appearance of a classy hotel rather than a bar. Mind you, with my background anything beyond the usual can be classed as up-market. A number of Ann's and her partner's friends soon arrived and more introductions took place for me. Then after a drink or two it was time to eat. And boy, what a wonderful meal it was, followed by my favourite dessert, apple pie, cream, and ice cream.

Well, that was a real treat for me with more to follow. About eight tables were placed near to where we were sitting. Then all of a sudden like the gust of a soft summer breeze enchanting music flowed to greet a number of beautiful women completely naked as they started to dance on the tables that had been placed before us moving their bodies to the music. Well that certainly took my breath away, but in no way did it arouse my animal lust as a situation like that is capable of doing. It was all carried out with an artistic sense of professionalism that left no room for any lurid thoughts to form in my mind. I felt nothing but admiration for the way they displayed their God-given figures. Later I was told that these women earned good money for what they did there. It would put some of them through university, and also help educate their children, or set them up in a business. I was on another wonderful learning curve, taking this poor old Irishman into a world he never knew existed.

Later that evening there was a small party in my honour at Ann's place. As the partying went on the men drifted into a corner to talk about sport and other so-called male topics, leaving the women to talk among themselves. Being younger than me, and into all kinds of Canadian sports and politics, the men's conversation eventually drove me to join the women who were seated on some soft chairs and a large couch close to me. I said, 'Make way for this old guy,' and squeezed in between those on the couch. Well what a fun time I had as they pampered me lift right and centre, and I lapped up every moment of it. That was another of those enchanting nights that were slowly to become very dear to me because of all the wonderful people that helped me to a higher level of understanding of what to be human really means. Emptiness has to be filled in some way or another. And I feel very strongly about making all the opportunities that are available to me to be put to some kind of use in whatever way I can. And if they led me at times into difficult situations at times which they have, then I accept the challenge and see where that leads me.

The next day, I caught the train back to my sister's house in Toronto a little wiser and more opened minded about the ways humanity preserves itself in whatever form it chooses. If you stop doing the familiar and try something new, you'll find you're that more of an asset to humanity than you once were. I was quickly finding that out.

When I got back I learned there was an Irish pub about a mile away from Ann's place, so off I went one evening after dinner for a Canadian Irish experience. I found the place without any trouble apart from my difficulty in crossing busy streets. I was used to looking right, left, and right again that I nearly got into trouble for not doing it the other way around. I heard later that another Irish guy wasn't as lucky as I was. He was sent home in a box instead of a passenger seat.

As soon as I arrived I ordered myself a drink and sat down to enjoy the music. I was soon in conversation with the character who was doing most of the singing and I told him a bit about myself. He asked me to sing, so I sang Danny Boy but didn't feel too comfortable as I hadn't yet made my singing debut. But at least the audience very kindly applauded instead of throwing things at me.

I went back to that pub a second time before I was due to fly out to New Zealand and the place was packed. I got myself a beer and looked around for a table. I must have attracted the attention of three young men sitting together at this table for one of them beckoned me over to join them. They probably felt sorry for this poor old guy looking like a lost sheep, little knowing that I was now becoming a wolf in Irish clothing. But it didn't take them long to find this out as we got talking, and I could have gone home drunk as an old fool if I'd let them buy me all the drinks they wanted to. I didn't fancy the thought of going home in a box like the other Irish guy I mentioned. I was enjoying life far too much at the moment

One of the guys had an arm in plaster. I asked him what had happened and he said he came off his bike. I said 'You're lucky that's all the damage you've done to yourself coming off a motorbike.' He said, 'No it was a bicycle.' Well I couldn't help but laugh as he came out with that because by now I had a few drinks under my belt and the very thought of it somehow burst that humorous bubble in me. And the other guys laughed as well, then gave him a bit of a hard time over it. They asked me where I came from. I told them I was originally from Ireland but now living in New Zealand. They had no idea where New Zealand was. One of them thought it an Island off the coast of Australia. I said you're somewhat on the right trail, but I wouldn't advise you to try swimming the distance between. My efforts to educate them as to the whereabouts of my second homeland made me the centre of attention for the rest of that evening, and of course I lapped that up. When you've lived out in the cold for so long as I had, it's only natural to grab at anything to warm the cockles of your heart.

On the evening before I left Canada Ann's son Tom invited me to join him in a game of snooker, so off we went to do battle. We were only able to play two games in. He won one and I the other. I said it was one for Canada and one for Ireland, and if God spares me, I'll come back to play the deciding game. Now rewriting my life story it looks like that game is about to take place somewhere between 2nd and the 17th of July. My daughter is taking me there on a luxury flight. That's one for the books if ever there was one.

The time came for me to depart so Ann and Tom drove me to the airport. We said our goodbyes and I boarded my flight back to New Zealand. I'd just sat down to await take off when this tall handsome man sat down in the seat beside me. He very quickly introduced himself as Terry Ross. I shook his and said, I have one advantage over you, I'm Terry as well, but it's Terry Robinson. I can be a smart arse at times but generally stupid and harmless. He laughed and said, 'You're a breath of fresh air, I believe that I'm going to enjoy our trip back to New Zealand.'

Terry told me he was on his way to Canterbury University to lecture in political science for ten months. His wife would be joining him at a later date. I had the most enjoyable plane journey that I've ever had chatting to him, as I openly told him of all the changes that were taking place in my life. I said, 'When you've been where I've been the weeds don't do anything for you anymore. I'm off to smell the roses, and so far the aroma has been fantastic.' I found Terry Ross a very good listener with an intelligent mind. There were no airs or graces about him but at the same time he was clever in the art of expressing himself about everyday life. When we arrived in Auckland my family were at the airport to greet me. It was the first time their old man had left New Zealand since we arrived here, so it was quite an exciting moment for all of us. I introduced Terry Ross to the family and told them he was stopping overnight before heading to Christchurch the following morning. My daughter Rachel said 'Why not stay with us tonight, and Dad can drive you to the airport in the morning.' I advised him not to argue with Rachel, saying I'd given that away a long time ago. So off we went to where Rachel was staying with her with her husband to be. They were renting part of a house from a lovely lady named Claire Balfour who was to become a very close friend to both my family and myself. On arriving Terry and I were introduced to Claire. She soon organized a sleeping place for us. Over dinner and drinks Terry entertained us with charming stories of his travels over much of the world, stimulating our minds. Later as I got to know Claire better she asked me 'Where do you meet all these interesting people?' I said, 'I don't find them, they find me, and only God knows the reason why.'

Terry wished everyone a fond farewell the next morning, and I drove him to the airport. On the way he said, 'This has been the best hospitality I've ever received in all my travels.' I replied 'Just put it down to Irish and Kiwi hospitality.' As he was saying goodbye he said he was hoping to be back this way in about six weeks' time to have a look at the North Island and would look me up. I told him I had no Idea of what was in store for me until I had spoken face to face with my wife about going our separate ways, and getting her to agree to a settlement. I told him that I could be contacted through Claire, and gave him her address and telephone number.

When I got back to Claire's house she said, 'Why not stay here for a week or so until you get things sorted out with your wife. It will give you some breathing space, and time to sort things out. It's a big move in both your lives, and the more calmly you approach things the less stress there will be.' I thanked her. I was soon to learn that Claire was a very special kind of lady. How fortunate I have been to have women like Claire in my life.

A week later I went to see my wife, and without any real difficulty she agreed to a separation. I slept in the room my daughters used to sleep in till I believed everything would be settled. I then found a solicitor to make the necessary arrangements for a settlement. It was now October and he thought it could be finalized by January. I informed my wife so she could find a solicitor to look after her interests. With time on my hands I once more involved myself with my lovely friend in Ward 11 at the North Shore Hospital. There is something very peaceful about spending time with such people who give you much more than you can give them.

I'd now purchased a cheap set of golf clubs and was trying master the public golf course at Takapuna. It soon told me who was master. Until I felt a little more confident I played on my own, but eventually got up enough courage to join others. "God", I said to myself, "I would really enjoy this game if the holes weren't so far apart, and they were bigger." As I felt uncomfortable being at home with things how they were between my wife and I, I would spend most of my time away from the house.

Just about all of my evenings were taken up playing snooker. I was a member of the R.S.A. at Birkenhead and had a lot of great times there making new friends, and enjoying the challenge that each game brought me in this new found way of life.

After playing snooker one night I arrived home one night to find the locks on the front and back doors had been changed. Well, I got the message well and square, illegal though it was. So without kicking up any fuss I drove to where Rachel lived, and Claire soon organized a bed for me. I won't repeat what I said about my wife, but we soon turned things around and ended up having a good laugh. The next morning I told Claire I'd find myself a room to rent until my settlement was finalized. Then I'd take off for two of three months to tour the South Island. She said, "Until you find somewhere to live, you're most welcome to stay here."

Well as I've so often said, God never closes one door without opening another. Quite a paradox there if there ever was one?

The same evening I got talking to a really nice guy I'd met called Logie Williams. He was around eighty years of age and had been the first to welcome me to the R.S.A. when I first joined. Whenever I spotted him I'd make it my business to have a chat with him. I told him I'd been locked out of my house. Straight away he said he had a spare room in his house. 'It's no palace, and you will have to fend for yourself but you're very welcome if it suits your needs.' I said, thinking to myself, as I have already mentioned, 'one door closes and another one opens.' So without even bothering to see his place I said 'I will gratefully accept your offer.' So we settled on a figure of $50 a week. I shook his hand and the deal was sealed, along with a thank you for being the friend I needed at that moment.

I lived with Logie for close to three months and enjoyed his company whenever our paths crossed. He had to be the most laid-back, humorous, interesting, and likeable character I've met in all my travels. Apart from my Uncle Harry, that is. Nothing bothered Logie. He could sleep on a clothes line. What really amazed me was his in built alarm clock. When the All Blacks were playing their international rugby matches overseas, he could program himself to wake up in the early hours of the morning to listen to the game on radio. He's passed on now, but his memory still lives on with me.

One day I was playing golf and I teamed up with a young Englishman and his girlfriend who was accompanying him. What a delightful lady she was, with a great sense of humour. The couple were doing a budget tour of New Zealand like most young people I came across in my walk.

During the course of the game I discovered the young man played snooker and tennis so I invited him and his lady friend to join me at the R.S.A. one evening. And to keep his friend from being bored we could include her in a game of pool after the game. One thing I've learned is that if you don't keep the women happy it will come back at you in some form or another. And, in many cases, quite rightly so. I wasn't concerned about myself, but for my young snooker friend. I'd given away my prison cell and no way was I going back there.

The couple had just over a week to go before they left Auckland. I asked the young man if he could give me a few tennis lessons before he took off as I'd always had a hankering to get into the game. He said no problem. I borrowed a racket and managed to get five lessons in before they left. Like my golf I learned that I had a long way to go before I would be able to play a reasonable game but I was determined I'd get there one day. And I did. Determination I believe is the driving force that can take you around many a corner where otherwise you would never have dreamed going. But then again what are those corners therefore if not to be ventured around.

My English friends came back to the RSA with me a couple of times before they left. On their last visit I took a raffle ticket for a dollar and asked the lady to pick a number. Lady luck was with us, I won fifty dollars, so I gave her twenty five dollars for the stroke of luck she brought me. We were as happy as Larry, though I have no idea who Larry is, but I'm sure he's a nice guy.

In late January I received a cheque for forty thousand dollars as part of my settlement for my share of our house in 58-James Street, Glenfield. My wife wanted to keep the house and took out a mortgage. My solicitor said that I could have gotten more out of it but I just wanted to get to hell out of it and hit the road. I felt that I had a lot of living to do with the years that were closing in on me. After buying my son Bernard a car and paying off my own car together with all the other hungry bills that had to be fed, I wound up with close to twenty-seven thousand dollars in my bank account. I said to myself, this is probably the last time you're going to have this kind of money at your disposal you old spendthrift. Maybe a little caution is called for. I admit I did think about it, but it didn't really appeal to my sense of rationality which, thank God I have very little of, otherwise there'd be no point in writing about my life. A permanent source of happiness is indeed a thirsty one.

So now all systems were on go. My tour of the South Island was no longer a dream. I equipped myself with the necessary maps that would help me to both find and lose myself as is customary to my way of reading them. And even though it was a bit of a hit and miss affair at times, there was nearly always a pleasant experience unravelled for my growth. With my now more opened mind things were being placed in my path for all sorts of various reasons. All I had to do was acknowledge them for what they were, and then see where they would take me.

So armed with a tape deck and a stereo I added a guitar and an amplifier to the music side of things. Mind you I had no idea how to play a guitar, but for the moment money was no object, and dreams were free.

At the beginning of February 1990, after saying goodbye

to my family, I gave Logie a big hug, then thanked him for his kindness, and hit the road. I had booked a ferry from Wellington to Picton for the car and myself. I planned an overnight stay in Whakatane, but when I got there I had difficulty finding accommodation close to Ohope Beach, so I drove on to the next beach at Waiotahi and found a lovely little unit right on the beachfront. After a bite to eat I began writing a letter to my daughter Rachel just to tell her how wonderful I felt having this great sense of adventure swelling up inside me moment by moment. I must have been halfway through the letter when the urge to go for a swim came over me, so off I went

Farewelling my family with only Faith in my pocket

The tide was well out as I remember it, and the waves seemed in a very restless mood, chopping and changing. Like an innocent dove, or maybe a fool, I worked my way through one wave after another till the water was somewhere around my chest. Then when I started to swim back to the shore I found I was getting nowhere fast and could no longer touch the sand under me. The current seemed to be slowly pulling out to sea. Off went the alarm bells inside telling me once again that my only chance of survival was to go over on my back and try to ride back to the shore on the crest of the waves. This had saved my life once before as I have already mentioned. But it was a different kettle of fish this time, I was fighting an ever changing current that I had never experienced before with no knowledge how to deal with it. I have no idea how long I battled to get a foothold on the sand. Just when I thought all was lost after taking in so much salt water, and having little or no strength left in my body my right foot touched the sand. Now just before this happened I had said to the Good Lord 'If this is my time to go, I accept it, let not my will be done but Yours.' Well as I made my way out of the water I thanked Him with all my heart. When you're so close to death with so much to live for, it is just about impossible to describe all those emotions that are taking place within you.

So very slowly I staggered up to the soft sand and lay there with my stomach heaving because of all the salt water I had taken in. I did raise my arm a few times in the hope someone might see me, but there was no one in sight but the seagulls, and as you can well imagine they had other things on their mind. I don't know how long I lay there, but I very distinctly recall giving thanks to God for once more coming to my rescue and saving me from a watery grave. I too must admit that I was reluctant to leave this life with all that money to spend, and the whole new life opening up to me. Well, there are only two reasons I can come up with as to why God plucked me from the sea. First, He loves a trier, and second, a fool who tries. And I believe I qualify for both those titles.

As I walked back to my unit it dawned on me that, had I not survived, my lovely daughter Rachel would have received, with all my other belongings, the unfinished letter I was writing to her, and what an injustice that would have been. You know that song, "You always hurt the one you love."

Next morning, after once more giving thanks to God for being so wonderfully alive, I decided I wouldn't tempt providence again by having another swim before I left. Under different circumstances I would have had a swim before I left because I love the being at one with the ocean. There is something about it that gives me a wonderful sense of satisfaction, as it still does to this very day.

After picking up a few hitchhikers at different points I arrived in Wellington and caught the evening ferry to Picton. It was quite a choppy crossing, but with some difficulty I managed to keep my stomach contents in place. There is one thing for certain, I'd never have had a snowball's chance in hell of becoming a stowaway. Anyway I went looking for accommodation to tide me over till next morning. Then, with a good night's sleep and a nice breakfast tucked under my belt, I looked at the map of the South Island and said, 'Where shall I go first?'

QUEENSTOWN, NEW ZEALAND

I must say I was very moved as the daylight gave me my first real glimpse of the South Island. My first impression was that of a fairyland, because just about everything seemed to glitter in the beautiful morning sun. As you well by now I have one hell of an imagination, and what I was seeing in front of me just kept adding to it. That moment was one of those that touched my soul in a way I pray never will be forgotten. Deep down inside something was telling me this trip would be the making of me. Any last doubts I had of myself would surface after I'd completed the trip, and as you read on I'm sure in some way you'll agree with me.

So after looking at the map in more detail I decided I'd take a drive to the area around Golden Bay and fill my lungs and mind with what it had to offer. Well, after taking in as much of the scenery as I could by stopping here, there and yonder, I got to a place called Takaka and had something to eat. Then something told me, 'No this is not where I really want to go.' Queenstown was rooted deep in my subconscious. I had to get to

Queenstown. Why I had no idea, but eventually I would find out.

So I turned around, and coming back I picked up three people, two men and a woman, who wanted to go to a place called Kohatu. As I was feeling a bit tired I asked them if anyone had a driving licence. One of them said he had. So without further ado I said, 'You're now the driver and I'm going to be the lazy one for a while.' And I've got to admit he was a good driver, and I felt quite confident that our lives were in safe hands. I would have taken the wheel off him had I thought otherwise.

A bit later I picked up a young couple at Kawatiri. The lady was Maori, and the young man Pakeha. They were really a lovely young couple. I said, 'I'm heading for an overnight stay in Murchison, if that's any good to you.' They said that would suit them fine. Just before we got into Murchison with the light failing, the heavens opened up. As the rain continued to pour down I asked them 'where are you going to stay?' They said, 'we've got a small tent, we'll be fine.' I said 'no way, I'll find you a motel and I'll book you both in along with myself.'

When I woke up next morning the sun was shining and the young couple had moved on. After a shower and something to eat I found out where the golf course was and played eighteen holes like the Lone Ranger as there was no one about.

Somewhere around midday I started off on the next leg of my journey. This would take me to Westport. Well I didn't get very far till I came across the same couple I'd picked up the day before. When I stopped they told me they'd been waiting for some time, so I said, 'Well, obviously I was meant to pick you again. Hop in.' Off we went and drove through the Buller Gorge, which for me was another breath-taking part of my journey. It was very warm on this particular day. Around three o'clock I said, 'God I'm hot, I would love a swim.' When we came to an open part of the gorge I stopped the car and said, 'I'm going in.' The young man said, 'I'll go too.' The lady said, 'No, I won't bother.' We swimmers grabbed a towel each, changed at the water's edge, and jumped in. Well, my God, my breath was completely taken away. I couldn't believe water could be so cold, especially on such a warm day. I was back out as quick as I went in along with my young friend.

But it didn't finish there. No sooner were we out of the water when we were attacked by wave after wave of sandflies. They seemed to come from nowhere. It was just unbelievable. We were covered in them. We rushed back to the car trying to fight them off with our clothes and towels. We closed the car and annihilated as best we could, but not without them leaving their calling cards on our bodies. I don't know about my young friend, but I had a few uncomfortable days after that.

I dropped the young couple off in Westport and found somewhere to stay for the night. After I had something to eat I took a drive up to the Golf Club. I was told they'd be having a twilight game quite soon and I was welcome to join them. Well, I can't remember how many stableford points I scored, but I won a pot of jam. Mind you, they may just felt sorry me and thought this poor old hit and miss golfer deserved a little something for travelling so far to take part in their twilight game.

Next morning I headed for Greymouth just taking my time as I took in the scenery. Eventually that evening I arrived in Greymouth and found myself a little self-contained hut to spend the night in. Next morning I had a walk around the town and spotted this shop with a variety of goods in it. I went in and had a look around and spotted this snooker cue that really took my fancy. It was made in Canada from Canadian Maple wood I was told. Well I just got a feeling it was there waiting for me because I still have it to this very day. And it has travelled with me on all my journeys since the day I bought it. And it will be accompanying me to Canada to play the deciding match against my nephew Tom in Toronto somewhere between 2nd and 17th of July of this year 2014. We won a game each when I was there in 1989.

I also bought a fishing line and some gear. Never fished in my life, but it seemed a good idea.

Later that morning after looking at the map I thought I would take a little run inland to a place called Rotomanu. As I knew I would never come this way again why not take in all you can. Not long after I got underway I spotted these two ladies looking for a lift, so I stopped and asked them where they were going. They said Reefton. I looked at my map and saw it was off the route I had planned, but without batting an eyelid, I said hop in. I was in no hurry to get to Queenstown, and their need I felt was greater than mine. They were from Germany, and both of them were nurses. From what I can remember of our conversation it was very interesting, and they were easy on this old man's eyes, and had a good sense of humour.

After I dropped them off I decided to leave Rotomanu off my calling card. So once more I pulled out the map and thought I would go back to Greymouth, and hit out for Christchurch. Well I got as far as Arthur's Pass, then something told me, stop messing around, and get yourself on the road that leads you to where you really want to go, Queenstown.

When I got to Hokitika it was that time again to eat and sleep. The next morning on my way to the Fox Glacier I picked up a young man from Denmark called Tomas Technik. He was looking for a lift to the Fox Glacier where he intended to spend a few days taking in its wonders. He told me he was born in Hungary, and lived there until about a year ago, until out of the blue, he was offered a job in Denmark. He grabbed it like there was no tomorrow because of all the problems he'd experienced in Hungary. His English was pretty good, but he was quite shy. After spending the best part of a day with me, I believe I'd taken some of the shyness from him as we tramped around the Fox Glacier. As I talk to almost anyone, whether it be good-day or Hello or whatever, I soon had him mimicking me like a parrot and enjoying every moment of it. I took him for a meal that evening and after that we said our goodbyes.

After an overnight stay in Haast I set off on the road that would give me a bird's eye view of two of the many beautiful lakes that lie down the South Island. Lake Wanaka and Lake Hawea. I hadn't gone all that far when another hitchhiker hailed me and said he was making his way to Queenstown. I said, 'so am I, but I'm not in a hurry as I need to take in as much of this breathtaking scenery as I can. If you're in a hurry you'll need to catch another taxi.' He said, like you, I am trying to do the same. I called him Bob in my last mixed up book, but his Christian name to me not long after I started this revised book of mine. It was Don. Refreshing your memory can bring to the surface some amazing things. I have proved that to myself beyond any doubt as I continue this story of mine. And at the same time I'm hoping it will make more sense than the last one.

Don I reckon was between twenty and twenty-five and hailed from Canada. He was a well-built young man and very fit. He told me he did a lot of rock climbing back home with no ropes. He just scaled up the rocks with his bare hands. He also had some scary stories to tell about bears that involved both his father, and himself. I found him very interesting because the word fear seemed to play little or no part in his life. And his manners left nothing to be desired during the short time we spent together.

Don had a fishing rod in his backpack so we stopped at Lake Hawea and made our way to the side of the lake. Being a young man with fishing experience Don took off his boots and let himself gently down the side of bank to test the depth of the water. With his feet planted firmly on the bottom he cast his rod out as far as he could. Brave little me was quite happy to cast my rod from the side of the bank. Well, we could only have been trying our luck for about twenty minutes when Don let out this unmerciful scream with some choice language to follow. I rushed to his side just in time to see a big black eel dislodging itself from his leg. That was the only time I saw fear in his eyes. The rest of our fishing was done from the bank. He caught three small fish, but as Jesus wasn't around we had to make do with some sandwiches we had with us. No I caught nothing, not even a cold I'm glad to say.

Just before we got to Wanaka a young lady hitchhiker hailed us down. She, too, was on her way to Queenstown. Like Don she accepted my lazy way of getting there. She was a skiing instructor from Switzerland. Her English was a little up and down so Don and I had a lot of fun putting two and two together. She was a lovely young women with a delightful sense of humour, and a very simple outlook on life. I think her name was Frieda, or something close to that. So off we went, stopping and starting whenever we thought it was worthwhile to do so. I have always been a person who loves to share things with others, so I considered my fellow travellers' stop requests just as important as mine. That way it puts no restriction on our friendship. Their enthusiasm to take in and experience as much as the South Island as they could was just as exciting to me as I felt sure mine was for them. Three pairs of eyes could see a lot more beauty than one pair, especially when we examined it under the microscope of our humanity.

As we neared Queenstown our curiosity was aroused when we came across a large group of people watching an event going on just ahead of us. I found a parking spot and off we went to investigate. Well, lo and behold, here was another eye opener for us. Bungy jumping off the Kawarau Bridge. Somewhere in the back of my mind I remembered hearing about it, but this was for real. After watching for a while Don said, 'God I'd love to do that.' The eighty dollar charge was a bit too expensive for him so I said, 'here you're fit here's the eighty bucks. Off you go.' Well I've got to say it was money well spent because he did it with a lovely sense of ease and grace.

I also had a lot of admiration for a young man who was partly crippled who also did the jump with the rope around his waist.

I also saw another guy throw up as he was about to jump into space. I thought to myself, could I do that. No. not for this old man. Little did I know what the future held in store for me.

Going back for seconds

As the sun was saying goodbye for the day we arrived at Frankton. I'd been informed that there were very comfortable cabins there but it was advisable to make a booking as February was a busy time of the year. But I was on a pot luck holiday and The Good Lord was doing an excellent job looking after me, as I have already mentioned, although I can be a right pain in the neck to Him at times.

So off I went to the reception office to book in and was informed that the only cabin available was a three-bedroomed one. Without the slightest hesitation I asked if I could book it for a week. The man behind the counter said, 'that's perfect timing for both of us. The day you move out I've got someone else coming in.' When we settled into our temporary abode we went shopping for some provisions to keep our hunger and thirst at bay. After sharing something about the events of the day, and about ourselves in comfortable cabin we hit the hay.

The next morning after breakfast Don said, 'I'd like to climb the Remarkables.' I'd noticed his eyes on them for some time. 'Off you go,' I said, 'but don't expect me to come along with you.' One escape from death in the short time since I'd started out on my journey has been more than enough for me. And if I have to die before it's over I would, at the very least, like to get to the finishing line with some sense of achievement tucked under my belt. We had a good laugh about that.

Frieda said, 'I'm going to make my way down to Queenstown, I'll be back later.' I said, 'well I'm going to have a look at the nine-hole golf course, and all going well I will play eighteen holes.' I had no bother getting on the enchanting course and joined up with a couple of guys. I thought it looked an easy course at first, but changed my mind when my score-card took a hammering.

When I got back that evening I asked Don if he'd enjoyed his climb. He said yes he had, but he'd got one hell of a fright just before he reached the top. He was putting his hand on a ledge to haul himself up when an opossum took a dislike to the invasion of its privacy and took some blood from one of his fingers. What saved him from losing his balance and becoming a victim of the Remarkables only God knows. I said to him, 'I think there's a message somewhere for you in all of this.

First that run in with the eel, now that opossum. Maybe you should go easy on the rock climbing and fishing till you get back to familiar territory.' From what I've learned about New Zealand it's not a country to trifle with, especially the South Island.

A few days later Don came back after spending the best part of the day in Queenstown and said he'd made friends with a few people from different parts of the world. He asked me if he could invite of these backpackers to join us for a few days. He said 'I'll ask them to bring their own beer and some food so that I wouldn't be taken advantage of in any way. I'd been more than generous already.' I said, 'the only reason for my being what you call generous is that I happen to have more than you at this particular time. And money, in the end, like life, comes down to two things, you either keep it, or you share it. So let's have the first of I hope many parties to come and new friends to share some part of our lives with, and if anyone has any kind of instrument to play ask them to bring it along. And as long as they have sleeping bags there is plenty of room on the floor. In that way they can relax while they are staying here.' What a great evening we had the day they arrived. We had one guy who could play the guitar so mine kept us all in some kind of harmony as we enjoyed each other's wonderful company.

With two days left on the rented cabin I had paid for, everyone went on their way to do whatever they had to do from there, I wished them well and thanked them for all those special experiences they'd shared with me. And, likewise, they returned the compliment. I said that I was going to stay in Queenstown for a while, and in all probability would run into them again.

That morning I made my way up to Kelvin Heights Golf Course. It was another of those wonderful sunny days that I was experiencing in this part of the world. I got talking to pro and told him I needed a new set of clubs that would suit my standard of play as a beginner. He sold me a brand new set but what I didn't know at the time was that they were blades, not intended for the amateur golfer just starting off. But never mind. When you're green, you're green.

I then asked him how much it was to join the club and as far as I can remember he said $250. Well, seeing that I was going to be in Queenstown for a while, and intended to play as much as possible, I thought I could save myself some money by joining for that amount. So that's where I got my first handicap. After putting in five cards I wound up with a 26 handicap.

But I must say the course, speaking for myself, was absolutely fantastic. The combination of the Remarkables, the Lakes, and layout of the golf course just about took my breath away.

That afternoon I went into Queenstown to see if I could rent an apartment for six to eight weeks. Within a couple of hours I'd signed up and paid for a lovely two-bedroomed apartment right across the road from Lake

Wakatipu. With a happy smile on my face I set off back to my cabin to spend my last few days in Frankton. About half way back I found a young backpacker looking for a lift to Frankton. I stopped and told him where I was going. I said, 'I've got two more nights left before I'm due to move out of my cabin so you're very welcome to stay there till the morning I leave.' He said, 'That would be fantastic. I'd be very grateful for that.I was looking to pitch my tent for a few days, then make my way back to Wellington to fly out to the States.' He'd done his tour of the South Island so now it was home time.

When we arrived back we got talking. He told me about his family. He said he was from Texas and told me something of the area he lived in. His name was Eric Coggins. He was a lovely young man, what I'd call a spiritual person. I told him about the bungy jumping that I'd witnessed and he said, 'Oh,God that sure would be great to do.' I said, 'would you like to do it?' He said he would, but his budget was rather stretched at the moment. I said, 'I'm not trying to embarrass you in any way, but here's a hundred dollars. Go and do it.' He looked into my eyes and said, 'I can see that you're a man of God. Would you mind very much if I didn't do the jump but used this money to extend my trip a little longer?' And I said, 'no not at all. As a matter of fact I think that's a more sensible idea.'

So I told him that I'd joined the Kelvin Heights Golf Club and he said, 'Oh, I'd love a game of golf, though I'm not much of a golfer.' I said, 'Well, tomorrow's our last full day here. What do way you say about a game tomorrow? I'll pay your fees and hire a half-set of clubs for you. And you can also use any of mine if you wish.'

Well, I've got to tell you that was the funniest game of golf I have ever played in all my golfing days. I was bloody awful but Eric in all fairness was bloody, bloody awful. But the highlight of the game was the way we laughed all the way around the course. He had this Texan expression when he hit a bad shot, 'Oh my God', and I'd just about double up with laughter. A day to remember. Yes, it certainly was.

After a nice meal that evening we talked about our feelings and emotions and so forth till it was bedtime. We said our goodbyes that night as he was to have a very early start. When I got up next morning there was a letter written out for me on the table for me to read. I still have it very tattered and worn.

'Terry what a fantastic game of golf. I can't thank you enough for your hospitality and generosity. I pray you will never be taken advantage of because you are a Christian. You are already one. God is with you. I pray for your safety in your future endeavours. Pray for God's guidance. Appreciate all the encouragement that you have been given. Please look me up if you ever come to Texas. Be more than happy to return it.

Yours in Christ.

Eric Coggins.'

Well that really touched my soul, but then that was the type of a young man Eric was. He was one of those special people who you adhere to the moment you come together. The vibrations of truth and honesty seem to reach out and envelop you because of a simple act of kindness.

That same morning I made my way down to Queenstown to collect the keys of my temporary accommodation and sign a few papers. I use the word temporary because nothing is going to be permanent. And when you come to terms with that I find it makes life so much easier, more interesting and challenging. More light will fall on this as you continue your walk with me.

SKIPPERS BRIDGE

After I had settled into my new place I went for a drive into the town centre to evaluate my new surroundings. The first place that caught my eye on the waterfront was a place called Eichardt's Hotel right on the waterfront. I parked my car and went in. Apart from my growing up experiences and during the time I was married I had now come to understand that that if you want to learn something about people, whatever it may be, go into a pub. Sooner or later all sorts of magic keeps popping out because people seem to let their hair down and expose their humanity over a few drinks. Now, I am not going to say this is the right or wrong way to expose your emotions for I really believe there isn't a right or wrong way, so long as you don't step on someone else's feet. And mind you that's a possibility as well! Anyway, this day, the following episode took place in this hotel. There were quite a few people occupying most of the tables when I walked in but I spotted one guy stuck at a corner table looking into his glass of beer as though he was trying to have a conversation with it. I said to myself, 'this could be an experience not to be missed.' I ordered a beer and went over and asked if he'd like some company or should I push off. He looked up at me and said, 'You're not an Anglican are you?' 'No' I said 'I'm Irish.' Well obviously that was the password. He welcomed me with open arms and I mean that literally because he got up and put his arms around me. I could sense some of the people in the background eyeing us so I said to myself, eat your heart out.

I have to say that he was quite a few drinks ahead of me, trying to drown out some of his sorrowful past I guessed as the story he was relating to me unfolded. He was born in Australia and spent most of his life there doing, from what I can remember, a variety of jobs. Then he met this woman and they got married. Sometime later he found out that she was two-timing him and the bottom fell out of his world. He decided to get away from his circle of pain, so he settled for Queenstown New Zealand.

Being a good listener I let him unload his pain and frustration. And as a certain amount of anger started to find its way to the surface I gently persuaded him to smooth it down. I ordered a couple of pies and when they came he began to relax more. Then I put the boot on the other foot and told him something about my life and the circumstances that drove me from my home to join the RAF, then come to New Zealand. I also spoke of my breakdown and my marriage break-up. After hearing all that he wasn't feeling quite so sorry for himself.

He then told me that he was going up to Auckland the next day, and said, 'I'd better go and sleep of some of my self-pity after hearing your story. Thank you for being a good listener and a good friend. I won't forget you.' And I said, 'Neither will I forget you.' We hugged each other goodbye.

Feeling a bit drained but happy I went back to my unit, had something to eat, and then relaxed on my bed listening to some of my favourite music.

Now, for the remainder of my stay in Queenstown I'm just going to touch on the people and things that keep this walk of mine alive, well from my point of view anyway. Someone once said, 'We don't remember days, we remember moments.' So if an excuse be needed I'll use that one.

A few days later I teamed up with an English guy called Kevin. We started playing pool together in my newfound hunting ground, Eichardt's so it was all go after that. Kevin was just about as crazy as they come. He was good looking and I'm sure he could charm a woman to jump off the Remarkables into his waiting arms, but doubt very much if he'd be still there when she arrived. Well meaning, but not the reliable type. Someone who could be classed as any woman's dream-boy if she was prepared to take the nightmares he brought with him. And of course there's nothing new about that. I asked Kevin where he was staying, and he said he was in some old room on the other side of town. So I said, 'you are quite welcome to use the second bedroom at my place for a while, but no women are allowed in your room or mine. I'm on an overdue holiday and quite willing to help out anyone I can, but there has to be a code of ethics. Any woman who visits my unit for a party or whatever must feel safe and secure. I have two young daughters in their twenties and I'd like to think someone might do them some good turn if ever the need arose.'

So Kevin was happy with that. Then I said, 'I need some new clothes. I can't remember the last time I bought some decent clothes for myself. At the moment I look like an old backpacker driving around in a car. It's time to upgrade while I've still got some money in the bank. And if you don't mind me saying so, you need them more than I do. So if you're not too proud I'd like to buy you some.' 'Not at all', he replied, 'I like to be pampered now and again.' So off we went to a shop that sold top quality menswear, and in about fifteen minutes to twenty minutes I'd parted with close to one thousand dollars. I'd never owned a leather jacket in all my life, not even a second-hand one, and here was a brand new, immaculate, brown, half sized jacket beckoning to me like one of the most seductive women I could possibly meet. So I took the jacket at five hundred dollars because I knew it would be less expensive than the lady in the long run, on both my pocket and on my heart.

Later that evening we showered and went into the town centre dressed to have a nice meal and some fun. I can't remember the name of the hotel we spent that evening in, but boy did we have a good time laughing and chatting with people.

From what I can remember Kevin stayed with me on and off for around two weeks. He'd made quite a few friends in town and knew a lot of backpackers. The ladies really took to him so he had to do his cat calling anywhere other than my place. And don't get me wrong, I like having women around me because they are a lot more alive and sensitive that most men I have come across. Having had to cling close to my mother's apron strings because of the hell my father put me through gave me a deeper insight into womanhood. Their sense of compassion and understanding has no equal apart from The Good Lord Himself. I won't be a hypocrite and say I'm not averse to some of them, but on the whole I feel comfortable in their presence.

One evening about a week later Kevin brought some friends round for a few drinks and a chat, and before I turned the TV off it showed a group of people bungy jumping off Skippers Bridge. Kevin said, 'God, I'd like to do that', and so did a few others. I said, 'I'll pay for you Kevin and that crazy friend of yours.' His name was Peter. He was from Switzerland, and was a ski instructor. And when Kevin brought him in to my place he was pretty pissed. He was completely hooked on doing it. Like Kevin he was crazy, but with a more simple outlook on life.

Anyway they both jumped at the chance of doing the jump. Then Peter put it up to me to join them, but I said I don't think I have the guts to do it. But he and some of Kevin's friends said, 'You can do it Terry. Go on give it a go.' So, after a few more drinks, I let myself be talked into it.

Next morning I went up to the bungy booking office to pay for two young, and one old crazy bastards to launch themselves into space off Skippers Bridge. And I have got to admit that even in my senior state I was just as crazy as my two young companions. If you haven't arrived at this conclusion in your walk with me so far just keep walking.

I was given a choice to go by bus or to fly by helicopter, which would be more expensive but would mean they could fit us in that afternoon. So I thought to myself, no way do I want to prolong the thought of jumping off this bridge, to hell with the expense. And I'll get some scenery in as long as I can keep my mind off the jump.

So we took off that afternoon, and just as we did so did the wind. That, of course, gave us a bumpy ride all the way to our jump-off point. Well, by the time the helicopter settled down on its landing platform my stomach was giving me a hard time. As I walked up to the jump-off point I was more concerned about the nausea that was creeping up on me than the fear of the jump. But not to dramatize the situation any further, when my name was called out I walked to the area where I was guided with tender loving hands through a small opening onto the launch-off platform. Even in my state of fear and nausea I felt moved by the concern and kindness shown to me as my two helpers prepared me for the moment when I may well be needing a change of underpants.

After tying the bungy rope on my ankles and giving me what reassuring instructions they could in my jittery state of mind which I'm sure they must have been well aware of, they stood me up on the platform and told me not to look down. My cue was to jump after one of them had counted from seven back down to one. Well, I did look down and God did it put the fear of hell into me! So much that I didn't wait for the count back to one; I took off on the count of four and hung like a wet blanket till I was eventually lowered into a waiting boat in the river below. I must say I felt quite pleased with myself as I sat in that boat being taken back to where the helicopter was waiting to return those of us who'd finished our jumps. My old stomach was more settled and the chills running along my spine turned into a warm glow. There was no turning back now. And if there was, it was only to regroup and tackle what had to be tackled. As I was the last to jump I watched Kevin and Peter give a brilliant display of how bungy jumping should be done, both vocally screaming out like crazy man as they left the platform.

That evening Kevin cooked a meal for the three of us, and over a few drinks we recapped on what that jump had meant to us. And boy, did we get a few laughs out of it. Later Kevin and Peter took off to fill in the hours of desire that the evening held for hot-blooded young men like themselves. I was quite content with what the day had already brought to my doorstep

SHOTOVER RIVER

Next morning when I woke up the sun streamed in through my lounge window the moment I pulled back the curtain, and it seemed to bounce off me. I really felt good. I felt great. And a great feeling of thankfulness went out to all those people who had encouraged me to do that jump. Spending time with these young people, and sharing what I could with them had brought a new sense of meaning into my life. And because I accepted them for what they were and made no judgments on how they should go about their lives in my presence, other than that they treat my unit as a place of friendship and not a lover's den, we'd all benefit from it in some way. And I'm very glad to say, apart from one instance which I quickly defused, my unit was a place of sanctuary for those who needed it. You could class it in much the same category as my car, which was given the title, 'God's Taxi' by one of the backpackers.

About a week later my right knee became badly swollen. I went to the doctor who asked me what I thought might have brought it on. I told him the only thing I could think of was that bungy jump. I can't remember what he said, but I got the impression he didn't suffer fools like me gladly. He said, 'you've got a lot of fluid at the back of your knee and I'm going to have to drain it off.' Well I couldn't believe the amount of fluid that came out of it, but a few days later it was as good as gold. Mind you, he warned me not to go bungy jumping again.

Three weeks later or so I was in Eichardt's Hotel and got caught up with around eight backpackers who wanted to go bungy jumping off the Kawarau Bridge. As only four of them had enough money to do it I said I'd pay for the other four. With nine of us packed into my four seater car we managed to avoid any police cars, thanks to the fact I was driving God's taxi. When we got there the others asked me if I was going to jump and I said, 'Since I screwed up on my first jump I've just got to have another go, leg or no leg.' Well, I've got to say that I really enjoyed that jump. I had no sense of fear whatsoever. And I had no ill effects after it. And who do I have to thank for that? Well, first The Lord Himself, and then all those young people He sent to encourage me. Without them my trip to the South Island could only be classed as another selfish tourist adventure, speaking from my point of view about myself.

As I remember it there were three main streets in Queenstown. I spent much of my time visiting restaurants and cafes in those streets with young people who crossed my path. They were wonderful centres for relaxation and communication, which I am still very much into today in different places I visit. And I never cease to be amazed at all the things I learn when I'm directly involved people, and that goes for people of all ages.

Books, TV documentaries, and so on, don't give me the same insights and vibrations great as they may be.

Anyway to get back to the point I mentioned about these three streets was the fact I could seldom remember which one I parked my car in because I was always moving from one to the other lost in my world of fun and laughter. For the moment I'd left the world of worry, dishonesty and discord behind me. I had found a reason to live again, and boy was I lapping it up. For those of you who want to really experience life before you move on I highly recommend you do something like this, and I believe that it will not only be a great gift to yourself, but also your gift to God.

So the fact that I could seldom remember where I'd left my car became an outstanding joke with my friends, and I'm sure it still pops into their heads from time to time as they go by in their lives.

As I was now learning to play tennis I bought four tennis rackets in Queenstown and they were put to good use in the public courts playing foursomes. Most of the young people I played with had more than an edge on me, but that didn't daunt me in any way. I knew I would improve in time. I was now quite confident that anything I set my mind on I could master to some degree. The only thing that could stop me was myself. Apart from my music and singing which had not really come to the surface, I had three passions in my life. Golf, tennis and snooker. As an RSA member I was able to play quite a few games of snooker with my young friends in the Queenstown Club.

And I must say a big thank you to that club for their hospitality to all the young people I introduced to the club. They enjoyed themselves, and not once did any problem arise.

As I began to come into contact with a number of the townspeople I thought I'd extend the hand of friendship by inviting them to a little party at my place. I put the word around and a yes seemed to be the response from most of them. I invested $250 on the food and drinks I thought would be needed to make the party an enjoyable one.

On the morning before the evening party one of the backpackers I'd befriended came to see me. She had a lot of stuff going on in her life and just needed someone to talk to, and as a father figure, she knew I would listen. But the core of her problems was too complex and sensitive for an inexperienced person like myself to deal with so I made her a cup of coffee, got her sitting comfortably, and used some home-grown psychology by telling her about the party I was putting on for some of the townspeople. I said, I could do with a woman's touch. Well that completely took her mind off her problems. She started helping me make sandwiches and giving me ideas on how to set things out with more enthusiasm than I was prepared to put into it. I let her have the floor completely. After she was happy with the set-up of things I said, 'I'd be very grateful if you could join my little party this evening as a small thank you for your artistic contribution towards it.' She said, 'I have a friend, could I bring him too?' I said, 'No problem, bring him along.'

She arrived back about 8.30 with her friend and introduced him to me. We sat talking over a drink as the time ticked slowly by. Nine o'clock, ten o'clock, but no one else arrived. I said, it looks like my party is a lost cause. Then out of the blue my very kind helper said 'It would be a shame to waste all this. Why don't I go down to the hostel where we are staying? There are lots of people of all ages and they'd love to get stuck into this.' Then like a flash I said, 'Go get 'em.' Then it suddenly dawned on my mind, didn't Jesus quote a parable in Matthew's Gospel that fitted close enough to the situation being presented to us by her? Matthew 22:8-10 if you wish to look it up.

Well, in about half an hour my unit was crammed with men and women of different ages and cultures. What a party we had! Music, singing, laughter, eating, drinking and dancing. It went on till around four in the morning, then gracefully fizzled out. But there are always a few after a party who find it hard to find their feet, as well as feeling a bit off colour. I gave them a blanket and a pillow each and told them to sleep it off and, if necessary, use the toilet not the carpet.

Before my friends left they found a writing pad on a small table in the lounge and everyone wrote a short message expressing their thanks for a wonderful time they had.

I shall I hope never forget that party that came together out of the blue, and how relaxed and happy everyone was. You could say it was wild in one sense, and tame in another. Everyone behaved beautifully. The following morning I got up around nine and made some breakfast for my three overstayers. Within an hour they were on their way.

The rest of my stay in Queenstown, apart from a trip to the Manapouri Dam and driving around some of the beautiful lakes, was concentrated on spending time with people. The need to be active in whatever department I could was very important to me. Golf, tennis and anything else I could do to stretch my limbs and mind was helping me to get right back on track again after allowing myself to exist in a world of fear, pain and loneliness. I don't believe I could ever find the right words to express how happy I was with my new lifestyle, even though I knew my bank balance was dropping fast.

I'd always wanted to do a parachute jump after my daughter Rachel told me how exhilarating it was. But I decided to leave her with the honour of being the only one in the family to do a single jump. I would go second best and with a tandem jump. Not so much because I might take the honour away from her, simply because I didn't have the courage she has.

I paid to do the jump in Invercargill, but the weather didn't settle long enough for me to do one. But where there's life there's hope. And if not, I may be able to convince my family to have my ashes strapped to a parachute and let them free-fall to the earth below. What a wonderful send-off that would be.

As my bank account was getting close to journey's end I thought I'd fly my youngest son down to join me for about a week. Due to his studies, however, he could only come for four days. So we both grabbed the opportunity to have some special time together. Bernard was a late arrival in the family so I wasn't able to spend as much time with him as I had with my daughters and eldest son. Here was a chance to bridge the gap a little.

When he arrived I asked him if he'd like to do the two bungy jumps that were on offer, and he jumped at the chance of this new experience. He did the two jumps with a lot more grace that his old man, and I was very proud of him.

During our four special days together we went whitewater rafting on the Shotover River. As we were coming around a bend on the river I got thrown into the surf. Like a shot Bernard jumped in and got me safely back on the raft with nothing more than a dent to my foolish pride. I will I hope never forget that moment because of how protective my son was for my safety. That is a very special feeling not too many fathers are privileged to have during their lifetime. And I say that with no type of judgment attached to it.

The rest of the four days we spent together I let Bernard do all the driving, which allowed me to take in more of the scenery than I could have if I was driving. The day after Bernard flew back to Auckland I checked my bank account and it told me the writing was on the wall. It said, time to start making plans for your new future. I had just over two thousand dollars to my name. Now's the time to see what you're really made of Terry was being expressed to me.

So three days later I said goodbye to Queenstown, and to whoever was around to farewell. In the early hours of that morning I drove out of Queenstown feeling like a million dollars I hadn't got. As I gazed at the beautiful mountains that add so much to the area's grace and tranquillity. I had a vision that one day I would come back. Well organised, I'd place large speakers on the mountain tops and play all sorts of music to give thanks to God for getting right behind me and giving me this fantastic opportunity to expose my humanity to all those whose lives I had touched, and who'd touched mine.

When I got back to Auckland I unfolded my experiences to my family, but I don't think they quite shared my enthusiasm because of my so-called extravagance. And I could well understand this because they were concerned for me. And of course they were seeing a whole new image of me and not the one they'd been used to for all those years.

It is so easy to let the grass grow under your feet, and this can happen if you let your mind get distracted from the course you're tuned into. I knew the odds were against me from the money point of view, but there was a deep sense of restlessness clawing deep within my gut. I was craving an even greater adventure than the one I'd already experienced in the South Island. I'd become inspired with a flame of happiness, enthusiasm and challenge that I'd never have thought was possible for me, especially at this late stage in my life.

To give up now would be nothing short of an insult to both God and myself. And though I didn't talk about Him very much on my journey, He was always my constant companion and always has been, even though I have failed to recognise it on so many occasions.

Looking back over the last few sentences I felt inclined to write this poem. I call it "Down Under."

We look at so many things to see
which will light our candle
and give us some sort of direction.
But yet we are bound by the choices
we make to keep that candle
burning or let it go out.
It's not down to the stuff the
candle is made of but to what
we are made of ourselves
that will keep our candle
burning or let it go out.

AUSTRALIA — LONDON — IRELAND

Not long after I got back to Auckland I decided to sell my car then have a quick look at Sydney and take a bus to Surfers Paradise just to say I'd been there. Then I'd make my way to Brisbane airport and purchase a one-way ticket to Dublin. No, it was not a very sensible approach considering my circumstances, but I'm sure that you are becoming well aware by now that sense was fast being replaced with such words as insanity and craziness. Mind you I love been told I'm insane or crazy because that tells me I'm very much alive.

When I got to Sydney I decided not to hang around but find a bus that would take me to Surfers Paradise. I had arrived around midday in Sydney and found a bus that was leaving for my destination somewhere close to six o'clock. Well I have got to tell you the journey completely put me off ever taking a long bus journey again. Not only was my stomach upset, well before we got there, but I was completely bored to death. Anyway I found somewhere to stay till I booked a flight to Dublin from Brisbane. Can't tell you much about the day I spent in Surfers Paradise because my holiday was no longer a spendthrift one, but now a pauper's.

The next day I was on my way from Brisbane to London, then on to Dublin. I had informed my brothers Tony and Ken that I was on my way. When I arrived they were there to meet me, and took me back to where my brother Gerald lived in Raheny. In due course I told them where my new life style had taken me. A few evenings later they began lecturing me regarding my extravagance, and the craziness of it all. Well I let them go on and eventually I said, 'Hey, guys, who was there for you when you needed somebody? All the years I took the brunt of Da's wrath when he was drunk. I know poor Ma went through her own hell, but she could lock her door when things got really bad, I couldn't. Small as it may be, who made a contribution to the family in those six years I spent in the RAF.' Very quickly they backed off and we finished up hugging each other.

A few weeks later my daughter Rachel wrote to tell me that my pension had been stopped because I hadn't let Social Welfare know I was going overseas. Seemingly the telephone call I made to advise them I was going overseas didn't carry much weight. She said unfortunately she couldn't do anything about it because I hadn't filled in the required forms. I sensed from her letter that she was a bit upset because she was concerned for me. I had also found out that Rachel had written to my brothers about her concern for me. Anyway a few things backfired in my mind and I wrote back to her more or less saying 'Sorry, love, but maybe it's time to just forget about me and get on with your own life.'

The following letter came to me out of this.

Dear Terry

Hi got your letter yesterday and it made me finally realise a few things. I'm sorry if I caused a rift between you and your brothers. It's just that so much has happened at once and I flared up. But I finally see why you went and just lived, and I hope you continue to always be happy.

I don't understand a lot of what happened years ago

between you and Sybil and your breakdown, but I do remember never seeing any demonstrative love between you two. Alex and I often talked about it. I would say: 'Why doesn't she ever give Terry a hug?' I never forget how hard you tried for us. Terry, I know you were always there. You always washed the dishes, made our lunches, took us to school when it was possible, and if I had a nightmare you were the one to come and comfort me.

Unfortunately, it's the ones you love most that you take for granted. I really hope you find the love you need and deserve. The only love I can give you is from my heart and head, but you are always in my thoughts. I guess it took a while to get used to how much you changed from a quiet bred Dad to a boisterous bungy jumper.

Well, Terry, I am really sorry if I put you wrong. Please don't ever stop writing to me and if you want to call, phone me collect. I insist. Bernard's always asking how you are. I think you know how deeply he cares for you. After you wrote in your letter that I would hear from you one day it sounded you were going for good and I felt very sad. So I had to write to you and let you know how much you're loved and cared for

   Rachel.

Well, that brought a few tears to my sad old eyes and it more than made up for the unfriendly words that had passed between us. It was, as I see it, something we both had to go through to bring us closer together and that's where we are to this very day, even with a few hiccups in between.

I could have asked Rachel to send me an air ticket to get me back to New Zealand when my money ran out, or stayed with my brother Gerald and settled back in Ireland, but neither of these prospects appealed to me. I was fast learning that the only way out usually ends up the hardest. I'd had already been placed in some tough situations in my growing-up years with my father, but between God and the will to survive I'd always managed to find a light at the end of the tunnel. But because of my circumstances I've got to admit I was going to do a lot of tunnelling in the next part of my walk before I'd even begin to see a flicker of light.

So I decided to enjoy myself as best I could till it was time to make my next move. Until that time when I had little or nothing left in my pocket. I'd then make my way to Belfast and throw myself at the mercy of the RAF. I'd ask them if they could get me to London, and then see what fate had in store for me. My daughter Alex lived close to London so I'd not be completely without a life support. My sister-in-law Eileen lived close to my daughter, but as I had separated from her sister I wasn't sure what kind of a reception might lie on that mat for me. But it wasn't necessary for me to cross that bridge till I came to it.

So I played golf in Deer Park in Howth till it was getting too expensive, then I reverted to pitch and putt in Saint Anne's Park which was less costly. I also played tennis there. Then I met a young man from England who was living close by. We became friends and many a hiding he gave me at tennis, but it was all part of the wonderful experience that was preparing me for an even greater one.

Then at last that experience arrived, as it does for those of us who have the courage, or maybe the stupidity of our convictions, to walk into the unknown more or less blindfolded. And I will admit there were quite a few butterflies running around in my stomach. I sold my camera, but in no way was I going to part with my golf clubs, tennis racquet or snooker cue till such time as my back was right up against the wall.

I said goodbye to all my family, who looked at me with concern in their eyes, and my brother Tony drove me to the station to catch my train to Belfast. Just as I was leaving he thrust a fifty pound note into my hand, which I can tell you I accepted gratefully. Men of Tony's charming personality and sense of generosity are few and far between. I saw much of my Uncle Harry in him.

As the train pulled out from the station I suddenly realised I'd been here before, the only difference being time and circumstances. Fifty three years ago I'd left this same station to escape from my father's clutches and join the Royal Air Force in Belfast. That seemed a lot more than a coincidence to my way of thinking. It felt as if I was being taken back in time to complete something I'd only half finished. And as the train got closer to Belfast things began to fall into place for me. This time I was not running away because I had been pushed into it. This time it was my own choice. No one had forced me to take this path. I can't explain in words what a wonderful sense of encouragement came out of that realisation. I no longer doubted myself. The will to survive and get myself back to New Zealand on my own terms, no matter what obstacles I had to climb over or crawl under, became the driving force within me.

And by this I don't mean that there wasn't a certain amount of fear and uncertainty lingering in the back of my mind. But I believe it was there only as a warning to be cautious of how I tackled the things that confronted me each day as I walked towards my goal.

Be careful with your words
Be diligent with your answers
Be courageous with your choices
And you'll succeed where millions have failed.

When I arrived in Belfast I found a cheap place to stay, then straightaway I made enquiries about getting in contact with my old saviour, the RAF. When I had located the reception desk and informed the lady there what my need was, she was able on the spot to make an appointment for me to see someone in a couple of days' time. I am a bit sketchy about all this, as I have and will be about certain parts of my walk, but it's not easy to keep everything in its place going back in time. Just to be truthful and sincere makes life into a means of getting somewhere. But anyway the outcome was that they very kindly made arrangements to fly me to London and booked me into an RAF accommodation centre across from Waterloo Station. This all took about nine days. To keep my mind and my physical being tuned up I started wandering around having a look at a few places. One day I was standing on a corner waiting to cross the road when I heard an explosion. When I looked to see what had taken place, I saw a van about two or three hundred yards away emitting all sorts of flames and smoke. I said to the guy waiting beside me, 'Well, obviously it wasn't meant for us.' He just looked at me as if I was a nut case. What did I say earlier about being careful with your words? That was a sharp reminder to me that I was in Northern Ireland, not Southern Ireland where you could get away with just about anything, except maybe robbing a bank or being a bad Catholic. Anyway, I'm very glad to say no one was in the van, and no one was close enough to get hurt.

That was about midday, so I thought I'd go back to my digs. That was enough excitement for one day.

While I was in Belfast I went to the Workman's Club and played snooker. I also had some interesting discussions over a few drinks with some of the people there, and was always treated with respect. There was only one occasion in Belfast when I was left to hang out like a wet rag. One Sunday morning I got this novel idea that I'd go to Church. You never know what's around the corner till you make the effort to go there. And of course a little bit of help wouldn't go astray in my particular circumstances. So I set off for this Presbyterian Church and as a new face I got a warm welcome. Then after the service as we were partaking in the usual tea, coffee and biscuits I was asked what had brought me to their church. Very honestly and openly I came out with my predicament. Well, there wasn't too much brotherly love coming my way after that. No one even attempted to offer any kind of help. As a matter a fact I'm quite sure they were only too glad to see the back of me. But it was very interesting, and laughable too, because if my mother, God rest her soul, had been alive and found out I'd attended that service she'd surely have thought my soul was damned forever, whilst my father would be smiling like a Cheshire cat.

A few days later I was on my way to London. From Heathrow I took the tube to Waterloo Station. The RAF had given me ten pounds and provided me with two nights' accommodation at the RAF club just across from the Station.

When I got settled in I rang my daughter in Watford to let her know where I was. She said, 'I'll pick you up on the morning you have to leave the club', so that put my mind at rest for a while. Alex duly arrived and took me to where my sister-in-law Eileen lived with her husband Hugh. They were on holiday at that time and by now I was very hungry as my money had run out. Very quickly Alex whipped up a lovely meal of bacon, eggs and fried bread. I don't recall having a better meal in all my life because I felt like I was literally starving. And those of you who've been there will know what I'm talking about.

I stayed there for a few nights and then Eileen and Hugh arrived home. I've had some uncomfortable moments in my life and this had to be one of them. Hugh wasn't very impressed at all because I'd left his wife's sister and he was worried about Eileen being upset, which I could well understand. It was a very embarrassing few minutes for me I can tell you, but Eileen was really very good about it. I think it was more the shock of finding me there that took her off her guard. She is no longer with us, but I will always remember her as one of the most humorous, generous and caring ladies I have ever met. I remember talking to Hugh on the phone one day and he humorously said to me, 'You married the wrong sister.' He didn't let me forget about that.

A couple of days later Alex arranged a bed and breakfast place where I could stay for a couple of weeks till faith had some other plans for me. This walk of mine was all about learning when to compete and when to yield.

So I took it easy for the first week, and the second week I went to an organisation something equivalent to Social Welfare here in New Zealand. I explained my predicament to them. I was told to take a seat and someone would talk to me later. While I was waiting I got talking to the guy beside me. I told him about myself and he said he had somewhere I could stay and it wouldn't cost me a cent. Naturally my ears pricked up. Where is this haven for this mad old Irishman? It sounded too good to be true, but I was in no position to ignore anything that was thrown my way. It was as though God sensed my need for help just as He had all those other times. And if you look closely at my walk you will get a better picture of what I'm talking about.

Eventually, the Welfare people told me to come back in two days and they'd have something for me. So when my new friend had got himself sorted out he took me to this street in Ealing, the name of which I can't remember. We went into an old, rundown, two-storied house where he showed me a large room with a double mattress on the floor. He said, "This is your home away from home if you want it. Then he showed me the kitchen where there were cooking utensils, mugs and dishes and said, all you have to get yourself is a knife, fork and spoon. The electricity is working and the gas stove is too. What more could you want? I couldn't believe my good fortune. Once again God was smiling on me. So three days later, for the first time in my life, I was actually squatting.

My fellow squatter told me that all the houses on both sides of the street were in for the chop and the only one that was considered habitable was this one. A couple have just moved out of where you are, as luck or faith may have it. It's yours till such time as you move on. I told him how grateful I was and he said, it will cost you a beer when you have the money. As far as I can remember there were four others squatting there. They seemed nice people except for one. There was something about that guy I didn't trust. Just call it a gut feeling that eventually proved to be right.

The day after I moved in I picked up some money from the welfare people and they told me to come back again in two weeks' time. For the time being I could relax and make the most of my new environment. There was only one drawback about the house. It was very near the railway line, and when a train passed by you could feel quite a few vibrations, but as the saying goes, beggars can't be choosers, especially when you're living rent free, with gas and electricity thrown in.

A few days before payday, with just enough money to for a half pint on beer, I went into a bar to relish it. Out of the blue a guy came over to me and started talking to me. I said to myself, Oh, God, what have I done to deserve this at such a low ebb in my life? Been there? I'm sure you have, and if not you still could take note of it.

Anyway his problems started to flow thick and fast. His wife had left him and he was still trying to figure out why. To cut a long story short he was a very boring person and I could understand with what little wisdom I'd collected over the years, why she'd done so. Mind you, on the other side of the coin I had to question why she married him in the first place. But then again love has many strings to its bow, weird, wonderful and stranger than fiction, to name a few. It seems that this man had been quite content to live his own sheltered lifestyle, and had expected her to do likewise.

Well, I tried as best I could to reach him but seemed to be getting nowhere. But I don't give up easily as you may have noticed. I took from my pocket three large sheets of paper that I'd been working on regarding my breakdown and my own marriage break-up and handed them to him to read. In doing so I had bared my soul to this man. He sat there reading for a while. Then he turned to me with moisture in his eyes, put his hand on my shoulder and said, 'Could I buy you a drink?' You're right, I didn't say no. Anyway, I believe I left him with a little more consideration for others than when first we met, and my thirst a little more satisfied.

EALING TO NEW ZEALAND

When I left my sister-in-law's house she said, 'If you're going to be around please come and have a meal with us', and gave me her phone number. So one day I took her up on her offer and everything went really well. I didn't tell her that I was squatting, just doing my bed and breakfast thing and was happy with it. Her husband Hugh also welcomed me. He hadn't been particularly fond of my ex-wife.

Then one evening before payday about five or six of us squatters got to together in the main lounge. We were all broke and feeling down. I said to them, I have a ring that cost me five hundred dollars. Another of those extravagant moments when my sense of value got the better of me. Then this guy I thought was on the up and up said. I could get eighty to one hundred pounds for it. So I said, 'Off you go, then we'll go out and do some shopping'. Well, that was the last I saw of my ring, but it was a lesson well learned.

One evening when I came this guy I'd had a bad gut feeling about asked me to come up to the lounge. When I got there two other guys were in the room. Then this little so and so who asked me up said, 'We want you out of here within the next two days'. He had a knife in his hand which he was toying with nervously. One of the other men about his size was sitting close to him with his head in his hands, leaning forward as though he was suffering from some kind of pain in his head. I wasn't too concerned about either of those two, but I had reservations about the bigger guy sitting in the far corner of the room. Rumour had it he'd just come out of jail. He didn't say a word, just sat there with a kind of sinister smile on his face. So once again I heeded the advice that discretion was the better part of valour. 'I'll be out of here in two days' time.' Without giving them any opportunity to gloat I turned and walked away.

Next day I went to the Housing Department in Ealing that caters for people in my situation. I told them about myself and got fixed up straightaway in a house run by this bowzy of an Irishman. And when I say bowzy, I mean not a very nice person. I was to share a room with another man younger than myself whom I found very pleasant but plagued with all sorts of problems. The room I wouldn't class as filthy, but it was making a name for itself in that direction. There was just one small window to let in some light and a little air, and my buddy was not too particular when it came to laundry time. So that gives you a rough idea that it wasn't even close to being one star accommodation. And the toilet on our floor was so small that anyone with a large arse would have a job getting in and out of it. It had been reduced to make space for another room.

Mind you, bad as it was, I was still very grateful for a roof over my head for the time being. I mention all of this only because I, like most people crave a little sympathy at times, and it also adds a little something to my walk.

On one of the days that Eileen and Hugh had invited me down for lunch I was walking through Greenford Park singing because it was a lovely day and I was in good spirits. As I was about to pass an elderly lady she looked over her shoulder at me and said, 'Oh, it's nice to hear someone singing.' I said 'thank you', and then I glanced down at the two pretty full plastic bags she was carrying. I could see that her hands were swollen with what seemed to me to be arthritis. I said, 'Please may I carry those bags for you?' She said, 'Thank you, I would be grateful. My arthritis is not so good today.' Then I told her where I was going and she said, 'I've seen and talked to the lady that lives there and found her to be very pleasant, and her husband keeps their garden in wonderful condition.'

So I walked with her to her home. She wanted me to come in, but I said, 'I would love to, but my sister-in-law and her husband are expecting me for lunch and I'm a little late already.' Then she made me promise that I'd come and visit her another day.

When I got to Eileen's house I told her I'd met a lady

who introduced herself as Molly Danger. Eileen said, I know her, she's a darling.

Four days later I went back to see Molly as promised. She invited me in and made some lunch for both of us.

She said her husband had passed away a while back and she lived on her own. Then I unfolded my story to her and she said, 'Terry, I've got a bedroom upstairs with a nice single bed in it. You are more than welcome to stay with me till such time as you get yourself sorted out.' Well that kind of blew me away. I could have been someone with all sorts of hang-ups, but this dear, kind-hearted lady was willing to accept me as I was after the very short time she'd known me. But at the same time I couldn't believe my good fortune.

I gratefully accepted her out-of-this-world offer of benevolence and thought to myself, 'Lord, what would I do without You?' And I'm sure as I can be that He was saying to Himself, 'what do I have to do to get this lost sheep of mine back in the fold?' And of course I would have to answer that by saying, 'Please Lord, I'm having such a good up and down time, bear with me for a while longer.' He must have heard me; I'm still here.

Late that afternoon I was making my way back from Greenford to my no-star abode in Ealing and as I got closer to it the owner spotted me in his car and pulled up along-side of me, opened his window and said I want you out of my place tomorrow. Mind you, it didn't surprise me, for I hadn't been very discreet in my choice of words about him or his makeshift premises. But now that I had a real ace up my sleeve I said to him, 'I would be only too delighted to be out of your place tomorrow. God has found me a paradise to live in, and it's got a lovely big toilet.' Well, for a moment I thought he was going to have a go at me, but he just said 'fuck off, be out of my place tomorrow.' Well, I don't often get the timing right, but that had to be the queen of them all. So, as Molly had given me her phone number I rang her and asked her if it would be alright to move into her place today. With the bad feelings that had developed between this guy and myself I did not want to spend another night under his roof. My philosophy is to keep the peace while you can, and challenge it when you have to.

Anyway, Molly said come as soon as you like. So I had to make two trips to get my gear to her place. When I came back for the second lot they were lying out in the front garden. I won't add to that other than to say it saved me climbing the stairs to collect them.

Now before I talk about my stay with Molly I'm going to indulge in a flashback. It's not easy to remember everything when you're living a crazy lifestyle such as I'd been catapulted into.

When I was squatting in Ealing I met a guy who'd been badly crippled in a motorcycle accident some years earlier. One evening one of his mates who was squatting with me asked me if I would like to come and visit him in a squat not far from where we were. He said, 'I told him about you, and he'd like to meet you.' I thought to myself, here I am just a few days living in what Barfoot and Thompson would shudder to be involved with, and my fame is starting to precede me. So off we went to meet this guy. Well, from the outside of building he lived in you'd shudder to think what the inside might be like. But when we reached that small area he lived in I was very impressed at how clean smelling and tidy this man kept his place. The bedroom wall was covered with a combination of pictures of all sorts of motorcycles and women dressed in fancy clothes, or no clothes at all. I don't think it would go down well in London's art galleries, but I was very impressed with it.

This guy could get around, but it was quite difficult for him. Yet a more humorous and cheerful person in his condition I still have yet to meet. He was also very intelligent and well read. Anyway that was a wonderful upshot to our chance acquaintance.

He told us that the Ealing Housing Council had made available to him a one-bedroom unit close to everything he needed for everyday life, and all that was required for it was some furniture. One of the guys where we were staying, who knew Ealing like the back of his hand, suggested that four of us take a hike around its streets to see what we could find to help furnish the unit. Two days or so later, on a nice bright morning, four of us took off to comb the streets of Ealing. Well, once again God seemed to be smiling on us. We collected a double bed mattress in very reasonable condition, four chairs, two tables and some carpet. All it took was a little dedication on our part, with fate or God's help, to accomplish our mission in less than three hours.

That evening we pooled what money we had to celebrate our friend's first evening in his new unit, and what an inspiring party it was. And although that was the last I saw of him, his memory is still fresh and beautiful in my mind.

Living with Molly in comfortable surroundings was like a little bit of Heaven. Her sense of humour and compassion left nothing to be desired, a real lady with all the trimmings to go with it. What she really enjoyed was her half-glass of whisky at night with not much water in it, and she insisted that I join her. She told me many stories about her life and family that both amused me, and touched my soul. I think a lot of her family members thought she was a bit of a nut case by what she told me about them. But I'd positively disagree with that, and say maybe the boot was on the other foot. Sometimes I'd sing Irish songs, other times we'd watch TV. I don't recall a dull moment between us.

On my first payday there I bought Molly a bottle of whisky as a small thank you for her kindness to me. I had enough money to buy my own food, but she insisted on spoiling me from time to time, and I've got to admit that I loved it. And I did manage to get in a few games of golf at the nine-hole golf course at Greenford. I tried to tidy up Molly's back garden as it was a mess, but unfortunately she lacked the necessary tools. I just did the best I could.

Then one day about three weeks after I moved in with Molly, my daughter Alex knocked on the front door and asked for me. I introduced her to Molly and we chatted for a short time as Alex had to go to work. She handed me a large envelope and said, 'that's from Rachel.' I opened it, and there was a letter and an air ticket that would get me back to New Zealand. The main message in the letter read: 'Terry, please come home before we all go crazy worrying about you.'

Well you could have knocked me down with a feather, for nothing was further from my mind.

After Alex had left, Molly said, 'I'm so happy for you, but I am really going to miss you.' That kind of choked me up as I returned the same feelings to her. But I also knew I couldn't go on living there on the edge of circumstances that surrounded me. Everything I needed to further my lifestyle such as it was, lay back in New Zealand. And not just my family and friends, but also the jumping point for the next venture in my life. I was now on a journey to God knows where, but to get there I knew I must not let anything stand in my way. The worst, or the best, that could happen to me is death, but as I know that is inevitable what have I got to lose. I had already let so many things pass me by, now had to be the time to try and rectify that to whatever degree I could and have as many wonderful experiences as I could.

As I was due to fly out in a few days' time we certainly lived up those remaining hours. With lots of hugs and a few tears I bid this lovely lady goodbye and said, 'I'll be back to see you one day Molly, and I will write.'

As I flew out for New Zealand I thought back to all those

crazy and wonderful experiences that had been dropped in my lap, and all the diverse people who'd drawn me to them or pushed me away. It also crossed my mind that I'd done a lot of living in a very short period of time. I must admit I felt on top of the world. Had I bought a return ticket when I flew to Ireland, think of all the experiences I'd have missed and the lessons I'd have failed to come to grips with. For the first time in my life I was starting to discover that self within myself. Getting to know yourself if that's possible, can take forever, but we don't have forever, all we have is the here and now. So I gave that a lot of thought as my sky bird took me home.

QUEENSLAND - COOLANGATTA

I had a great welcome home from my family and friends when I arrived back in New Zealand and Rachel had a bed waiting for me. The next day I went to see Social Welfare. As I was two days over the six months you're allowed to be overseas while on the pension, they refused to pay me for the time I'd been away. Very quickly I went to see my MP Peter Hilt and explained everything to him. Within two weeks I was reinstated on the pension payroll and received back pay as well. You might say that I was lucky, but I think I deserved it, but I did give a big thank you to Mr Hilt.

I bought myself a little car and joined the Pupuke Golf Club. It didn't take me long to find out what a hard course it was, especially on my old knees. But I will not forget the first day I played there. I was about to hit off from the first tee when I saw two young men in their teens about to hit off on the second nine. So I went over and asked them if I could join them. Without any hesitation they invited me to join them. We'd completed the tenth hole and teed off for the eleventh when one of the young men hit a sliced his ball and it landed on the tenth putting green. Behind us four men were attacking the tenth green so the young man had to wait until they were finished, then lift his ball off the green and drop it on the fairway before he could take his next shot. Then one of the men went up to the young man's ball and kicked it off the green. Of course straightaway my Irish came up. I went over to him and said, 'that wasn't very good etiquette for those young men to witness.' Well, he started to rave on and on and said that he was a committee member, and this that and the other. I just looked through him and walked away knowing his mates would back him up. Not one of them had the courage or the sense of etiquette to agree with me.

It wasn't long before I found out what an unsavoury person this guy was. For me that didn't say a lot for the rest of the committee at that particular time. Mind you I know that one rotten apple in a barrel doesn't necessarily mean that the rest are contaminated, but it still leaves a big question mark.

I played there for almost two years, then began to feel restless again. Mind you, I'd kept myself pretty fit through golf, tennis, swimming and snooker, and my voice well aired in the folk clubs. But I needed more challenge in my life. I felt I was just fulfilling my own selfish needs. What I enjoy more than anything else is giving and sharing, because through them my personal fulfilment is no longer a selfish one. I exist for a purpose and that is to try to explore everything that offers a challenge for my spiritual growth. And the more unselfish risks I take the freer I become to soar to new heights.

I had already programmed my mind on going to Australia not too long after I returned to New Zealand. Well, the timing was right for that as my car had packed up. Rachel had bought herself another car and given me her Mini for which I was very grateful, but it needed an engine job done on it. So I decided to sell the car, and with the money I got for it hit out for my first port of call, Brisbane.

The best offer I could get was $500 so I settled for that. Then I went to Social Welfare in Takapuna to tell them I was planning to live in Australia for a while or longer, can you give me a form to fill in. I didn't want a repeat of my last experience. Then this lady said to me all you have to do is show them your pension card when you arrive there and you will be transferred onto the Australian pension, she said.

A few days before I was due to leave I arranged for a farewell party to be held in Kitty O'Brien's pub close to Victoria Park. Many a wonderful night I'd spent in that pub when it first opened. Anyway it was a fantastic farewell party made possible with the support of my family and friends, How much so I hadn't fully appreciated until that night.

Before I took off for Brisbane a good Dublin friend of mine, Connor McSweeney, recommended a backpackers there called the Sly Fox. When I arrived it was late at night so I took a taxi from the airport and asked the driver if he could find me a cheap motel. The next day I made my way to the Sly Fox.

I was well pleased with the recommendation Connor had given me. The place was really nice and tidy. I got myself a room then took a walk around the area. I decided that I didn't really want to stay in Brisbane for more than a couple of days.

That evening before I left the Sly Fox they had organised a pool knockout competition and first prize was a dozen beers, or two bottles of wine. With a lot of luck I won. I gave the beer away and shared the wine. I paid the price next morning for drinking wine instead of beer, but it was one of those nights to remember, and my young competitors gave this old guy a great reception when I won.

I wrote this poem about the game and titled it "Make It Happen.

> *When I arrived in Brisbane*
> *I was very much at sea*
> *Where the hell was I going?*
> *What was going to happen to me/*

I had the address of a backpackers
A friend had given to me
One night at a cheap motel
Then the backpackers it had to be.

I got there the next day in the rain
I was made to feel at home
The room was small but cosy
So things were going rosy

That second night there was a party
With a pool competition thrown in
First prize a dozen beer or two bottles of
wine
The glory of the win

It was a knockout competition
And everyone played well
I got into the final
And with lots of luck I won

The wine was flowing fast that night
I gave the beer away
And paid the price next morning
For drinking wine instead of beer

When I left the backpackers I made my way to
Coolangatta and found myself a one bedroomed
apartment. It was a on the expensive side for my small

bank roll, but as I planned to go to Sydney as soon as I received my Social Welfare cheque I decided not to worry about it too much. Fate. However as fate has many surprises in store for us, little did I know once again I was about to get my arse kicked.

The day I arrived in Coolangatta I went along to Social Welfare with high hopes of receiving my first Australian pension cheque within a couple of weeks. In the office I was given the necessary papers to fill out. When completed I was then interviewed by a very nice man who asked me for my letter of introduction from New Zealand. Quite taken back I said to him, I don't have one. Then I went on to tell him how the lady at Social Welfare in Takapuna had told me all I had to do when I arrived in Australia was to show you my New Zealand pension card and then you would get in touch with them to sort things out. He said, I'm sorry, but it doesn't work that way. For a New Zealand citizen to receive the Australian pension we need a letter of introduction.

Then like a flash it all came back to me, a repeat of what happened to me in 1990 when I went back to Ireland. The only differences were the distance and the smaller sum of money in my pocket.

Well, what I didn't say to myself about that women in Social Welfare in New Zealand, and my own stupidity for not doing my homework after getting caught out before, would be censored if I were to write it down here. Then my interviewer said all we can do is to get on to our main branch in Hobart and get them to sort it out with New Zealand Social Welfare. But in the meantime there is nothing we can do for you. Well, that completely took the wind out of my sails. My adventurous trip to Australia was already falling apart at the seams, and I even got a suntan.

I was told to come back in few weeks' time to see if there was any news for me. I rang Rachel and asked her if she could get in touch with Social Welfare in New Zealand and make a plea on my behalf. Well, I thought to myself, there's no use crying over spilt milk. I've been through a lot worse, so let's get on with the living.

About a week later I was having a drink in a pub when got talking to a guy who was living in a Caravan Park nearby. We exchanged stories and he invited me back for a bite to eat. I told him of my plight and he very decently offered to put me up until I got myself sorted out. Any helping hand offered had to be grasped in my position. My experiences from the past were already telling me that. And whatever the consequences might be I'd have to deal with them when they arrived on my doorstep.

A week after I moved into this man's caravan the consequences did arrive. Actually they started building up the day after I arrived. You know that old saying, "If you want to know me, come and live with me. All this guy could think about was winning lotto, and then what he would do with the money. And do you know what was on the top of his list? A four-wheel-drive Pajero. He drove me to all sorts of car yards between Coolangatta and Brisbane just to look at Pajeros. And when we weren't looking at them, he was talking about them. I said to myself, 'I know I'm pretty desperate, but am I this desperate?'

After suffering in silence for seven days I slipped out early one morning and left a thank you note and made my way to the backpackers in Coolangatta. I now had in my pocket $150 to last till I hopefully might receive something from Social Welfare. Well I can't speak highly enough of the backpackers. What was most satisfying of all was that I was no longer at the mercy of a man who wanted to win lotto and buy a Pajero. Those words were no longer ringing in my ears. I promised myself if I was ever in the position to buy a four-wheel-drive vehicle a Pajero would never get a look in.

A week later, still no money from Social Welfare I pawned my beloved golf clubs for eighty dollars. As much as it hurt my pride, it kept my head above water for a while longer. Then lo and behold I got a cheque for $200 from Social Welfare. Nothing had come through about getting my pension finalised, but at least it was a helping hand for the moment. And I said to myself surely another two weeks should sort my pension out. So I put my trip to Sydney on hold. There comes a time when you have to believe in all sorts of illusions. But then again, what's the point of living a life that doesn't give you in some way what you want, what you need. Apart from the rough seas, there was still plenty of calm water to paddle my canoe through. And speaking of water, I was in it swimming almost every day. I also had an exhilarating time playing volleyball which I never played before, and if you'd seen me you'd have worked that out very quickly. But the team from the backpackers wanted the numbers, so they couldn't be too particular who they took on board.

On most of my evenings I played snooker at Twin Towers RSL, and pool and chess at the backpackers. And I played some of the best snooker I've ever played. I won chickens and meat packs which helped to fill my stomach. Yes, someone was once again smiling down at me, as He had so many times before. On one occasion, when I was playing in a snooker competition against a very good player who had to give me a 24 point lead, I beat him on the black ball. He was just about fit to be tied up. All through the game, by playing safe, I had this guy so worked up I thought he'd have a fit. I don't usually play that way, but this big, pig-headed individual was someone I really wanted to beat. It went down really well with the rest of the players.

There was an incident of a different kind on the backpackers' pool table, the difference being I wasn't out for blood this time. I'd finished playing a guy by potting the black ball when another guy challenged me to a game for five dollars. His words, as I remember them, were 'You're not a bad player, but I'll beat you.' I thought to myself, 'what am I doing to attract all these strange people to me?' Anyway, I took fifteen dollars off him in three straight games. Now in all fairness, I have to say he was the better player, but he lost his cool when I beat him in the first game. A week later he got his revenge as I handed him back his fifteen dollars.

A few days later this same guy got himself badly messed up by trying to force his drunken self on the daughter of the backpackers' manager. On the morning he was leaving he said to me, with his good looks still not in good shape, that trouble was his middle name. He lived in Canada and earned his living driving trucks he told me. Before we said our goodbyes I told him I knew he was a good pool player the first time we played, and he proved that in our second encounter. He said, 'No Terry, you are the better player. You won with grace and lost with grace. You are something I would love to be. You're a gentleman.' There will always be a soft spot in my heart for him.

Another moving incident during my stay in Coolangatta was the time I got involved with a group of school children. Not long after I arrived I went to the Baptist Church one Sunday morning. Before I knew what happened I was involved in entertaining young school children from 3.00 till 4.30 several afternoons a week. Along with the parents and teachers I helped to organise games for them to play, and I'm sure I must have been the biggest kid of the whole lot. I get on really well with kids, but I don't think my views on Christianity fitted in quite so well with the adults. My childlike sense of curiosity and humour seemed to be somewhat out of their range of understanding. The children understood me because they had not lost their sense of honesty. They'd not yet arrived at the gate when they would eventually find themselves, or lose themselves.

There was a lovely lady whose name I shouldn't have

forgotten, but have. She was one of the teachers. I was still having problems trying to get my pension sorted out and decided Sydney was my only option. I could go straight to the New Zealand Consulate and ask them to help me. My stumbling block was the train fare, roughly one hundred dollars. This lovely lady knew of my predicament because she was someone I could confide in. After I'd finished my duties with the children one day she invited me out for a coffee. After we'd had the coffee and something to eat, which she kindly paid for, she put an envelope in front of me and said, 'Please go to Sydney and get yourself sorted out. Your train fare is in that envelope along with a little extra. We'll be sorry to lose you, but it's time for you to move on.' After I thanked her tears came as we gave each other a big hug.

SYDNEY

Two days later I went to Byron Bay to catch the train to Sydney. I arrived early in the morning with my suitcase and went down to sit on the beach. I began reflecting on what I'd been through since I landed in Australia. Seven weeks had elapsed with all kinds of highs and lows testing my weaknesses and my strengths. It would have been easy to ask my daughter Rachel to send me an air ticket and fly back to New Zealand to all the comforts of home. But that would be the coward's way out and I would miss a part of what life's education had in store for me. All those messages that smile on me from my past are all those actions I was forced to make, willingly or unwillingly.

The train to Sydney was not due to leave till around midnight so I had time to kill. About ten hours. After a few lazy hours on the beach I made my way to the pub for a light meal and a beer. I'd only been sitting down for a few minutes when a guy with a backpack began chatting to me. I'd say he was about thirty to thirty-five years old. Our conversation flowed very freely, and down came any age and personality barriers. He was one of those nice people you meet when the timing seems right.

After we exhausted a certain amount of conversation we spotted a vacant pool table and got engrossed in a game. He was very good with the cue so I lost two games in row. Just as we finished the second game two guys came up and challenged us to a game of doubles. Well, between the two of us we hit a winning streak. For around about three hours we took on challengers from every direction. What beat us in the finish was my partner getting so drunk. But, boy, did we have an audience while we were on top, and they gave us a good cheer when we left the table. I never had a chance to thank my pool partner before I caught my train. He'd fallen asleep, and boy did he need it.

My train journey to Sydney was one I could forget very easily. Apart from getting no sleep, and developing an upset stomach I had to try and shave in cold water at the railway station in Sydney. It must have been about midday when I arrived at the New Zealand Consulate. I took the lift and made my way into a small office. Very quickly I gave the lady behind the desk a short rundown on my situation, but don't remember any sympathy forthcoming. She said, 'If you would like to take a seat outside I'll get someone to see you.' I went outside into the corridor hoping to collapse into a chair, but there wasn't one to be seen. It looked as if the burglars had been there before me, or that woman had taken an instant dislike to me. I must admit that I was angry as well as feeling pretty miserable, but I had enough sense to know that it wouldn't help my cause if I pushed any wrong buttons at this particular time. So I just stood there with my back against the wall and gave some kind of a prayer I felt had a mixed side to it. Well, I don't know how long I'd been standing there, but I do remember starting to feel light in the head. That's the last thing I recall until I woke up in Sydney Hospital. When I came to I found myself gazing into the face of an angel. Well, that's how it seemed to me at the time. This lovely smiling face was uttering these words to me, 'Wake up, Mr Robinson, wake up.' Then I started to realise that I must have passed out back in that corridor with no chairs. A good analogy to that pub with no beer, seeing I was in Australia...

Anyway, a little bit of notice and affection was just what I needed to help me get back on my feet again. The next morning a gentleman from the New Zealand Consulate put to rest any future problems to my receiving the Australian pension. I don't often congratulate myself for sticking to my guns, but that day I did.

Two days later, with a new mischievous sense of adventure under my belt and money in my pocket, I headed for a backpackers at Cremorne Point that had been recommended to me. As I stood at the wharf at Circular Quay waiting for the ferry to take me across to the Point I was captivated by the scenery all around me. The Sydney Harbour Bridge was an awesome sight to take in as the clear blue sky added to its majesty.

Shortly after my first ferry ride in Australia I got myself booked into a small single room in The Cremorne Point Backpackers. It was more expensive than sharing a room, but with a few unwelcome experiences in the sharing department I decided it was more of a necessity than a personal luxury. Besides I was really enjoying my own company since I'd left my marriage. My needs for survival were really quite simple, but the need to be at one with myself was something of a far more serious nature, as you will see for yourself as you keep walking with me.

I had a very relaxing five nights at the backpackers. I say nights because I spent my days cruising around Sydney, exploring the city that was to become my home for three years. What really turned me on was the fact that it cost me only one dollar a day to go anywhere I wanted by ferry, train or bus. 'God' I said to myself, 'they know how to look after their old folk in Australia. What took me so long to get here?'

When the five days I'd paid for in advance were coming to an end I decided to look for something of a quieter and more permanent nature. Well, little did I know what fate had in store for me once again otherwise I might have missed its trials and tribulations. Even in the grimmest moment a new hunger is born. Every day we stand before the gates of Heaven or Hell.

A few days before I was due to leave the backpackers I spotted an advertisement in the local newspaper for a room to let in a hotel in George Street in the city. I looked at the room and decided it would be my next refuelling station till such time as fate dictated otherwise. Well, life's lessons were coming thick and fast. I arrived for my stay on a Thursday and was screaming to get out by the weekend because of some very loud and uninspired music that rocked the whole building, and made sleep something you could only dream about!Once again my eyes were searching the Accommodation Offered columns to keep my sanity intact. The following Thursday was a payday so I thought I'd be better equipped to make my move sometime after that. In the meantime I suffered in some sort of silence. Then after I'd drawn my money from the bank on the Thursday I had to go to Social Security to receive my medical card details. While I was sitting there waiting to be interviewed I got talking to the guy who was sitting beside me. Being honest and very green, besides being Irish, I was about to get my first lesson on what a tough and unscrupulous place the beautiful city of Sydney could be at times. I told this guy something of my circumstances and said I was looking for a room to rent. Very convincingly he described a small, self-contained unit that could be rented in Bondi for a hundred dollars a week. He said the owner was a friend of his and that I needed to put the money up front. Without giving it any thought, other than grabbing this wonderful opportunity I gave him two weeks rent. We then caught a bus to Central Station to catch the train to Bondi. When we got to the station he said he had to go to the toilet. I said '"Okay', without the blink of an eyelid. Well, I waited and I waited, till all of a sudden the penny dropped. I'd had been taken to the cleaners.

Or maybe for the fool I was. I'm sure if the streets of Sydney could laugh they would have split their seams that day. As the truth dawned on me I began to laugh. What was the point of doing anything else? I got exactly what I deserved. I need a wakeup call and I got one. But, without my realising it, this was to be part of my destiny. This was the setting for the next stage of my journey. Knowing that I wouldn't have enough money to rent a place till next payday, I made a few enquiries. A few days later I was a guest at the Matthew Talbot Home for destitute men in Woolloomooloo, run by the St Vincent de Paul Society. What a culture shock that was for me to start with. The three free meals a day were fantastic, but the sleeping quarters were something I hadn't bargained for. It's very much improved since then, I hear. I remember on the first night being told to sleep with my necessary belongings under my pillow and to take them with me if I went to the toilet. My suitcase with my tennis racquet and snooker cue they put in storage for me. But I hadn't reckoned on someone being in my bed when I returned from the toilet. I could have asked the man to leave, but he was a lot bigger than me, and looked a lot meaner. So once again I reckoned discretion was the better part of valour and camped in a chair instead. The other eight days I spent in that dormitory passed okay.

About five days elapsed before I started to survey my surroundings with a deeper sense of awareness. A little voice in my head began telling me, there's a need for your services here, as well as a wealth of experiences for you to sample. Fate hasn't dumped you at the Matthew Talbot for no reason. You have enough money to live on and lots of free time so put it to some sensible use. Two days later the Matthew Talbot was set to become a fantastic milestone in my life as I became one of its volunteer workers.

My duties involved cleaning up after the morning, midday and evening meals, and I could always get something to eat myself. The kitchen staff were a great bunch of guys who'd been through some rough times themselves. As the days went by I began to realise that I was involved with men who unfortunately had tasted all kinds of whiplash that life had dealt them for one reason or another. And they were still licking their wounds. In all probability they would be for most of their lives.

THE MATTHEW TALBOT HOME

Not long after I started work at the Matthew Talbot I had

my first and only run-in with one of the kitchen staff. On this particular evening I was removing plates from the table after the men had eaten, and then leaving them on the bench for two other volunteers to scrape of the leftovers into bin bags. They would then put the plates on a ledge for the dishwasher to put them through the washing machine. As there'd been a lot of men in for this meal, and a shortage of volunteers, an unusual build-up of plates was hampering progress. I mean no bad reflection on one of the guys scraping the plates, but he was never cut out for this sort of work. So, I delicately asked him if he'd let me take over, and I'm very happy to say he was quite relieved to do so being a new boy on the block. It hadn't taken me long to realise that speed, humour and a sense of craziness were the important tools of the day if you wanted to make an impact at the Matthew Talbot. For that matter I could say the same applies to most things in everyday life.

But something got misconstrued about my attempt to speed things up, and word got back to Jerry who was in charge of the dining room that I was trying to do his job. With a real bee in his bonnet he tackled me after we'd cleaned up. I told him I was only trying to speed things up, not trying to do his job. Well, it took me a day and a half to convince him, but I finally got there and we became the best of friends. I knew that if I was to become a worthwhile volunteer at the Matthew Talbot I would need all the cooperation I could, and vice versa. Now maybe you're wondering how I got through his thick coat of armour. Well, I humbled myself a little and said, 'If you believe that I was interfering in any way, I apologise.' He said, 'You're apologising?' I replied, 'Yes'. Well, that took him off guard and for a moment he was lost for words. I got the impression that no one had ever said to him, 'I'm sorry.' Jerry was a Maori, so eventually we had we had a few things to relate to about New Zealand.

One day not too long after that incident Jerry asked me if I'd like to join him and a few friends to play darts at the Rugby League Club in Redfern. I said would, and that I enjoyed a game of darts. Well, we must all have had a few drinks that night because I remember winding up in front of the dart board while one of the better players placed three darts neatly over my head. I'm not sure how the dare came about, but I'm sure I wouldn't have done it had I been sober.

Later that evening after we'd had a lot of fun and got our marching orders at closing time we headed for Shane's lodgings. Shane was a friend of Jerry's. His lodgings comprised of one room, with all the mod cons necessary for a man on a low income. Mind you, that scenario suited the six of us there that night. We all lived in rented rooms, though I'm sure how the others felt about theirs, but I considered mine to by my castle. Anyway about an hour later Shane and Jerry became involved in an argument that eventually began to turn very nasty. Two of the guys held on to Shane while the other chap and I held on to Jerry. What a job we had to keep them apart. Nothing we could say or do would bring any kind of sanity into the picture. Eventually, I had one of those flashes of inspiration that comes just when you need it. I told Jerry, in the most sorrowful voice I *could muster, that I* wasn't feeling at all well and asked him if he could please take me home. That was enough to momentarily take his attention off Shane. We were only half-way down the stairs, however, when he started to flare up again. So again I pleaded with him and managed to make it to the front door of the building. When I opened it we were greeted with the heaviest downpour that Sydney could possibly have dropped on us. Well, that did the trick. It took Jerry's mind completely off his run in with Shane. He stood there dumbfounded, with the rain pouring down around us. I told him I'd go and hail a taxi and that he was to stay there under the awning. I managed to close the door so there could be no repeat of his performance with Shane, as I was just about exhausted with the whole episode and couldn't handle the curtain going up again. Well, God is good to sinners like us, and before I got completely saturated a taxi seemed to come from nowhere. I grabbed Jerry by the arm, and hauled him into it, and got him back to his room. All he could talk about was the rain; everything else was forgotten, including the fact that he was supposed to be taking me home. When I got back to my room I took off my clothes and had a good rubdown. As I lay on my bed I thought about that crazy evening, and fell asleep laughing.

The next day at the Talbot Jerry thanked me for taking him home. He seemed to remember nothing about his encounter with Shane, so I let sleeping dogs lie.

The accommodation I found to live in was a mixed bag with all sorts of ups and downs attached to it. Being open about my life with a good sense of humour, and happy to listen to other people's woes, and nearly always singing or humming along with keeping to myself when I was in my room, seemed to make me an object of curiosity more than anything else. I'm sure a lot of the men who frequented the Talbot thought I was crazy or high on something. I got some weird looks at times that soon taught me to be careful about my actions and responses. Because of what many of these men had been through in their lives, some of them were like time-bombs waiting to go off.

There were a number of fights where tables, dishes and chairs left a mess for us volunteers to tidy up, but no ambulances or police were called in. Though broken, angry and hurt they were still very much aware that if they really soiled their copy books they would be banned from the Talbot.

I recall one occasion when two guys got really worked up. Both of them picked up table-knives and began circling each other. I knew some action out of the ordinary was needed. As calmly as I could with my heart rate working overtime and underpants ready for just about anything, I said to what appeared to be the meanest looking guy, 'Those knives are not very sharp, let me find you some good ones.' Well, this guy just looked at me for a moment, one of the longest moments I've ever experienced, and said, 'You're a crazy bastard', and threw the knife at me. I was waiting for the worst, but he turned on his heel and walked away. The other guy looked at me, put the knife on the table, and also walked away. I guess sometimes you have to put your head in a noose and hope it won't get too uncomfortable.

The first room I rented after I got involved with the Talbot gave me a unique experience. It was in Darling Harbour. The guy who owned it was renovating it and I doubt if I'd have ever escaped with my life had I ever come home drunk. I had to climb two flights of very narrow stairs that seemed to moan painfully as I walked on them. There was no banister on either side to hold on to. Had I been a sleepwalker I'd have stood no chance at all. The bedroom was very comfortable, I must say, as well as the other amenities, so I guess there's a price to be paid for just about everything.

Now that I was settling in Sydney I started to look around for the thing that turned me on the most, music. I was told about a good Irish pub in the Rocks called the Mercantile that might be able to satisfy my music needs, as well as my thirst. I wasn't disappointed. On my first visit I was greeted by some of my favourite melodies from the lovely voice of Shaylee Wilde, accompanied by two other musicians. Shaylee was from my home town and had quite a following wherever her band performed. I got to know her and her husband, within the limits of what you could term an honest friendship. One of those friendships that stand out in a different circle than others.

It was still a few weeks before my first St Patrick's Day in Sydney. After Shaylee had performed at the

Mercantile one evening she told me she'd be performing at the St Patrick's Day breakfast in the Mercantile, and invited me to come along. I said I would love to, but I can't afford the twenty dollar entrance fee. She said, 'Just be down there to help us carry our gear in and we'll see that you have all you need to drink and a free breakfast.' What a morning that turned out to be. And that was the beginning of my dancing sessions. I never got into the art of dancing because I thought I had two left feet, but the moment I began to feel the music going through my feet I found no trouble responding to it. That was one of the greatest confidence boosters of my life. There was no stopping me after that. Thank You Lord and Shaylee for opening another door for me.

That morning was also my first appearance on TV. A few days later Jerry and a few others told me, 'we saw you on TV dancing with a lovely woman.' I was quite amused and thought to myself, 'So long as I'm only dancing with them I can't be a problem to them or myself.'

The second strong memory of our friendship stems from the time when Shaylee and her husband invited me to dinner and an overnight stay in their home in the Blue Mountains. I was really intrigued by their magnificent recording studio which they talked me through that evening. Then we had a wonderful night with some other superbly talented musicians also invited along to share the occasion. I thought to myself as my head hit the pillow, 'isn't music a wonderful form of communication? It brings people together from all walks of life, and from its seeds grow all kinds of relationships.' I really believe that music has a stronger appeal than religion because it is not tainted in any way. It brings freedom to the mind instead of doubts and all sorts of unanswered questions.

SYDNEY PUBS

Now I had found this new zest for living through walking away from my inadequate past, I sensed that I needed to be in at the kill of every opportunity that was offered to me. I wasn't put on this earth to be strangled by man's stupidity, or my own. God, I'm sure, has little time for fools who miss themselves and their capabilities. No use praying for something you can't do for yourself, you might as well be a snowball in hell.

I was really beginning to enjoy Sydney and had nothing but praise for the rough and ready circumstances that had brought me to its doorstep. On the pension I could travel on the bus, train or ferry the length and breadth of Sydney for one dollar a day. All my medical needs were free. I soon joined one of the RSLs, and the Bondi Rugby League Club which had seven or more snooker tables plus cheap meals and drinks. But what really appealed to me was the challenge that was being offered to me, as well as all the experiences I was deriving from it. I was learning fast that even on my pension I could live the life of Reilly as long as I was in control. All I had to do was let my feelings and common sense take me where they would. And God, life, or whatever, would do the rest.

I now had become a graduate in the greatest university of all, life itself. And better still, I didn't need any of man's self-styled education or a thick bank roll to join that student body. All I needed was myself and the courage to participate. I was now learning more about people and life than I'd ever dreamed possible. I'd finally come to realise that life was not about fame or fortune or even education, it was all about how you lived it, every God-given moment. I had nothing to prove to anyone else, only myself. We miss ourselves because of those who think they know what our answers should be. Eventually we become lost, a burden not only to ourselves but to all those whose lives we touch.

I could see a living example of this around me, but had no wish to become involved in something that could be both useless to others and myself.

You can't live life backwards with the idea of bringing something meaningful into the present or the future. It won't fit. The past is a wonderful learning curve, but to let it get in the way of discovering new learning is like trying to climb a ladder with no rungs. Perhaps this poem may add a little colour to the point I'm trying to make.

Capturing the essence of the unknown
Arouses my lasting curiosity
From it I get infamous, unreserved

encouragement
Full of enthusiasm
As I expose myself to the venomous
And the beautiful channels
That test my capabilities.

Wonderful
moments

I can't remember who introduced me to a pub at the Rocks called The Hero of Waterloo, but I will always be very grateful to him. I've been to quite a few pubs since I changed my life around, but the Hero of Waterloo will always be at the top of my list because of the people and the music it enriched me with. The moment I walked into the place I was captivated. I was filled with a sense of belonging. Straightaway I felt at ease. The music, the atmosphere, the people, all seemed to blend into one happy family. I spotted a vacant chair in front of the band and soon myself talking to one of the band members who was taking a break from playing her trumpet. She said her name was Val and the guy playing the piano was her husband John. In no time I was being introduced to all sorts of people who frequented the pub. I'd walked into the pub a complete stranger and in less than half an hour I was being accepted as one of its family. From that moment on another part of my education was to be fulfilled.

Later that afternoon I had my first encounter with a guy called John Cross. John hailed from Cork, but now lived in Minto in Sydney. We became good friends and spent some crazy, and wonderful times together. John introduced me to another pub, another happy hunting ground for me. It was situated in the Hilton Hotel in Pitt Street and was called the Henry the Ninth. We agreed to meet there, and when I walked in a few weeks later on a Thursday evening I was greeted by a band calling itself The Irish Drovers. Once again I said, thank you faith for bringing me here.

I soon realised The Henry the Ninth was another training ground for my education, just as the Talbot and the Hero of Waterloo were. When John arrived he was later joined by his two sisters with whom I had the pleasure of making their acquaintance and dancing with. What a wonderful evening we had, the first of many more to follow. I who'd never been shown a step of how to dance, did some of my best footwork there to some great Irish music.

One of the lovely friendships bestowed upon me at The Henry the Ninth was born in its own unwritten fashion just as all the others were. On this particular Thursday evening I'd arranged to meet some friends there so we could get into another enjoyable evening where just about anything could happen, and usually did. Not long after I arrived and got into conversation with my friends I happened to glance across the table, I found myself captivated by an attractive blond lady sitting at a table close by. I can't remember how many times I glanced in her direction, but on the last occasion I got the cue for the curtain to go up on what could be another friendship.

I saw this guy I'd taken a dislike to go up to her and make a nuisance of himself. Like a shot my new found intuition went to work. *I walked straight up to the lady, completely* ignoring this guy, and asked her for a dance. She looked straight up into my eyes and with a lovely smile said, I would love to dance with you.' As we began dancing she told me my timing was perfect. She said, 'that guy was beginning to bug me.' I said, 'Yes I noticed that because of the type of individual he is, but I'm quite sure you could have handled the situation. I just thought a little help wouldn't go astray.' The lady laughed and said, 'My knight in shining armour.'

After we'd exchanged names and so forth I invited her to join us at our table. She gracefully accepted and soon had us all captivated with her charm and lovely sense of humour. Joyce said she was an air hostess and lived in California with her husband and daughter. She said she had a horse named Maggie that was her pride and joy. Once she began talking about her horse everything else was forgotten, and each time she visited the Henry the band would make a point of playing Maggie for her. I believed she looked forward to that more than anything else. I really enjoyed Joyce's company and she said she enjoyed mine, but we were both sensible enough to know that a solid friendship would last longer than an entangled romantic one.

SISTER YVONNE HEFFERNAN, OAM

About six months after I'd become involved in the Talbot I met a lady who was to become a big part of my life. Just before lunch was served one day I noticed a nun walking towards me. She stopped and introduced herself as Sister Yvonne Heffernan. She said we hadn't met before because she'd been in hospital having a heart bypass. I can't remember how many years she'd been looking after the men's welfare at the Talbot as well as all the prison work she was involved in. I was straight away captivated by her amused smile as she listened to something I impulsively said after introducing myself, 'I don't claim to be religious, or anything other than what I am'.

She said, 'I am of much the same opinion.'

From that moment on our lasting friendship was born. Whatever creases had been in my sails Sister Yvonne helped to iron them out, and no matter what I say about her in my Walk those words will never do her justice. I hope one day the people of Sydney will give her the full recognition she really deserves. And if not, I have no doubt in my mind that God will.

A little later Sister Yvonne told me that she had a small room just off Burke Street where she invited those whose needs required a sympathetic ear or a little friendly advice. I told her I'd like to be involved in some way as I am always looking for new experiences for my growth. She said, 'I'd love to have you on board', and that's where it all began for us.

When I arrived at the room I was greeted with a hug, tea and biscuits. There were three other men there enjoying her hospitality and I was soon in conversation with them. As time went on my eyes unconsciously began photographing the room. It wasn't a big room, but it had a lovely cosy atmosphere. Just all it needed to be. Everything seemed to be in its rightful place. If my memory serves me right the faded blue paint on the walls offered its own nostalgic feeling of homeliness. The pictures on the walls stood out, the fridge, and the dresser with a number of cups and plates on it added their own sense of being to it. But what put the icing on the cake for me was Sister Yvonne herself. Without her presence it would just have been another room for me.

After her visitors had left Sister told me about her work over the years, and what it had involved her in. I'm not going to talk about it as that's her story and I would make a very bad presentation of it, and do it no justice whatsoever. I then told her about myself in greater detail, and the

Sister Yvonne Heffernam O.A.M.
'The Lady of the Talbot'

circumstances that had brought me to the Talbot, and she said, 'The Lord works in mysterious ways.' 'I fully agree with that' I said. I've had the privilege of conversing with a few lovely nuns in my lifetime but Sister Yvonne was something special. She has what I call class, and what's more I recognised it almost straight away. And apart from mother, my sister Ann, and my daughter Rachel, I've found no one to equal her smile, her sense of humour, her intelligence, honesty, compassion, and her great love of life.

As I could not afford to buy a set of golf clubs, my next outdoor love was tennis. I bought myself a second-hand tennis racket from a pawn shop in Williams Street. I was now equipped with a tennis racket, snooker cue, table-tennis bat, chess set, darts, and a small stereo. I'd managed to hold on to them through all my ups and downs. Now I felt ready to take on whatever fate would throw my way.

But after saying that, there was just one more thing I needed to complete the picture. I knew it would come in time, and that was a cassette recorder so I could record my newfound philosophy. I wanted to share with others the sayings and other things that had helped me reshape my life. What could be better than putting it on tape and handing these tapes to people to listen to without looking for anything in return? Anyway, I knew it would happen when the time was ready. First things first.

My introduction to tennis in Sydney came through an ad in the local paper. So off I went to Jensen's tennis courts at Prince Albert Park, near Central Station, to start another chapter in my life. Not having much tennis doubles experience and even less at singles left me open to some doubtful glances and remarks, but I was determined nothing and no-one was going to alter the new course I'd charted for myself. And I had no vision to become any kind of a top player even in my age group, but rather to be able to hold my own with some of the best of them. And even though it took a bit of time I believe I got there. One thing I soon learned was that the Aussies love a trier. Once I was accepted and made feel at home, those courts were a great training ground for me because of all the wonderful people I met and the sheer exhilaration of the game itself.

I'll never forget the day I was walking down Williams Street with my tennis racket to catch the train at Town Hall to take me to Jensen's tennis club, and a man approached me from The Church of Scientology in Pitt

Street. He asked me if I could spare the time to go into a nearby building and fill in a questionnaire. There were times when I would have said 'Sorry', and left it at that, but since I found the courage to open the Door of Life and let curiosity come beckoning to me in all shapes and sizes, as you will already have gathered, caution was no longer a word in my dictionary. In its place I inserted challenge, to whatever degree I was capable of. What was the point of my dying before I'd made some sense of living?

I said yes, I'd be quite happy to oblige. The man took me into the building, sat me down at a desk and placed the questionnaire before me. He said, 'When you've finished put your hand up and someone will look after you.' With a sense of amusement running through me I completed the questionnaire and held my hand up.

Well, they mustn't have been too busy that day because no sooner had I put my hand up than a lady came over and sat in front of me. She had a lively smile and the trimmings to go with it. She introduced herself then proceeded to decipher my answers. When she'd finished she said, 'from my calculations, based on these answers, your self-esteem and love life seem to come in on the low side of our chart scale. Everything else is good.' As she was an attractive woman I said to her with a sheepish look on my face, would you like to sleep with me. Well the guy sitting next to me heard what I said and nearly cracked up. The lady gave me one of those strange disarming smiles that could have said, yes, no, or, you cheeky bastard, as I bowed to her and took my leave. My tennis wasn't the best that day. I kept remembering the look on the lady's lovely face and I couldn't stop laughing. I'd even go so far as to say we both got a few laughs from it, and I'll always respect her for not making a big deal out of it. A top rate lady in my book.

I had now left my dangerous staircase lodgings in Darling Harbour and moved into the Rex Hotel in Kings Cross. Mind you two to three months later I decided it was not one of my better choices. Climbing three sets of dirty stairs, plus the cockroaches and uneven floorboards in my room, soon told me to get on my bike. So I moved into a cosy clean room in Darlinghurst which was not too far away from The Talbot. I soon got to know a guy in the room next to me who enjoyed playing chess, and before long I became one of his victims. I can't say how good he was, with my lack of experience, but Icouldn't beat him. Mind you, I never really felt frustrated about it because he was such a nice interesting guy who never tried to rub it in. But one day I was rewarded for my patience. With a lapse of forethought on his part I struck gold. Well, the praise he heaped on me was heartening. I learned that day you can be a better loser than a winner. I never got the better of him again, but then I didn't need to.

One day I was asked by The Talbot if I could help with forming a volleyball team. They were putting a team together to play against the Salvation Army Hostel at Moore Park. I've already mentioned that my volleyball experience left a lot to be desired, but this time it was indoor volleyball. Maybe I'd make a better fist of that.

At the worst I had nothing to lose, which has been the story of my life to date, and I feel will continue to be.

Well I don't think I've ever enjoyed myself so much playing a new sport as I did indoor volleyball. In all, I played about eight games, but there was one little incident that really highlighted the sport for me. We were close to half-way into the game with a team from somewhere around the Coogee area when a guy called out to me from the sideline, 'Close your fist more when you're hitting the ball.' Well, like most people I too have a variable degree of tolerance, but as this wasn't one of my better days I went right over to him and said, 'Excuse me, what gives you the right to dictate how I play my game and my feelings towards each shot that I make.' He stood there looking at me with his mouth partly open, at a loss for words, as I re-joined the game. I was then applauded by my team mates. Not long after that I scored eleven straight points with my serving, mind you, the opposing team wasn't all that strong. But I must admit I got a lot of satisfaction out of it. After the game that same guy came over to me and apologised. We became quite good friends.

I really believe that pushing one's ideas of what ought to be into the face of another should be classed as an embarrassment to the human race.

One payday I acquired the last item to fill my needs. A cassette recorder. Once again the pawn shop came to my rescue. I was well known there by now. Before payday arrived I'd often pawn my snooker cue for twenty dollars just to keep my head above water, a few beers in my stomach and maybe something rich from the dessert shelf.

Anyway they gave me a good deal for being a steady customer and I was over the moon because my voice sounded so clear on the tape. If you want to build up your confidence and really get to know a little more about yourself I highly recommend this, I'd already worked out how I'd present myself on the tapes I wanted to hand around to people. All systems were set to go. And I have to say it was one of the best decisions I've ever made because of all the feedback I got, even if some of it wasn't too appetising. We've only a certain amount of time to make our presence felt, and believe it or not your measure of joy or sorrow is found in those around you.

I thought the best way to present myself was within the medium range of knowledge I already acquired, and what was in store for me. So as well as tuning into all sorts of music I also attended all manner of talks and so-called lectures, some questionable, and some wonderful learning experiences. As the old saying goes, you can't have one without the other. The learning wasn't so much derived from talks and the lectures themselves but through the debates and people I met there. At the same time you can't have a fire without a match or some other means of ignition. But I do respect those who have the courage to start the ball rolling. We are all teachers in some way or another, but there is no satisfaction in just being like somebody else. Be different and you'll always be noticed, and if your motivations are unselfish you will produce good seed. Jesus put a great meaning to that.

As my great loves were philosophy, music and humour they became the format for my tapes. I must admit that at first I was very apprehensive. It was with mixed expectations I waited for some reaction to flow from the people who'd received them. The first thing to really amuse me was the wary look I got when I said there was no charge for them. Freely I have received, freely I give. People tend to get suspicious when you offer them something for nothing. 'Surely you have some ulterior motive behind this', and so on. People, I believe, feel more comfortable when they pay for what they get. And it did come to my mind that the people who listened to my tapes could have such doubts running through their minds, which might prevent them receiving some of the benefit from them. But all going well you're really only going to reach out and touch a few people in your lifetime. And that's all you need to do. The Great Man Himself said that.

The first reaction I got from one of my tapes came about in the Menzies Hotel piano bar in Sydney that I frequented on a number of Friday evenings from around five-thirty to any old time. I'd get there early so that I could get a seat around the grand piano and get lost in the music of the accomplished musician that played there. When I arrived it was Happy Hour so the drink prices were pretty reasonable, later they would drain a hole in the pockets of people like me. Well, I don't know if you've ever been involved in singing around a grand piano, but I highly recommend it. Some of the most wonderful evenings I've ever spent in Sydney were around that piano, and I met many fantastic people. And when I couldn't afford to drink liquor I drank water.

There were two things offering their own uniqueness to me because of my participation around that piano. The first one was the music, and the second was sharing myself with all sorts of people from everyday life. And making these tapes to hand around to people meant that my Walk was never going to be one of least resistance. What makes us human in my book is our willingness to be challenged for our beliefs. If your motivations have other people's interests at heart, just about everything you do is honoured by the fullest attention you give to it. I don't try to be too careful about how I present myself because that would destroy its naturalness.

One evening, not long after I arrived at the piano bar, I got into conversation with a guy and eventually ended up giving him a tape. A few weeks later I met him again in the piano bar. He told me he thought my tape was full of shit. I said to him, 'I'm so sorry, but there's a lot of it around when you get stuck in its corridor'. Well, he stood there looking at me, trying to work out what I'd said, and as fate would have it, the timing was perfect for me to leave as I'd been invited to a party. I left him, I believe, looking after me as I made my exit with a big grin on my face. I met this same guy a few months later and found I was no longer on his hit list. He said, 'I take back what I said about your tape. I may not understand it to its full value, but at least you've the guts to speak your mind and that's what I admire.' He told me a bit about his life. It was like so many of the sad stories that I have heard echoed through the halls of the Talbot.

Another little story relating to the piano bar came about when I began talking to a very well dressed man who could have been in just about any profession. When he learned that I was involved in the Talbot he fired all sorts of questions at me. He soon knew more about me than I knew about him. But now that I had chosen to become quite open about my life, I also found a closer bonding with people. Granted it had its moments of embarrassment from time to time, but in general it made things easier for others and myself.

As this man was getting ready to leave he said, 'Terry, I would like to make a donation of one thousand dollars to the Talbot'. You could have knocked me down with a feather. But I gathered my sense very quickly and said to him, 'Please send your donation to Sister Yvonne Heffernan as she badly needs it to spend on the men there'.

Eventually Yvonne did get the money, but there were so many strings attached to it that I often wondered if it was worth the trouble. If you can't give without expectations of any kind, keep it in your pocket, or wherever.

Then I went outside to catch a bus to take me to the party at Kings Cross. There was hardly anyone on it so I sat down just across from the driver. Before we got to the turn that takes you up Williams Street, a guy smelling like Guinness Brewery got on the bus. He said to me,

'I'm drunk, can I sit beside you?' 'Of course you can' I said. I could see the driver laughing his head off as the man staggered up the steps and sat down beside me. Then the man said, 'I went out this afternoon to attend a meeting for alcoholics, but I couldn't find the bloody place so I went into a pub instead'. Both the driver and I nearly broke our sides laughing. About six stops later I was still laughing and nearly fell down the stairs as I got off the bus. Just think what I would have missed had I not taken my chances and gone to Australia.

Readers, I don't know how many of you have been in the fortunate position of making a snap decision when an opportunity offered itself, and then found from its fruits grow weird and wonderful things. Here's another one of mine.

I'd left the Talbot and was making my way up Williams Street after the evening meal when I noticed a guy staggering towards me. The people ahead of me were trying to avoid him as if he had the plague. I said to myself, I'd better get into the scrum here or no one's going to score a try. So I walked towards him wondering what fate had in store for me this time.

As I stopped in front of him he put both his hands on my shoulders to support himself and then, through the thick cloud of alcohol fumes and incoherent vocabulary, I eventually pieced together that he was trying to find the Matthew Talbot. A place to rest his weary, self-afflicted body. That place where people cared about people with no strings attached. I got him to put his arm around my shoulder, then looking like two drunks we walked back to the Talbot. After I'd settled him in I went back to my room with a smile of satisfaction on my face.

After the evening meal the next day, as I was cleaning up plates from one of the tables, a hand grabbed my wrist. The same guy I'd guided back to the Talbot looked up into my eyes and said, 'Aren't you the guy who brought me back here last evening and got me fixed up?' I said, 'Yes, and you look a lot better now'. He laughed and said, 'I shall never forget you, my friend'.

Before I left that evening my friend Jerry came to see me and said, 'would you like a small part-time job here, two hours a day, five days a week, making the tea first thing in the morning?' I couldn't believe my good fortune. I said, 'Jerry I'd be very grateful for anything'. Several months later I was able to add a few more luxuries to my simple lifestyle. A new stereo, tennis racket and a better cassette recorder. And I put it all down to just offering a helping hand when the opportunity presented itself.

COOGEE TO ARNCLIFFE

A short time after I took up my part-time job I was offered accommodation in the suburb of Coogee. The Matthew Talbot owned a building with very reasonable priced rooms for the not-so-wealthy like myself. I did hear a whisper it was only temporary as it would eventually be sold. Anyway I never look a gift horse in the mouth. So with new experiences around the corner I moved in.

Well, I have to say in all sincerity this accommodation in Coogee topped all the others. Even though the building was rundown I was enriched with the brightness of my two small rooms — a kitchen and bedroom. It also contained a very comfortable double-bed mattress on the floor, an armchair to relax in, two chairs and a small fridge. But the best was yet to come as I started to explore my new surroundings. As I hadn't paid a visit to Coogee before it was all new to me. I'd accepted my new lodgings without even looking at them, just like I accept people in my life till I learn otherwise. I can only be persuaded by what I experience, not by what I'm told. If you need a why for everything, what will surprise you?

After I settled in I walked down to the beach and watched the sea move gracefully backwards and forwards on the soft inviting sand. Then I walked round the cliff heads to inhale the sea air and drink in the scenery. Yes, I liked Coogee. I could stay here for a while.

I soon found where the Coogee Tennis Club was situated, and after a few enquiries learned that the annual membership fee was one hundred dollars. Briefly, I told them about my situation and they very kindly gave me a month in which to pay my sub. Well, I can't speak highly enough of the people who made up the club and all the enjoyable games I played, and the parties I was invited to. They gave me some beautiful memories to take away with me.

With my new part-time job at the Talbot I had to catch the bus at five-fifteen to get me into work for six o'clock. My job was to make up two big urns of tea, then help with the setting up of tables for breakfast. Then after breakfast I helped with the cleaning up. The only hard thing about all this was having to get up so early in the morning, but having that said that it was well worth the effort.

I must admit I really did enjoy my new job and the comfort of feeling those extra dollars in my pocket. But even more important were all the new experiences it was gradually presenting me with. Every corner I turned I found something new to deal with. The hundreds of men who passed through The Talbot each day carried scars of some kind from the past, and many of them seemed beyond healing. I'd been warned not to get into areas that were outside my job, but for people like me that's easier said than done. But at the same time I was fast learning that when it comes to helping people limited rescues are about as close as you can get. Only a degree of intelligent compassion would keep me in a lesser conflict area.

I got pushed around, scowled at, cursed at from time to time but I also got smiled on and received a pat on the back, so I fared a lot better than Jesus did.

There were times during my off-duty moments when I'd sit at one of the tables in a little room listening to what someone had to say. I even held the hand of a few who poured out their pain to me. I really believe you can learn a lot more about humanity by just listening. Even ugliness needs to be loved.

Not long after I moved into Coogee my friend John Cross told me he'd found a Council flat in Coogee. Now we could see a little more of each other. Shortly after he moved in he showed me an ad in the local paper that read, "Anybody interested in reading poetry". We rang the number and a week later were involved in poetry reading. There were three ladies and us two.

Once a week from ten till twelve noon we'd read out poetry from books and discuss what turned us on.

One morning a little later I suggested we should write our own poetry and see what we could come up with. That didn't go down so well with the three ladies, but I was determined to carry it further. Meeting a challenge had now become the dominant factor in my life. Being very nice ladies they finally agreed, and boy did we have a lot of fun. Here's one of the poems I wrote. I call it "Carry On"

My sights are set on justice on the railroad
of my dreams
Each sleeper symbolising my strength to
carry on
With music all around me I draw from well
to well

A flowing combination of my strength to carry on.

Our little get-together didn't last long due to a run-in with a member of the Coogee Council who'd allowed us to use a room in one of their buildings. I can't give you any in-depth explanation of what brought this to a head, so I won't try, other than to say some people love to share their misery with others. But I must say I received a lot of inspiration from the poetry group and to date have written a few poems.

One day I was asked if I'd like a change of duties with another two hours attached. Start at eight and finish at twelve. My main task was to look after the bread department. Hundreds of loaves found their way to the Talbot daily and they had to be sorted and sliced for meals each day. I of course said yes, with the nice thought of not having to get up so early and extra money in my pocket.

In no time at all I had a second-hand set of golf clubs from my favourite pawn shop, and shortly baptised them at The Public Golf Course at Moore Park. Being a Public Golf Course I got senior citizen rates. I can't tell you how good it was to be playing golf again. My patience had once again been rewarded. If you really want to enjoy another set of values just turn up at any Public Golf Course. Now that I was equipped with everything I needed to keep me active and motivated, golf clubs, tennis racket, snooker cue, table-tennis bat, chess set, cassette recorder and my stereo if there was a man in Sydney as rich as me I had yet to meet him.

But the highs must have their lows to keep an even balance. I was told that because I was working at the Matthew Talbot, I'd have to leave my haven in Coogee. Having moved to a slightly higher income bracket I was no longer classed as poor enough to warrant cheaper lodgings. It was company policy. I felt sad when I got the news, but this kind of thing was fast becoming like water off a duck's back to me. My new life style is always telling me never to get too comfortable otherwise you may find it difficult to overcome difficult situations. Addicted to any kind of security you're no better off than a drug addict.

A week after I had received my walking papers I found myself a room in Redfern. I said to myself, 'another little culture shock, but a few steps backwards won't do you any harm. Just another learning step to toughen you up and teach you a little more about humanity'. And I did learn that in my short duration there.

A lot of Aboriginal people live there under the roof of harsh circumstances, which I won't even try to elaborate on for its picture can never be painted to please everyone. If people did more and said less we could learn a lot more about each other.

My room was at the front of the building on the ground floor, and my window looked out on to the street. I was now used to noise so the busy street didn't bother me too much. The toilet, shower and cooking facilities were reasonable for eighty dollars I was paying and I was pleased that the cockroaches, or most of them, were on holiday. And I was also close to my work. Jensen's tennis courts were very close, and two bus rides would get me to the Coogee tennis club in about thirty minutes. I was close to Moore Park golf club as well.

I seldom used the kitchen facilities as I could eat at the Talbot or treat myself to a meal whenever the necessity arose. I'd purchased an electric jug when I arrived in Sydney so I could always make a cup of tea when needed. I kept cake and biscuits in a containers in my room, plus bread, butter and jam, so I was really self-contained.

My privacy was very important to me. Because of my happy disposition and always being on the go, as I may have mentioned before, I seemed to attract attention and it did land me in a few unfavourable positions. So once again the old thinking cap went on again and cleared the air for me. Mind you I would talk to anyone, but kept it at low key.

Every so often as I was coming home in the evening there'd be a few boys playing or fooling around by the front door of the building I was living in, and a few smiles and a nice chat never went astray. I'm a great believer in showing your true colours. That way you can keep them flying at full mast.

Joseph Campbell puts a better colour on this way of thinking I'm into. "We're so engaged in doing things to achieve purposes of outer value that we forget the inner value, the rapture that is associated with being alive, is what it is all about".

One Saturday I walked to Jensen's for a round of tennis, then made my way to the Hero of Waterloo to meet John Cross and enjoy the rest of the evening. This had now become a regular pattern with me. I'd arrive in my tennis clothes to be greeted by my newfound friends and the music the band was playing. My new lifestyle raising a few eyebrows with both approval and disapproval. But I always say, be different and you will always be noticed, especially if you're a Mr Nobody in the eyes of the world.

I was really enjoying this newfound attention and was using it to the best of my advantage. If you don't move beyond the familiar you will always remain its victim. Apart from John and the musicians, two people stood out more than all the rest for me. The first of these was a lovely Aboriginal lady called Alice. Soon after I was introduced to her I asked her for a dance. She said, 'I'm not the best on the dance floor'. And I said, 'You will be. Just let's do it'. Well nobody could keep her off the floor after that. Alice became Queen of the dancing floor. Every time I arrived she would have me on the dancing floor and we'd do all sorts of weird and wonderful steps to great music. Thank you Alice wherever you may be, and for being a part of my life, and for all the encouragement I received from your personality.

With Alice, one of my favourite dance partners

The next angel to arrive on my doorstep was a lady called Sue. I walked into the Hero one Sunday afternoon to find the place packed, but good fortune smiled on me again and found me a seat at one of the tables. I got talking to a lovely couple from England who told me they were visiting their daughter Sue. They said she'd had gone out to meet someone and would be back soon.

And, eventually, she did arrive. So began another wonderful friendship for both of us. Although I didn't know it at the time, Sue would be there to support me in my hour of need.

After all the introductions were over and a deeper communication set in, the rest of the evening was one of the most enjoyable I've ever had. Not long after Sue's mother and father had gone back to England I gave Sue a phone call and asked if she'd like to join John and me in the Henry the Ninth one Thursday evening. I'd already introduced John to Sue and her parents in the Hero. Our friendship grew from there and we became good friends.

As it was coming up to Christmas I was informed by one of the guys who worked in the Talbot that he was leaving his flat in Arncliffe if I would be interested in taking it over. The landlady wanted someone who was responsible and tidy. I said to myself, I don't know about the responsible part, but I am tidy so it must be time for me to move again. When I went to view it I was captivated by its charming appearance and the rent of one hundred and thirty dollars a week with no bond attached looked like home sweet home for me for a while. The lovely Italian lady who owned it said when I went to see her that Michael, the guy who was leaving, had provided her with good credentials on my behalf. After she had given me the third degree and placed two weeks' rent in her hand I was set to move in.

The evening before I left my old room I met a guy in the kitchen who had just moved in and we started talking about ourselves. Well, actually, I let him do most of the talking because that's where I felt the greatest need lay. As we talked I felt drawn towards him in a way few people could ever draw me. He touched my inner being with his soft, honest nature. He told me he'd received severe spinal injuries when he fell off a house he was helping to build in Fiji. When he'd recovered enough to travel he was sent to Australia to complete his treatment and now resided here. He was looking for a job that wouldn't involve him putting too much pressure on his spine. But there was no self-pity in his words or attitude such as I'd heard so many times before. Every word he spoke had a ring of truth to it.

Through my sense of curiosity I found out that he had little or nothing to his name. So I gave him a few things to help him out over Christmas and told him about the Matthew Talbot.

As I was leaving on the next morning he knocked on my door and said, thank you for making my Christmas such an enjoyable one. Please drop me a line and tell me how you're getting on. I did and here is the letter I got back from him. I still have it. It goes like this.

Thanks for your letter, mate, it's quite encouraging.

It's 10.41 pm (Thursday) and I finished work at 9pm

Yes!! Thank God I've got a permanent job and the shingles are almost gone.

I feel a lot better.

It's good to hear that you like your new place. Thanks for sharing what you have learned and your thoughts. Hope to hear more. It's good not to blame God or anyone else for our failure. I am glad that we can always learn and improve.

I work at Martin Place in a seafood restaurant (kitchen hand) and I like the job because my workmates have now become my friends. It was hard for them to accept me at first, but The Lord has His own ways of getting people together. The Lord's ways are unpredictable, but they sure work.

Looking forward to reading the book. I used to have cappuccino at the coffee shop at the end of Bayswater Road in Kings Cross so I may see you one day.

Be happy. Stay smiling.

Just looking at his letter at this moment I noticed the address we both lived in was 81 Redfern Street.

I never did catch up with my friend again, but the mere fact that we did meet was I believe a blessing to both of us. One without the other brings anything of little value.

After I'd moved into my new flat I soon found that Arncliffe railway station was only ten or so minutes' walk from where I was staying so transport presented no problem. Mind you, Sydney's transportation system must be one of the best there is.

BONDI

I'd only been in my new flat about six weeks when fate thought it was time for me to be tempted once again. I had a morning off work on this particular day so I decided to go to Moore Park and play a game of golf. As I was making my way to the station I felt an awful pain in my lower stomach. It then made its way right up into my rib cage and stopped me dead in my tracks. I must have stood there for about five minutes, breathing heavily. When it started to subside I began walking again, but didn't get very far. I knew then that something was very wrong. So I set off back to my flat. Well, I knew it only took me around five minutes to reach where I was when the pain first grabbed me, but it must have taken me a painful three quarters of an hour to reach my flat.

When I got home I made straight for my bed, and must have lain there for about an hour. When I got up to go to the toilet thankfully the pain wasn't so bad, but I knew I needed to see a doctor. As I didn't want to upset my landlady who lived next door, there was only one quick and sensible way around that, ring for a taxi and ask to be taken to the nearest doctor. About thirty or so minutes later I was in the doctor's surgery being politely informed that I had angina. The doctor prescribed little white tablets to put under my tongue when the need arose and said he'd arrange for me to see a heart specialist.

Oh boy, those little white tablets did the job. Not only could I work and play golf, but I could also play tennis. I was still a member of the Coogee tennis club and twice a week I played evening tennis there. Once I popped a tablet under my tongue I was good for at least two or three hours.

Three weeks later I was examined by a heart specialist in Bondi. He told me I'd need to have an angiogram. He explained the procedure and said that I'd be admitted to St Vincent's Hospital as soon as they could take me in. Around two weeks later I was admitted to St Vincent's. I went in on a Saturday and came out on the Sunday. I was treated like a king and the food was first class. But there was one hiccup for which I claim full responsibility. A meal tray was placed before me that evening on my bed after I had my angiogram, and as I was starting on my meal the plate slid along the tray as I moved to a more comfortable position, so I reached out to grab it, and the clamp on my groin, knitting my flesh together after the operation came unstuck, and I started to bleed like a pig. After all the commotion was over, and the flow of blood stopped, and the bedclothes replaced, I got a telling off from the nurse on duty. I'd been warned to stay quiet, but being a tidy person as I have already mentioned my natural reaction was to react first and think later. I must say that's got me into a bit of strife at times, but how do you get a leopard to change its spots? I tried to explain to the nurse, but I feel it fell on deaf ears God bless her.

But I have to add without a doubt Sydney's medical facilities will always remain high in my estimation.

When I got back to my flat and lay on my bed I could feel my heart pumping as though someone was using a road drill inside me. It was really a weird feeling. Apart from that I was in good shape and very grateful to all those who had participated in my recovery. Writing this story gives me another opportunity to thank them.

Three days later I was back at work and playing tennis. A few weeks later after that little more work had been thrown my way, I was now living a more comfortable lifestyle than I had for some time. Looking back, I felt a sense of temporary achievement by sticking to my guns. As I said before, it would have been so easy to return to New Zealand and the easy comfort zone that even lower income people like me live in. But look at all the fun, the challenges, and the spiritual growth I'd have missed. How shallow my Walk would have been. There'd be no depth to my story and I'd be less than half the person I am today. The drive-on lessons of life are the ones that give you an opportunity to move on or remain where you are.

About a month later opportunity once again knocked on my door. Fate was about to present me with a set of wheels. One of the guys who worked at the Talbot told me about a two-door Holden Torana that had broken down in Kingsford. The owner was asking one hundred and fifty dollars for it. So I was given an address to go and see him and the car. Apart from what I could see, it looked as good as you could expect for that price, but being unable to drive it of course is another story. He told me I could pick up a second hand engine for about two hundred dollars. So my ears pricked up and crazy ideas above my station started running through my mind. I wouldn't have to drag my golf clubs around any more. That in it itself would be a luxury. If any of my friends or anyone else in need wanted to move a few things from one place to another I could help them, as well as all the other things I could do for myself.

I had six hundred dollars in the bank. That would cover the price of everything, including insurance and tax, cutting it fine which of course is the story of my life.

Two days later it was in the wrecker's yard in East Putney having a second-hand engine fitted. Now there was only one thing needed before I added more pollution to the atmosphere, a driving licence. Well, I surprised myself how quickly I passed both the theory and the practical test. It must have had something to do with the incentive that promoted the whole thing. You know that old saying 'Where there's a will, there's a way'.

A week later I went to collect my car from the wrecker's yard, and as I drove out with a silly grin on my face, it was soon wiped off when the accelerator hit the floor with no response from the engine. I lifted the bonnet and found the throttle linkage had come adrift, not a very good start to what I considered to be my new upmarket lifestyle. I walked back into the yard and told the boss what had happened and they soon put it right. Off I drove again minus the smile on my face. That was soon justified when the exhaust pipe started to play ungodly tunes of its own. I returned to the yard again, with a sinking feeling that all was not going to plan. That was reinforced when I saw them jack up my pride and joy and endeavour to realign the exhaust without putting any heat on it. Having been a mechanic myself it was all I could do to keep my mouth shut. Once again I drove off wondering where the next pit stop would be.

Well the next pit stop happened two weeks later in Cleveland. The engine decided to give up ghost and came to halt. By now I was having second thoughts about my future behind the wheel. There was a garage close by so I went in and told the owner my tale of woe. He said, 'I'll get the car into my garage and arrange for the wreckers to send me another engine. They won't charge you anything, but I'll have to charge you one hundred and twenty five dollars to remove the old one and fit the other one'. Well I'd come this far, I may as well go the whole hog. Four days later I was back on the road again with my fingers crossed and a prayer on my lips.

A few months later my daughter Rachel wrote to me to say she was coming to visit me with her second son Conor who was four months old. The timing was perfect. I now had a car that seemed to be going as could be expected, and a cosy flat. Rachel could have my bed, and I could sleep on the large couch. I stood waiting for her to arrive at the airport, but completely missed her till she stood right in front of me with Conor in her arms. She said, 'Don't you recognise your own daughter?' She had her hair cut short and I was used to her long flowing hair. I'm still trying to live that one down.

We spent a wonderful four days together covering as much as ground as we could, plus the lovely bonding I had with my new grandson. One morning I took Rachel and Conor to meet Sister Yvonne and show her where the one of the new chapters of my life had begun, the pages written, and yet to be written. Rachel was very impressed with Sister Yvonne and they got on like a house on fire. That will always be one of the special memories of Sydney for me.

I also took Rachel and Conor to The Hero of Waterloo. They were both made very welcome there. Looking back I now suddenly remember the number four played quite a significant part in my life. First those four days my son Bernard spent with me in Queenstown. Then Rachel and Conor coming to visit me. Then something I came across a while back which goes like this.

The Cross

Although the cross is best known as the supreme symbol of the Christian faith, cross symbolism itself is much older than Christianity. The oldest examples are those engraved or painted on flat pebbles, dating from 10,000 bc, found in a cave in the French Pyrenees. These 'ancestors stones' were believed to contain the spirits of the dead.

The Cross symbolises the four roads; it is derived from quartering the circle through the omphalos at the centre. The Cross in the wheel has been used as a symbol for the

Sun, and Christ's rule over all things — length, breadth, height and depth.

When the wonderful four days had played their part in our lives, I took Rachel and Conor back to the airport for a memorable goodbye, and drove away a very happy man.

Sister Yvonne had now moved into the Matthew Talbot from her room off Bourke Street, so I started to assist her on Wednesday afternoons. She had told me she'd be moving into a room in the Matthew Talbot building as soon as it could be arranged. It would be a lot more convenient to operate from there.

So began another important part of my education in what I hoped would be developing into a better human being. Sister Yvonne's years of experience with those from many sorrowful walks of life made her a wonderful example of what it is to be fully human. The men loved her. That mischievous smile on her face and the twinkle in her eyes are her trademark. Good humour written all over her.

When I started to liaise with Yvonne she'd invite four men or five men into her little room. She'd talk to them while I boiled the electric jug. I'd make tea or coffee, and she would give them a few biscuits from a jar she had there. Sometimes she would be called out of her room for some reason and I'd chat with the men. When the session was over and the men had departed we'd relax with something to drink and eat. Then we'd discuss where there was room for improvement. That was typical of Yvonne, always looking to improve her wonderful skills.

Eventually, we decided on a one-to-one basis. This way she could use her valuable time in a more positive direction.

She'd send into the room one man at a time and I'd entertain him for around fifteen to twenty minutes. Mind you I was nowhere near the popularity bracket Yvonne was in, but I served a purpose.

One day a young man came in I'd say close to his thirties. He was quite good looking, and appeared well educated. As I listened to him he started pouring out what he thought was the rough edge of life for him. After I had listened to him and put two and two together from my own past and elsewhere I said to him 'What the hell are you doing in a place like this? You've got everything going for you. Good looks and you're obviously well educated, and capable of moving in just about any direction you wish to go in. All you're doing here is taking up space'.

I told him briefly of the dark place I'd come from. And I could have made excuse after excuse but where would it have got me. Then I waited for some kind of retaliation, but it didn't come. I guess I was lucky enough to reach the vulnerable spot in him that needed to be reached. He got up from his chair, held out his hand to me, said 'thank you', and left.

A while later Yvonne came in and said, 'that young man you talked to came to me singing your praises'. I told her what I had said to him and she said, 'good on you'. We never saw him again.

My association with the Matthew Talbot brought all sorts of challenges for my mind to tackle. Men full of anger, disillusionment and sorrow. Getting thrown right into the middle of all this, with no experience, tended to put my faith in humanity under a lot of pressure.

But now that I'd crossed over the threshold of what it is to be human I had to go with the fact that anything that intrudes into my personal space needs my deepest consideration. Faith can only move its hand if we move first. So gradually I learned to turn a deaf ear and a blind eye, and place an extra shield over my heart. By all means give a hand to whatever you can, but remember you need to take it back.

Once again opportunity came knocking on my door. Call it change, challenge, whatever you like. My lovely friend Sue told me that she was off to England for three month to visit her parents and some relations. The only problem was she didn't want to have someone she couldn't trust take over her apartment as she would need to have some money coming in to cover her expenses. So I said if you can reduce the rent to a hundred and fifty dollars a week I'll take it over for you. Here was an opportunity for both of us. Although I liked where I was living it was on a busy main road, and the traffic was quite noisy. So I ask you how could I refuse such a generous offer of a lovely apartment only a short distance from where I worked, even if it was for only three months. I already had a few shorter stays under my belt, so what the heck. I'd become more of a modern-day tinker than a permanent resident of anywhere. Maybe I should have called my story, "A Move with an Irishman, rather than a Walk.

When I told my disappointed landlady about this she offered to reduce my rent to one hundred dollars a week, but I told her I had a friend in need. She said, 'Where am I going to get someone like you who cleans up my right-of-way without accepting anything for it, and all the other little chores you've done for me'. As she was a good Catholic I said 'The Good Lord will find someone for you'. I didn't give her a chance to reply in case she had me down on my knees there and then.

Being back in the heart of Kings Cross was familiar territory for me. I had joined the Aquatic Club in the Cross and used to drop in from time to time to listen to the music they provided several nights a week. I went there one evening after I'd settled in Sue's lovely flat where everything was above the tide mark of some of the places I'd lived in and had to be classed in the four to five-star bracket.

When I walked into the Aquatic Club on this particular evening I was treated to some of the loveliest piano playing one could wish to hear. I made my way to the piano and sat in the only vacant seat. Well, what a wonderful entertaining evening I had, as well as the new friendship that blossomed between the piano player and myself. Terry King was a really nice guy as well as a fantastic pianist. I clearly remember our first humorous encounter. He asked me if I had any requests and I couldn't think of any at the time. Next time I came back I handed him a list with twenty pieces on it. He said 'that's the last time I'll ask you. Your tastes are far too expensive!' Boy, did I have an enjoyable time listening and dancing to his playing during the time I frequented the Club.

GERALD

One day I received a phone call from my brother Ken in Dublin to say our brother Gerald's health was starting to cause concern. He'd had an operation for cancer about two years previously and it hadn't been as successful as they'd hoped. Ken said if things got any worse he'd let me know. A week before Sue got back, I found myself a room in Surrey Hills so that became my next move. I'd been there only a month when Ken rang to say Gerald wasn't going to be around much longer. Naturally I was very upset because I loved Gerald dearly, as did all the family. And what seemed worse at the time was the sad fact that I couldn't afford the plane ticket to say goodbye to him.

I then got in touch with my good friends Yvonne, Sue and John. Just talking to them helped me unload some of my pain and sorrow. Then Sue invited me out for coffee and a chat. After some touching exchanges regarding the low ebb in my life, Sue said, 'You've got to go back and say goodbye to him. Please let me help you'. That was typical of Sue, always upfront with her concern for others. And she herself had been through some rough times herself which she shared privately with me.

I said 'we are looking at around two thousand dollars or more for an air ticket and I don't know how or when I could pay you back. I'd have to give up my job at the Talbot because there's always some poor person waiting in the wings for my job. Not that I'm concerned about that, but trying to pay you back on my pension would just about take forever'. Yes, I would love make the effort to go back and see him. Gerald and I have always been very close in our beliefs and understanding growing up together, and anyone who knew my brother and what he stood for couldn't help but be drawn to him. His Irish wisdom and compassion reached to the stars and beyond. On my two visits to Dublin in 1989 and 1990, I stayed with him and we opened up the last old cupboards from the past and put a few meanings into them.

Sue said, 'It doesn't matter if you pay me back or not. Money is not the issue here, just your brother. You've done a lot for others, let me help you now'.

Next day she took me to a travel agency and bought me an open return ticket to Dublin. I told Yvonne what I was going to do, and of the lovely warm hand Sue had extended to me and she said, 'Where would we be without people like Sue'.

The day before I was due to fly out Yvonne came to me just as I was finishing up. She handed me an envelope with one hundred dollars in it. I have no idea who helped to top it up, but I was very touched, so touched that I wrote this poem and gave it to her to share with those who'd laced it with their feelings. It's called good friends.

As I walk the path of life, I'm not only assisted,
but gifted, by the influence and suggestions of good friends I meet.
They place a vision of near-perfect clearness that reveals that I am not alone in my quest for truth and knowledge.
And for this I thank them with all my heart.

I was ready for bed after packing all my gear and putting what I didn't need in the boot of my car. I'd left my stereo and a few other things with John Cross. I had a parking permit for my old car so I could leave it outside the building where I rented my room. I had a few days left before the rent was due again, but I told the rental agent that I would not be coming back due to the circumstances that were hanging over my head. That way he was free to let the room again, and I was free to make other arrangements to suit my pocket on my return.

The car wasn't worth stealing, and the stuff I'd put in the boot was low-priced possessions that accompanied someone in my station of life. But that again was in my favour. The less I have, the lighter I travel.

As I put my head on the pillow, and went into dreamland, the telephone launched an attack on my eardrums. Half awake and half asleep at that unwelcome hour I reached out and put the receiver to my ear. My sister-in-law Maureen was calling from Dublin to say that Gerald had passed away. For a few moments grief took the place of speech as the tears rolled down my cheeks. Maureen sensing my grief waited till I'd gathered myself together. She said he was in the Hospice at the time, and had gone to the toilet. When he didn't return they went looking for him and found him dead. I thought afterwards, that was typical of Gerald not to want to be an inconvenience to anyone. I got the feeling he knew it was time to go and he did it as gracefully as he could.

After I'd gathered my wits together I told Maureen I was to fly out from Sydney airport at eight in the morning. She said because Gerald had died at the Hospice their policy was that he'd be buried as soon as possible. I said, 'it's in the hands of The Good Lord as to whether I'll arrive in time for the funeral or not, so let's leave it up to Him'.

Well, there was very little sleep for me after that. I don't know how many cups of tea I drank as my emotions attacked me from just about every direction. I guess the first of any family of brothers or sisters to die tends to have a greater impact. Well, that's how it seemed to me at the time.

At five o'clock the alarm woke me up from a pitiful sleep. The taxi was due in about fifteen minutes so I had a quick cup of tea and waited. Right on the button it arrived and off we went.

What a nice guy that taxi driver was. I needed someone to lay my sorrow on and he more than fitted the bill. Not only did he listen, but he never charged me a cent. He just said, 'Go bury your brother, this one's on me'. After he'd gone I looked up in the sky before I entered the airport terminal and said, Gerald, somebody besides me down here loves you.

As I was checking in I was told that a senior management person was waiting to see me in an office upstairs. Somewhat bewildered I made my way to the office and was greeted by a lovely lady who informed me that she'd had a telephone call from my daughter Rachel in New Zealand saying that she needed to speak to me. She said, 'I'm sorry to hear about the sad mission you have to undertake and we'll try to accommodate you in any way we can'. I said 'thank you that's very kind of you, and my first need is to contact my daughter in New Zealand'. She said, 'give me her telephone number and we'll ring for you'. When Rachel came on the phone she told me that Maureen had rung to let her know that Gerald had passed away, and that it would be a race against time for me to get there for the funeral. Then she said, 'I'm so sorry for your loss, Gerald was a good man, I too loved him dearly'. I said, 'sorry I couldn't let you know myself, but I didn't like to ring you in the early hours and maybe wake the kids'.

So after a few more sorrowful sentences I hung up and told the lady what had transpired. She took me into another room, sat me down and asked if I'd like a cup of tea or coffee and a little something to eat. I said, yes, I'd be very grateful for that.

After I'd put a little consoling nourishment into my being the lady returned with a new schedule that might enable me to arrive in Dublin in time for the funeral. I'd booked a short overnight stay in Singapore because I find it so hard to sleep on a long plane journey. Anyway, that would have to go by the wayside, as now the time factor had become first priority.

She said, 'I've arranged to have you first off the plane after the first class passengers have disembarked at Heathrow and you'll be escorted to the Aer Lingus terminal for your flight to Dublin'. One thing's for certain, I shall never forget this lady's kindness to me, or Singapore Airlines for all the attention they provided on my very emotional trip to London.

Not long after we were up above the clouds my thoughts were again washed in tears as I returned to the days of my childhood with Gerald. We probably knew a little more about happiness and freedom than our other two brothers and sister did. Dad hadn't really got into drinking at that time and we did have a few more luxuries to play around which gave us a closer bonding. So with my memories flooding back and forth in my mind, my journey to London was a sorrowful and very long one, as I'm sure you can gather.

As soon as I disembarked from the plane at Heathrow there was someone to escort me to catch my flight to Dublin. My niece Ann spotted me as I cleared Customs, gathered what she could of my belongings, and had me and them in her car in no time at all. From that moment on she pulled all the stops to get me to the church in time. I'm happy to say there were no police cars around. I don't believe I would have been able to pay the fine. Boy, can those Robinson women drive!

Thirty-two hours after leaving Australia I arrived at the church in Raheny with five minutes to spare before the funeral service took place. I was completely exhausted, as you can well imagine. My two brothers Ken and Tony and their wives along with the rest of the family were there to greet me with looks of astonishment, joy and sorrow on their faces. No way did they think I'd make it in time. Mind you, neither did I. After the service was over Gerald was buried in the same grave as our mother. And in my book nothing could be more fitting than that as Gerald was the one who looked after her.

Later on when all the goodbyes were said, we made our way to a hotel just down the road from Raheny to toast Gerald on his new journey, and to share the memories of our love for him. He'd left behind an emptiness that would never be filled till we all came together again. Although my sister Ann had emigrated to Canada, and I to New Zealand, I don't think you'll find too many families with bonding as close as ours, considering the battleground we had to walk through as children and into our teens. I can never speak highly enough of my sister and my brothers, but then I don't have to do that by the way they live their lives.

I stayed with Maureen and Ken for a few days, and then went back to Gerald's house. I spent around six days there with only Gerald's ghost to keep me company. Trying to get to sleep at night could be both a terrifying and sad experience. I was sleeping in what we called the box room. The smallest of the three bedrooms. My father had died on the bed I was trying to sleep in and the mattress felt as if it was packed with lumps of straw. That only added to the extremes I was going through.

Mind you I had slept in that bed on the two occasions I stayed with Gerald when I first revisited my family and thought no more of it. But this time because of the circumstances I felt like I was going through an endurance test. I guess when you're in a happy or pleasant situation things don't bother you anything like they would when you feeling sorry for yourself.

And waking up in the cold morning to the sound of silence brought new tears to my eyes. No longer would I hear my brother's humour, laughter and wisdom echo through his house. His artistic touch that had made the house come alive was no longer there. I guess I was in too sad a state to take in the more colourful memories we'd all shared together. Only time could do that for me.

BACK TO AUSTRALIA

After a few visits to my two brothers and their families the time came for me to return to Australia. Tony had been made executor of Gerald's will in which he'd left his house to be divided between us. At the airport, as they were seeing me off, Tony said, 'If you need any money to tide you over till everything is settled I can arrange it through the solicitor'. They all knew that I was the spendthrift of the family.

When I boarded the long leg of my flight to Singapore, Gerald's passing felt a lot lighter on my shoulders. I think the most trying thing living in Gerald's house was trying to cope with the intense sense of aloneness. It had indeed taken its toll on me. It brought back memories of that feeling of uselessness I experienced when I had my breakdown. One thing I'd learned through all my experiences was that you're very much alone on your journey through life. And how capable you become in dealing with that will I believe determine the outcome of it.

When I got to Singapore I had to wait in transit for only one and a half hours before we took off for Sydney. I was feeling a lot better now. I'd come to the terms with the reality that Gerald was where he needed to be, and I was where I needed to be. Nothing could take away those memories of our childhood and the years that followed. The love, respect and devotion we had for each other. Not even death could take that away.

I must say the last leg of my journey from Singapore to

Sydney was a very comfortable one because there were not many people on the plane. I had three seats to myself and managed to stretch out and get some sleep. After breakfast was served I felt a sudden desire to write this poem in memory of Gerald, and here it is.

Not of a big build was our brother Gerald,
But, oh, what strength that frame held
If you wanted something done the response
Was cheerful, and it was done.
He was too intelligent to be a politician
And too humble to be a preacher
If you needed someone to listen to you
Rest assured you were wiser when you left
Than when you came.
There was something about our brother
I couldn't put my finger on,
His pain and laughter graced his presence
And made him what he was,
Our brother Gerald.

It was shortly after eight in the evening when I cleared Customs at Sydney airport and caught a shuttle to take me to where I'd left my car. No one had been desperate enough to steal it, I was glad to see. I put my belongings in and went off to draw some badly needed cash from the nearest hole-in-the-wall. But once again the cards were stacked against me. The day before I left for my brother's funeral I drew out all but twenty dollars from my bank account, with the knowledge that another pay day was due before I arrived back. But something had backfired along the line, much to my disgust, for the same twenty dollars was still all I had to my name.

It was now around ten o'clock and I was feeling pretty close to rock-bottom after the initial shock had set in. 'God' I said to myself, 'have I not been through enough emotional strain without having to take more on board'. I'd planned to rent a room in a cheap hotel for the night and then drive out to Coogee and stay with John Cross for a few days till I found a room to rent. So once more I had to put on my thinking cap on my sorrowful head till I regained some presence of mind. So as it did, the obvious choice made its presence felt. The car might not be the most comfortable place to spend the night, but at least I'd have a roof over my head. Then I got another brainwave if you'd like to call it that. I'd taken the passenger seat out before to help a friend move some of his things from one place to another. So with a little bit of handiwork with some tools I took out the passenger seat and was able to be reasonably comfortable for the night. It seems to me that things are not there to fit into me, but I into them.

I don't know whether it was the tiredness or the makeshift bed I'd designed that gave me a good six hour sleep, so I gave a thank you to them both.

About seven next morning I made my way to the

Matthew Talbot, had a shave and tidy up, the joined the queue for breakfast. One of my workmates spotted me and hauled me into the kitchen and gave me a more upmarket breakfast, with a welcome back attached to it. I was told by the top man of the kitchen that I might be able to get my old job back at a later date. I said, 'thank you all the same, but I'm looking at going back to New Zealand in a few months' time. When the money comes from the sale of my brother's house I am going to blow it on another adventure'. He smiled and said, 'saving for a rainy day was never on your list of options'.

My friend Jerry then told me that a room had become vacant in the building where he was staying in Victoria Street in Kings Cross, so he put in a good word for me. A few days later I moved in. Now as I wasn't working I had to use a little more discretion in the spending department. But with lots of experience under my belt it wasn't very hard to adjust. I had lots of free music and interesting and uninteresting lectures to immerse myself in, plus snooker, tennis, table-tennis and the use of transport to take me to wherever I fancied to go. I decided to give golf a rest so it left me a little more money in my pocket. I could pick that up again when I got back to New Zealand.

My membership at the tennis club at Coogee had run out, but I was lucky enough to find three guys who wanted one more to play on a Saturday afternoon in Bondi. It was a private court that the owners rented out to the public. When I rang the guy who had put the ad in the paper he said it was a hard court, but he never told me how hard it was to play on. Mind you I've seen worse but that's another story. But I've got to say we four guys did have a lot of fun on it, and it only cost us five dollars each for three hours.

On certain occasions when the well was running dry I'd take a train from Kings Cross to Martin Place in the evening. Then I'd walk down to Circular Quay, buy myself a thirty-cent ice cream cone at McDonalds and board the ferry to Manly. When I got there I'd head out to the beachfront and enjoy what scenery the evening had to offer to my imagination. On the way back to Circular Quay I'd take the Jetcat and enjoy the beautiful balmy evenings, if it was that time of the year, and the glimmering lights of Sydney. Just a little imagination and you can just about make anything out of anything. And at times I'd have some wonderful conversations on the ferry crossing. Mostly, when I got back to Circular Quay, I'd walk home. I may not have been rich in my bank account, but in all other ways I was more fortunate than most men.

I remember walking up William Street about eleven thirty one evening and a lady-of-the-night approached me and asked if I had change of twenty. I felt in my pockets and came out with two ten-cent coins. She said to me, 'You bloody fool, I meant twenty dollars'. And if looks could have killed that night you wouldn't be reading, A Walk with an Irishman today. I don't know where my mind was when she asked me, but every time I think about it I grin from ear to ear. I saw the lady occasionally after that with some of her friends, but she must have put the word around for they all avoided me like the plague.

About a month later the clutch packed up in my car, mind you the engine was only a stone's throw behind it. When I moved into my lodgings in Victoria Street I'd got a parking permit so there'd be no cause for concern. Still I hadn't used the car very much since I got back from my brother's funeral.

Well that really made up my mind to return to New Zealand. I wrote to my brother Tony and said I'd take him up on his offer to ask the solicitor dealing with Gerald's will if I could have an advance on my share of the settlement. That way I could buy a cheap car in New Zealand to tide me over until Gerald's house had been sold and everything settled.

Two paydays would give me enough to purchase an air ticket and cover other expenses. I informed my daughter of my intentions and she said there was a bed ready for me at her place.

Sue said she would be sorry to see me go, but understood the necessity for it. I told her when everything was settled I would pay her back for her kindness to me. Mind you, you can't really pay back that kind of kindness, but maybe something towards the effort of it when you really think about it.

A week or so before I left Sydney I was crossing on a street that runs parallel to Elizabeth Street when I got picked up on one side of a car bonnet and dropped off on the other. As I lay there on the ground I thought to myself, 'lady, if you're trying to make an impression on me that is certainly not the way to go about it'. The lady was quite attractive, but I'm wary of women who play it rough.

Very quickly a number of people gathered around. A couple of them started to abuse the lady. As quickly as I could, while nursing my right leg, I came to her rescue and said to them, 'I'm okay; it's just one of those accidents that fits into the category of human error'. Then a guy came up to me and said, 'I'll be a witness, here's my card'. Judging by his aggressive manner towards the lady you'd have thought he was the victim. I won't tell you what I said to him, but I'm quite sure he'll have nothing good to say about me.

With a week to go before my departure from Sydney I committed my one and only crime during my stay there. I didn't have enough money to have my old bomb towed away so I removed the number plates, cut each one of them into three, and late one evening, dropped them all into the sea beside the Opera House. They say confession is good for the soul and hopefully I'll get away with a fine instead of a prison sentence when this all comes to light.

The day before I was due to fly out I had one of those soul touching experiences. One of the older guys I'd befriended at the Talbot saw me walking down Victoria Street. He stopped me and said, 'I hear you're going back to New Zealand'. I said 'yes, I fly out tomorrow'.

Then he said, 'I'm going to miss you'. Then he put his forehead against mine and said, God bless you. As I walked away a tear trickled down my cheek. No one could have given me a better going-away present. Well, no one but Sister Yvonne. She gave me one of those special goodbyes that few could match.

AUCKLAND

Rachel was there to meet me at the airport in Auckland with the welcome that only a daughter could give a father, and drove me home. My son-in-law Paul and my two grandchildren were there to greet me and I quickly settled in to being a grandfather to them.

I must admit it took a little time to get adjusted to my new living conditions. My ability to adjust to all sorts of circumstances was no longer being tested to the degree that it had been. I was now having to adjust to a more comfortable lifestyle, something that had become foreign to me. Making snap decisions brought out the best in me, even though they did bring certain regrets at times. But then again I was never in one place long enough to let them tie me down. In Sydney, I could catch a train, bus or ferry to just about anywhere. In Auckland, without a car, it can take forever to get to places, and it's more expensive. Don't get me wrong, it's a very pretty city, and if they had listened to Sir Dove-Myer Robinson years ago when he urged the city to adopt rapid rail it could have been an even greater one today.

Gradually I adjusted to my new lifestyle, knowing that my restless feet would find more ground to cover in the not too distant future.

As soon as the cheque arrived from my brother's solicitor I bought a cheap car to last me till I received the main settlement for Gerald's house. And now that I had transport I was soon back into golf. Chamberlain Park public golf course in Western Springs became my happy hunting ground. If you want to experience everyday people, with all sorts of stories, I highly recommend Chamberlain Park golf course. And it's seldom you will be left playing on your own unless you're that way inclined.

I just about always went there on my own, then joined up with others to make a twosome, threesome or a foursome. And if you're open to people, you'll have an enjoyable round of golf on what I consider to be a top public golf course. And I can't speak highly enough of all the people who look after its well-being.

And I've received a wealth of education from some wonderful people I've played with there over the years, people from different parts of the world as well.

Having my car, my evening entertainment needs could be also fully satisfied. I'd been a member of the Devonport Folk Club, the Titirangi Folk Club and the Irish Club so I soon became involved with them again. Then I added another string or two to my bow - The Birdcage, and an Irish bar called The Dog's Bollix. Conor McSweeney who pointed me in the right direction at the Sly Fox in Brisbane, was now a part-owner of The Dog's Bollix. He was always kind enough to ask me to sing a song or two at the Tuesday evening sessions.

I was introduced to the Birdcage through people who were involved in the Baha'i Faith. My friend Paul Bennett entertained us with his enchanting voice and guitar playing, and we supported him with some of our best footwork.

As I have alluded to before, I consider constant change to be one of the greatest teachers of all times, and throughout the universe. If I can't change my goals, how will I change to discover the better qualities I have to offer others and myself?

In May of 1996 I received my share of the sale of Gerald's house. The first thing I did was to send my good friend Sue the money she'd lent me for the ticket to fly home to Dublin. Then a few days later, very excited, I went into a travel agent in Glenfield and drew up plans to launch myself once more into the unknown. I had a little under seventeen thousand dollars in my bank account, but I knew when I returned it would only be a shadow of its former self. At the same time, once you give yourself a mission, you have a thousand alternatives which are worth much more than the value of money.

With one more purchase left to make I bought a new set of golf clubs. Ever since I was unwillingly forced to sell the first new set I acquired in Queenstown I'd kind of hankered for a new set. Now my moment of glory had come it might help me to bring my handicap down a notch or two. And if not, surely I could impress someone with my new clubs. Yes, we just about all have that little bit of ego running around at times within us.

About a week later, with all my goodbyes said to my family, Rachel drove me to the airport to begin the first leg of my flight to Sydney. Since 1989, no one could have left home as much as I had. Maybe I should have said, no one was as crazy as me. As my bag was checked in I struck my first and only hiccup. Apart from my first flight to Dublin, I'd always taken my constant companions with me, my golf clubs and never had the problem of being overweight. This time I was relieved of one hundred and fifty dollars. Well I suddenly realised I had one thing in my favour. This time I'd more money so that had to be a plus. No use crying over spilt milk, unless you are forced to lick it up.

After Rachel and I had said our goodbyes I made my way through the usual formalities and boarded the plane to Sydney. Once more I was walking down memory lane. Those three years in Sydney had made a strong impact on me that I believe will stay with me wherever I go. I really feel in my own humble way that wonderful significance of Jesus' teaching was born there for me. Not from man but from the great Teacher Himself.

I timed my stay in Sydney to cover four days so I could catch up with Sister Yvonne and a few close friends. A game of golf at Moor Park golf club was also on the cards. My stay in Australia was planned around four days in Sydney, then ten days touring around in whatever direction took my fancy. I had already pre-booked and paid for a rental car. I had arrived on the Thursday and would leave on the Monday. On Friday I caught up with Sister Yvonne. We had a very enjoyable meal and shared a lot of our past memories as well as a few dreams of the future.

I phoned Sue a few times but could not get hold of her. On Saturday afternoon I met up with John Cross at the Hero of Waterloo, our old hunting ground, where we indulged in a joyful drinking spree and a nice meal.

With my head a little out of shape on Sunday morning I took my time getting out of bed. Sometime after midday when the liquor fumes had subsided in my brain, I had a shower, shave and something to eat. A little later I made my way down to the Hero for some soothing music. It turned out to be one of those special evenings as I danced with a number of entertaining ladies, as well as my lovely friend Alice.

As I had to be up early next morning I took off around seven o'clock. I ordered a taxi and got talking to him about my short tour of New South Wales. He said go to a place called Wellington and you won't want to go any further. You'll fall in love with it. I'm going to retire there next year. I thanked him and said I'd certainly put it on my agenda.

When I woke up on Monday morning I was quite excited about the new adventure I was about to experience. I'd only once ventured outside Sydney when a friend I used to play table tennis called Shane hired a sports model car for a day for me to drive him and myself a few hundred miles South of Sydney. All the details are very hazy in my mind except that I really enjoyed putting the car through its paces, and Shane with a worried look on his face from time to time. I guess the racing genes of the Robinson family had something to do with it.

Apart from that we had a very enjoyable day, and stopped at some nice cafes to indulge in some lovely food.

Anyway, here was an opportunity to see a little more of the wonderful continent of Australia. The only thing that brought a shadow of sadness was that my brother had to die to give me this opportunity. I don't know if he frowned on me from time to time because of the reckless lifestyle I'd adopted, but I got a feeling he was smiling down on me this time.

When I went to collect my rental car I was informed that the four cylinder car I'd requested wasn't available. They said they'd let me have a Falcon at no extra charge. Well, that didn't bother me. By now I was used to not getting what I expected. You know that saying, 'Blessed is he who does not expect for he shall not be disappointed'.

Getting out of Sydney was a bit uncomfortable for a novice like me, but after a few wrong turns and some dirty looks, I hit the open road. The Falcon handled like a dream, especially after being used to driving vehicles that tended to leave the hair on your head a lighter shade of grey before its given time.

Before I left Sydney I'd pulled into a side street to decide where my first overnight stay would be and out jumped a place called Nelson Bay. Typical of my new lifestyle, feel it, do it, then look for the reason why at a later date. Then you can either applaud yourself, or look for a reason why you didn't make a more suitable choice which sometimes can be a great learning experience.

I drove to Newcastle, with one eye trying to take in the scenery and the other on the road. This massive but very enjoyable highway, which just seemed to go on and on, was quite different from driving on New Zealand roads.

Eventually I got into Newcastle and stopped for something to eat and drink. I was going to spend a few hours there giving it the once over, but the vibes I got just after arriving seemed to point me in the out-of-town direction. Probably my loss, Newcastle's gain, or maybe Sydney had spoilt me with its tantalising charm.

It was around four o'clock when I arrived in Nelson Bay and was seduced right away by its peaceful charm. There wasn't a ripple to be seen on the calm waters of its small harbour. An invitation to swim was being offered to me on this warm May afternoon. I found myself a cosy, reasonable priced apartment on the beachfront, dug out my togs and fulfilled the invitation. You've heard that saying, "A day to remember", well that's an afternoon I'll remember for a long time to come. Next day I found out where the golf club was and enjoyed a very up and down game with a pleasant member of the club.

When I informed the owner of the apartment where I

was staying that I enjoyed a game of tennis, he said 'There's a tournament taking place at the tennis club tomorrow, I'll ring and see if they can fit you in'. They very kindly did, and I spent a very enjoyable day in their company. Unfortunately, there were no booby prizes so I came away empty handed.

During the five days in Nelson Bay I swam every day and got in two games of golf along with the tennis. I felt very satisfied with the choice that had taken me there.

I decided my next port of call would be Wellington. I'm not sure how long it took me, but I couldn't help noticing how parched the surrounding countryside looked. Everything appeared brown and burnt. As I got closer to Wellington it seemed to get worse, but just before I drove into the town I was impressed with its fairyland appearance. The sudden change of scenery gave me the impression that I'd driven through something that looked close to desert, and ended up in a beautiful oasis. The taxi driver was right, it was a lovely town that you could give more than a second glance to.

The next item on my agenda was accommodation so I headed for the main tourist office. Well, it seemed that I'd arrived on one of those very busy weekends when some sort of festival was in progress and accommodation hard to come by. I think it was a flower festival. Had it been a music one I would have certainly remembered it. No disrespect to all you flower lovers.

When I got into the tourist office the lady behind the counter said to me, 'would you like to take a seat and I'll ring round and see if I can get you fixed up. It may take a little time as you've arrived on one of the busiest weekends on our calendar'. Well, the power of persuasion and patience brings its own rewards. Just before closing time, with what seemed to be only one possibility left, that possibility became the answer. The lady phoned a couple who take in people for bed and breakfast. Unfortunately, they were about to depart to visit their son and his family, otherwise they said they'd have taken me in. The lady then said to them, what a pity. This poor Irish Gentleman has been on the road since early morning and I can't find any accommodation for him. Well I can't say in all sincerity the word gentleman did the trick, but I feel the Irish part of it may have hit home. Then the lady on the other end of the phone said, if he's prepared to look after himself, send him around. I thanked the lady very sincerely at the Tourist Board Centre for her persistence, and ten minutes later I arrived at my temporary lodgings.

As I alighted from my car in the car park just outside the house I was greeted by a tall, friendly man who introduced himself then guided me into the house to meet his wife. After I told them something of my background they shared something of themselves. Of course they were from the Irish scene. Over a cup of very welcome tea, they said to me, 'If you're prepared to look after yourself the place is yours. We're off to visit our son and his family for three days'. I was very moved by their trust in me, a complete stranger, and I expressed that in no uncertain terms. I said, 'I plan to stay for two or three days, and if you're not back I'll leave the key and the money in an envelope in the drawer where the knives and forks are kept'. After they left I got my head down for an hour or so, then later refreshed, had something to eat. I spent the rest of the evening relaxing and watching television.

Early next morning I found out where the golf club was, and with mixed enthusiasm and expectations made my way there. Well, I've played on some sunburnt fairways since I took up the game, but none of them could hold a candle to this one. The only thing that represented the word green were the greens themselves. There was no such thing as taking a divot, but there was such a thing as creating a dust storm. Well for a novice like me who played off twenty five, there was.

The gentleman who played with me didn't seem to have too many problems, so it was obvious that I wasn't a good desert player. After the fourth hole I gave up marking my card for fear I'd get disqualified from the game altogether. The only thing I want to remember about that game are the few drinks and a pie I had in the clubhouse. Mind you, the gentleman I played with was a very nice person and very discreet. He didn't embarrass me in any conversation about the game. I guess he thought I'd suffered enough. Mind you, he must have suffered himself just watching me play.

Later that afternoon I took a stroll around the town and admired the park and the lovely layout of the town. I could see a lot of care and pride had been put in by all concerned for its development. Eventually, with my curiosity close to its peak I needed one more question answered, what does one do for the kind of entertainment I need in this beautiful sleepy town?

Well I won't go into any details because my needs were far too great to be filled. Wellington was a really lovely place to retire to because of its friendly atmosphere and good people, but for someone like me, with my new found hunger for living life to what I call its potential, what would I have to offer it and what would it have to offer me. But thank you, Wellington, and to those good people who made my short stay there a very happy and memorable one.

Next morning I wrote a letter of thanks to the two lovely people who'd offered me the use of their home while they were away. I left the money that I owed, and told them I'd give them a phone call when I got back to Sydney to make sure everything was in order.

When I arrived in Sydney I went to the motel I'd stayed in and booked a room for three nights. Then I returned my rental car. It was now Friday and I was due to fly out to Los Angeles on Monday. When I woke up on Saturday morning I decided to spend most of the day revisiting some of the places I'd always held dear to my heart. I'm a great believer in walking down memory lane every so often letting its warmth take me wherever it will.

It was about seven-thirty when I arrived back in Kings Cross. I then went into this coffee shop that had not only aroused my taste buds, but also aroused my mind with the people who shared their light and dark secrets with me.

After breakfast next morning I took myself off to St John's Anglican Church in Darlinghurst to give thanks for my trip to date, and hopefully receive a blessing for the future.

Later that afternoon I made my way to the Hero of Waterloo. Good fortune was there to greet me once again. An air hostess named Tori whom Joyce had introduced me to in The Henry The 9th arrived shortly after me and we filled in the gaps since we last saw each other. I said, 'I'm off to your part of the world tomorrow evening for a week, then on to England and Ireland'. I told her about the money my brother had left to me, and said 'no way do I want to let it burn a hole in my pocket'. She laughed and said it's your call. Then she said, 'I fly out in the morning and then I'm off duty for eight days. Would you like me to show you around?' I said, 'that would be brilliant. It would make my stay just about perfect'. Then she said, 'Joyce is also within visiting distance so I'll give her a ring and let her know you're coming. I know she'd like to catch up with you'. I said, 'it gets better all the time!'

After an enjoyable evening of dancing and catching up with other friends we said our goodbyes till fate should bring us together again. As I made my way back to my motel my mind took me back to the church that morning. I'd asked for a blessing, and here it was laced with all sorts of trimmings. No, I am not a regular church person, just someone who needs a bit of guidance as I walk the tightrope of life.

LOS ANGELES

As I hit the unclouded skies of Sydney next morning my thoughts were reaching out for all those questions that would remain unanswered till the time was ripe. I guess restless people like me live one foot in the moment, and the other in the future. Tricky as it may be, I feel it gives us a better sense of balance.

When I passed through Customs in Los Angeles I used my Irish passport. It had stamped on it, Indefinite Visa into the United States. Talk about that another time.

I'd booked a small unit for six days at the Holiday Inn complex close to Disneyland, and without too much confusion boarded the bus to take me there. I like to be up front where I can see ahead, and was lucky to get a seat close to the driver. I was soon engrossed in conversation with this lovely dark-skinned bus driver whose sense of humour was right up my street as we shared a little something with each other. That had to be the quickest and most enjoyable bus trip I've ever taken.

It was about five-thirty in the evening when I arrived at my unit, so I wasted no time in settling in. Across the yard from me was a restaurant and a swimming pool. I thought to myself, food first then maybe a swim. After a nice meal I went back to my unit and lay down for a while. Then after a shower I spent the rest of the evening collecting my thoughts and watching TV. The swimming pool became another of those forgotten inspirations that disappeared as quickly as it had arrived.

After breakfast next morning I rang my newfound tourist-guide-to-be Tori. She said 'I'll collect you tomorrow morning and give you a guided tour of Disneyland'. Later I took myself off for a good walk, and on the way back called in to a shop just across from the Holiday Inn to get a few provisions to fill the gaps between meals. As I came out of the shop I spotted two guys who looked a bit down on their luck. I dropped ten dollars into a dish beside one of them who was in a wheelchair. Then I got talking and I introduced myself and told them what had brought me to Los Angeles.

As we chatted away I felt myself drawn back to the Matthew Talbot. The lifestyle of these men bore a close similarity to those who frequented the Talbot. I was on common ground here, familiar territory. As we talked the men sensed my deeper sense of humanity and opened up to me. Like so many before them they'd got caught up in the unrealistic chain of life, and by the time they'd released it, the essential part of their lives had passed them by. It's a hard road back when you miss a part of yourself. I should know.

Next morning Tori gave me the promised guided tour of Disneyland and the enchantment of her company. When we parted that evening she said she'd pick me up next morning and show me some of the sights of L.A.

When she first arrived she'd suggested I should pack a

bag and stay with her till the day before I was due to fly out to Heathrow, she said it would be a lot less time consuming for her as she lived a two hour-drive away. Well, anything that makes life easier for someone else or myself I'm into, especially when that someone is bestowing so much hospitality on me.

What can I say about Disneyland that hasn't been said before? What would I say if you were to ask me how much I enjoyed it?

Well, on a rating of one to ten I'd have to say about five. But without taking anything away from it, or the amazing talent of those who designed it, or who worked there looking after it, it was just not my cup of tea. I guess the simple old fashioned pleasures of life had won me over. But at the same time I wouldn't have missed the golden opportunity that brought me to its doors. Fate doesn't always place you where you want to be, but where you need to be.

Besides having Tori's delightful company to keep my spirits in good stead, there was a lovely friendly atmosphere that seemed to bounce back and forth in just about every direction we went. I guess the children were the editors of that.

But the sun never sets without rising. The next day Tori drove me to a place that really lifted the roof on my next stay there. Mission San Juan Capistrano was its title and it just about blew me away. I felt as if I were being taken back in time as I allowed it to seduce me. It had to be one of the most beautiful feelings of Spirituality that I've experienced. I felt as if I'd been here before, and was being lifted into another dimension to search more enthusiastically for things I have not yet attempted. I can't enthuse enough over the old Bell Wall with its four Bells, each in its separate arch bordered by roses and bougainvillea. And even though the Mission was ravaged by time it still gave me a feeling of serenity and peace as I strolled through its beautiful gardens and frail buildings. Time seemed to stand still and you were at peace with everything around you.

I read in a little leaflet that the swallows of Capistrano return every spring to nest throughout the Capistrano Valley. They make nests with mud and saliva, built in rocky cliffs or under the eaves of buildings. Swallows feed their young on insects plucked from the air and therefore are beneficial to agriculture.

As the old mission town has grown the swallows have increased, but their food supply has dwindled because there are fewer open fields. The legend of the swallows is that an innkeeper, tired of the chattering of hundreds of swallows, destroyed the nests and drove the birds away. A Mission padre happened to be standing by. 'Come swallows', said the padre. 'Come to the Mission. We will give you shelter, there is room enough for all'. Recognising the padre as a brother of St Francis the birds began nesting in the old Mission. Doesn't that touch your heart strings no matter how you might view it?

After Tori had allowed my imagination to go where it needed to go she said, 'it's time we had something to eat'. She took me to a small Mexican centre dotted with tents, stalls and lightly framed buildings where all kinds of things were being sold, and all sorts of dishes were being cooked. But what really dazzled my eyes and imagination were the costumes the kids were dressed in. The children's lovely copper-coloured skin blended so beautifully with everything they wore to cover, or at least partly cover their bodies. And the different designs of headgear they wore was another breath- taking spectacle. Then, to top it off, was all this wonderful music that the different groups of musicians were playing.

Then Tori said to me, 'They serve the best potato skins in San Diego here or probably anywhere else for that matter, but choose what you like'. I said, 'you haven't put me wrong so far'. So I ordered them. And how right she was. I have tasted quite a few tasty dishes in my life, but those potato skins at that present moment had to be out on their own. What a fantastic day it was. If I'd seen nothing else in LA during my stay, that would have satisfied me more than enough.

When we got back to Tori's house another pleasant surprise awaited me. Joyce had left a message on Tori's answering machine to say she'd like to catch up with me, so could we give her a ring. After I'd told Joyce some of the hows and whys that had brought me to LA she invited Tori and me to a barbeque the following day to meet her husband, daughter and some of her friends. Winking at Tori I said to Joyce, have you told your husband about us. She said, if something had happened I wouldn't, but seeing nothing did I told him about you. I nearly split my sides laughing. They don't come much smarter than Joyce.

Around midday we drove over to Joyce's home in Laguna Hills. I've seen some lovely houses in my time, but the one Joyce and her family lived in had style written all over it. I'm not going to try and describe what I can remember of it just in case I get a lawsuit thrown at me for defamation. I'd never have made it in the real estate business, except perhaps for selling rundown places that didn't take a lot of enthusiasm to describe.

Joyce greeted me with a big hug and introduced me to her husband, daughter and the friends she had asked around for the occasion. After a tour of the house we sat in the garden beside the swimming pool with refreshments and caught up with the time since our last meeting. The sad news was that her horse Maggie had gone to greener pastures. The last time I saw her Joyce had mentioned that Maggie was going through a rough patch, and said she'd spared nothing to provide the best treatment available for the horse. How much she loved Maggie was written all over her. Whenever Joyce spoke about the horse in the Henry the Ninth her eyes would light up. The wonderful thing about animals is their unconditional love and affection – I'd say one of the nearest things to perfect love.

I can't remember how many people turned up for the barbeque, but I was busily engaged in conversation for the rest of that very entertaining day. Joyce knew I was planning to write my life story and asked how it was going. I said, 'at the moment it's not going anywhere, but at least now I will have something more to put in it'. She said, 'you're very much a dreamer, but I've got a feeling you will write it'.

Later that night as Tori and I were leaving I thanked Joyce, her family and friends for allowing me to share a little of myself with them to further my education as a human being. And they returned the compliment.

As we drove home I thanked Tori for another trump card she'd placed in my hand. With a little over a day left before I was due to fly out to England and catch up with my daughter Alex, I asked Tori if she could help me purchase a small stereo and a few other things I needed for the remainder of my trip.

The following day Tori drove me to a massive building that a golf cart would have been very handy to drive around in.

It seemed to me at that time what you couldn't buy there wasn't worth buying. The only problem, as I saw it, that by the time you'd walked so far with the aches and pains setting in, you'd probably have forgotten what you went there for, or maybe lost interest. That's why I mentioned the golf cart, especially for those of us with the years fast catching up with us.

Anyway, I got what I needed and headed for what I like best about shopping, a coffee shop. Nobody I feel goes into a shop to buy something and comes out faster than I do. When I go to the supermarket I buy between four or seven items so I can get out in a hurry. Even when I punch the numbers in after I've zapped my EFTPOS card I'm usually told, 'you're too fast, do it again'. My mother never told me, but I guess I must have been born in a hurry.

The next day around lunch time Tori drove me to the airport to catch my flight to London. I said to her as we parted, 'I'll never be able to thank you enough for your kindness. My stay here would have been very empty had you not made it otherwise'.

She gave me a big hug and said, 'I had a lot of fun watching you go through your paces. Good luck wherever you go'.

The flight to London gave me a chance to reflect on my stay in LA and naturally it was full of very pleasant thoughts and emotions. Quite the reverse from the last time I flew out for my brother's funeral.

BEGINNING OF MY IRISH TOUR

When I arrived at Heathrow Alex and her son Cosmo were there to greet me and take me back to where they were living in Watford. It was really good to be back with family again, especially when they lived so far away.

During the eight days I spent with Alex and Cosmo, one day was taken up with a visit to my ex-wife's sister Eileen, and her husband Hugh. As I mentioned before, Eileen was one of those lovely people who always had a welcome on the mat for you. She'd put a smile on the devil himself with her Irish sense of humour. Hugh was a nice guy too, but I'm sure he wouldn't mind me putting her on a pedestal. After spending a wonderful day with them Alex drove the three of us back to her place with my stomach echoing praises for Eileen's cooking.

The next thing on my agenda was to purchase a car under one thousand pounds. That would hopefully fulfil a dream I'd planned to bring to reality since the first time I visited my Green Shores in late 1989. About the third day of our search our efforts were rewarded. A two-door Fiesta with 90,000 miles on the clock stood in this driveway as though it was expecting me, and I fell hook line and sinker for it. Do you know that feeling, when you see something come out of the blue and you feel drawn to it, you know it's meant to be? Ever since I left New Zealand to venture into this tour I've been blessed with all sorts of good fortune. Around every corner fate seemed to be smiling at me. It was as though this whole trip was pre-planned from the moment I put the thought deep into my subconscious in 1989. That I believe was the year that life had really awakened in me. The interior unfinished things of the house within me I was at last redecorating. And all it took was that major decision to say yes to life, and to hell with the consequences. Until you like who you are, you'll do anything to become something you can't, and that way you become lost.

A quick look over the car and a short drive round the block brought a smile of satisfaction to my mind that told me, go for it, this car is just what you need. So I handed over the eight hundred pounds the owner was asking without trying to beat him down. He said he liked my style, and handed me back fifty pounds.

I said to Alex later, 'I'll wait until I get to Dublin and get my brother Ken's mechanic to give it a service before I start my Irish experience'.

A few days later with a map drawn up for me, and a few dry runs on how to reach the A40 that would take me to the M40 I headed off once more into the unknown with feelings of nervousness and excitement. But somewhere along the M40 I screwed up. I got stuck behind a bloody great truck that obscured my vision of the off-ramp I thought I had to take, so I took a gamble and vacated the highway. Well, as soon as I did I knew that I had backed a loser. I said to myself, I suppose it had to happen sooner or later, knowing what sort of a navigator I am. No wonder I was ground staff in the Royal Air Force. And even then I don't think they were too happy about that.

I realised there was only one way out of my predicament, scream for help in every direction I could. I drove a mile or so down this deserted country road and, as doggy faith would have it, I saw this woman walking on the footpath. I stopped and went over to her and said excuse me but I'm lost my way and looking to get back on the highway to take me to Holyhead.

Well I don't know if she had anything against the Irish or not, but she just looked through me with not a word to offer. So I hastily got back in the car and took off before I got arrested for indecent assault. I said to myself, I'd better be careful in my next approach, or I might never get back to my native shores.

But as we well know one door never closes without another one opening. Three or four minutes later as I cruised around I spotted a big truck parked by the roadside. I stopped behind it and walked up to the driver's door and tapped on it. The window came down and a man with a very pleasant smile on his face said, 'what can I do for you?' I started to tell him about my plight and he said, 'get in the other door and share a flask of tea and a sandwich with me and I'll set you right'. Well, that made all the difference in the world to my situation. One minute I was down in the dumps and the next I was on cloud nine. As we ate and drank we shared a little of our lives and beliefs with each other. It was as though we were destined to meet for whatever the reason. A little later with fond farewells to each other, and me equipped with the directions I needed, I was once again back on target to Holyhead. Mind you, I did have to make a few little detours before I got there, but nothing major.

When I arrived at Holyhead I had forty minutes to spare before the ferry was due to depart. Not too bad for someone who can get lost on a merry-go-round. As I settled in a nice easy chair in the ferry's comfortable lounge I thought to myself, 'this is a far cry from the rough and tumble boats such as the Princess Maude I used to travel on when I came on leave from the RAF'. I could have something to eat and drink on this luxurious ferry without having any real fear of throwing up, as I'd done before without even taking a bite.

As we got underway I felt really impressed with myself for having reached this stage of my journey, as well as feeling a great sense of gratitude to all those who'd helped to make it possible. As I had nothing to do I thought I'd put the time to some use so I wrote this poem. It's called, My Coming Home.

Here I am on the ferry bound for my home town
The sound of native tongues is a pleasure to my ears
The waves are soft and true with a bright blue sky above
And as I scribble in my chair I'm as happy as a king.
The whisky and the soda went down like a treat
The pleasant taste of alcohol is a mixture of all things
My journey to my native shores

has been both up and a little down
But a pleasant set of values is what really
makes the man.

As we approached the mainland somewhere between seven and eight that evening the rain began to fall and the daylight started to hand over its tour of duty to the sweet scent of darkness. Approaching Dublin by sea and by air are two very different experiences in my book. I don't think I could describe approaching Dublin by ferry with more enthusiasm than this poem written by my daughter on her first trip to the land where she was born. Rachel was only three months old when we left for New Zealand and she was returning to find that sense of belonging that is so strong in many of us who were born there. And no matter how poor you might have been or how harsh you might have been treated in your growing years, your Irish heritage has the capacity to overcome those injustices. I put it down to faith and forgiveness in ourselves.

Rachel called her poem "Remembering Ireland"

I saw a black sea so dark, so cold
I saw a stretch of grey land so hazy, so bright
I saw a brown port so tall, so wide
I saw a smokey town, so alive and drunk
I saw the rolling hills, so lush and sweet

I saw the mountainside, rocky and covered in mist
And I saw my home.

How could I add or take anything away from the deep feelings and emotions that surface from that poem. It's the kind of stuff that's born and bred in us Irish. We belong to no one, only ourselves.

Although it was dark and raining as I drove off the ferry my spirits were high, knowing I was completely independent of anyone else to take me here, there or yonder. With my vehicle, spending-money in my pocket, and no one to please, I was as free as an eagle on the wing to get into whatever fate had to throw at me. So just keep walking with me and judge for yourself.

I'd already booked into a bed and breakfast in Clontarf before I left Watford. Driving down Clontarf Road to reach my destination brought back flashes of the past both good and not so good. One of the not so good incidents was that time when I was driving the first old Morris Minor I had on that road when a child fell of his bike in front of me. I jammed on my brakes and a Volkswagen ran up my butt. There was little damage to my bumper, but the Volkswagen was not a pretty sight. The woman-owner tried to blame me for stopping too quickly. Then I pointed out the reason why. Then she took a look at her car and started crying. I didn't have the heart to make any kind of claim for my bumper. As a matter of fact, if I hadn't been married who knows where we could have wound up? She was quite attractive.

The other incident involved a taxi and me. It was around nine o'clock on a winter evening with ice forming on the road. I was turning a corner to get me on to Clontarf Road with a taxi in front of me. He moved off turning to his right, and I started to follow him. For some reason he almost stopped before he completed his turn, and silly me tried to brake as I followed him but the ice on the road put paid to my chances of avoiding him. Anyway he started ranting and raving. So I said 'I'm sorry, I will ask my insurance company to fix up the damage to your bumper'. Mind you the damage to my bumper was more visible than his. Then he said 'give me twenty pounds and we'll say no more'. I said 'I'm sorry I don't have twenty pounds'. So with a sense of very bad grace he took my particulars and went on his way. The dent I had put on his bumper was very slight, and showed really nothing on my bumper. Those are the only two little incidents that could be called a little upsetting for me, and of course the lady and the taxi driver in the Clontarf area.

I received a great welcome when I arrived at the B&B. Over a cup of tea and sandwiches I gave the family there a rundown on what New Zealand is like. I rang my brother Ken next morning, and arranged with him to have his mechanic service my car the following day, and spent the rest of the day revisiting old haunts. My boyhood memories of Yellow Walls in Malahide were always a big draw-card for me. Saint Anne's Estate and

Ringsend also rang their own bells.

After I'd satisfied myself with memories of the past I hit the sack. Next morning I drove up to Ken's business in Smithfield and he took me to see his mechanic. The man said, 'give me a couple of hours and providing nothing is amiss you're on your way'. Two hours later the car was given a clean bill of health, so the only thing that stood between me and where I was going was the open road.

Ken had arranged a farewell game of golf at Bray golf club. When I arrived he was already there, then my other brother Tony joined us soon afterwards. I drove off first, then Tony and Ken. But I must tell you before I go any further that Ken is the real golfer, and Tony and I the hackers. But even good golfers have their not-so-good drives so Ken's ball along with Tony's went left into some trees, and that's where the fun began.

When my two brothers hit off they hadn't checked to see if their golf balls were the same, which can make the game a lot more difficult than it needs to be. Anyway, Tony and Ken arrived at the spot where the balls had vacated the fairway. The ball Ken thought was his was playable back onto the fairway without getting too much distance on it. Tony would have to drop out. I just happened to look at Tony before Ken hit what he thought was his ball and Tony's face had a strange doubtful look on it. It was as though he wanted to protest and yet was afraid to do so. Very quickly I sensed what was going through Tony's mind, but was in no position to add my voice as Ken went through his shot. The Ken waited for

Tony to drop out, but Tony just looked at him with his mouth half open and a silly look on his face that no one but Tony could produce. Then the penny dropped as Ken read the message portrayed on Tony's face. I won't say what Ken said to him, but I just doubled up with laughter. Mind you, I came in at the tail end of the three of us, but still had more than my money's worth, and the great privilege of playing with two of the nicest guys God ever put on this earth.

After the game we had a few drinks and a few laughs, then decided to have a farewell meal in Killiney. Ken said he needed to put some petrol in his car so we followed him and parked outside a petrol station in a place called Shankill. I was parked behind Tony on the road outside. A number of minutes elapsed, then Ken drove out and proceeded in the direction of Killiney. But Tony made no effort to follow so I jumped out of my car and found him half asleep behind the wheel. I shouted through the window, 'for God's sake, didn't you see Ken pull out?' He sat up with a jerk and said, 'oh, my God, I'm really in trouble now'. I said, 'off you go, I'll catch up with you and ran back to my car fit to be tied with laughter'.

Well as expected Ken was nowhere to be seen so Tony headed in the direction of Killiney. When we arrived he cruised around a couple of restaurants that he thought Ken may have in mind. But no Ken. Tony then parked outside one of the restaurants and I parked behind him. He said to me, as I joined him on the footpath, 'I'll never live this down', and I just burst out laughing again. We must have been there about fifteen minutes wondering what we should do when, lo and behold, Ken appeared. What he said to Tony didn't leave much room for anything else to be said, as Tony stood there like a dog with his tail between his legs. And of course I again doubled up with laughter. I thought to myself, it doesn't get much better than this. And I'm sure if Gerald was looking on from his resting place he too would have enjoyed it as much as I did.

About an hour later we were enjoying a lovely meal and sharing memories of our beloved Gerald and whatever else came to our minds. With our stomachs and spirits satisfied a while later we said our goodbyes and headed off to get some shuteye. I thought to myself as I drove to my accommodation, 'what a fantastic day I've had with those two lovely brothers of mine. What a great lead-up to the rest of my journey'.

GALWAY

The next morning I had a late breakfast to give the early morning traffic a miss. I'd roughly planned in my mind the places I wanted to visit, but at the same time I was open to change if something of more interest appeared on the horizon. My years of confinement were well behind me and that was where I'd decided they would stay. I think this poem of mine fits in here.

It's called God's Gift To Me.

To live each day with hope and joy
I must always be on my toes
And each new friend I chance to meet
Is an enlightenment to behold
Each sunrise and each sunset
Sends heaven's comforters to me
While around the willow banks
The wind echoes to me its call.
The travel bug that drives me on
Rash dreamer that I am
Lays my suffering past to rest
As I triumphantly march on.

Set firmly in my mind was to hug as much of the coastline of Ireland as I could. Keep out of the cities where possible so I could drink in the simplicity and the beauty its people and its countryside had to offer me. With Galway set as my first port of call I headed off in that direction. It was a fine day when I left Clontarf, but when I reached around the halfway mark I ran into the weather pattern I was so used to when I lived there. But this time I welcomed it because I was in high spirits and felt in my bones it would get better as I got further into my journey.

To make my journey as comfortable and as sensible as possible I'd purchased a brochure which listed bed and breakfast accommodation throughout Ireland. As I entered the city of Galway I pulled in to one side of the road and ran my eyes over the accommodation available. Very quickly one popped out at me. It was in a place called Salthill, which is not far from the town centre, so I made my way there. After a few friendly greetings I settled in for a three-day stay. It was now about four in the afternoon so I thought I'd go and have a bite to eat in a pub I'd seen nearby. As I wasn't feeling all that hungry I ordered one of my two favourite desserts, apple pie and ice cream. The other is blackberry pie and ice cream, which in my book can't be matched outside of my native land. When I'd just about finished my dessert two men and a woman came in and sat at the bar. I didn't pay much attention to them at first but gradually I got caught up with their enthusiasm for life. One of the men had a guitar and soon the three of them started to sing. I turned my chair in their direction to enjoy the performance. They soon sensed my interest and invited me to join them at the bar. After an exchange of names and other formalities that bring people together, they asked me if I'd like to sing a song. I said, 'I do sing, but mostly unaccompanied'. And if someone can pick me up with a musical instrument it's always an introduction to something else. Our circumstances either tie us down or set us free. I said I'd sing the first song I ever learned in my growing-up years.

When I first heard the song Kevin Barry and was told of this young man's great courage, I had to learn the song.

Well, it was all go after that. We must have exercised our lungs for close on two hours and put away a few pints of beer.

Then one of them said, 'let's go back into town, have a meal and go to a disco'. I'm not a disco person, but I'm also not a person who lets an opportunity go by. Today there's only so much of me, but tomorrow, next month or next year I could surprise myself. They said, 'leave your car here and we'll run you back later'. So off we went and had a lovely meal and later wound up at a disco. There was dancing, drinking and talking for a number of hours till suddenly the age factor reared its sense of intelligence and told me that their younger vitality was too much for my ageing body. Mind you, my newfound friends were pretty much intoxicated by now. So I gracefully slipped away and left them to it. The circle had been completed. What was meant to be had been fulfilled. Though they may forget me, I would not forget them in a hurry.

I went outside, walked down the street and hailed a taxi which was always going to be on the cards as none of my new friends would have been capable of driving me back to my car. During the ride back I had a very pleasant conversation with the taxi driver before he dropped me off. As my head hit the pillow I said to myself, what a wonderful introduction to the first part of my journey, and fell asleep.

After breakfast next morning I looked up my map to see where the day would take me. It was raining at the time but my spirits were high so it didn't bother me. As I studied the map I suddenly remembered I'd always wanted to visit Connemara again. I'd never forgotten how captivated I was with its beauty when I first drove through it in the late 1950s. My ex-wife, her sister Eileen, my brother Gerald and I had hired a Morris 1000 for a week to cover as much of the countryside as we could, and take in what scenery and experiences were available to us, so now the timing was ideal to do just that.

It was still raining as I drove off, but about half-an-hour later the sun burst through the clouds and I started to sing. I don't have the talent to describe the beauty of the countryside so I won't even try. You need to take the trip yourself. And how lucky I was that day as the rain kept away. Connemara is one of the wettest places in Ireland. I think they make the rain there, a lot like the product of Guinness' Brewery.

As I was in no hurry I stopped several times to fill my lungs with the fresh air that only the countryside can bestow on you. Eventually, I got into Letterfrack which is the main town in Connemara and headed for Kylemore Abbey. In 1868 the Mitchell Henry family built Kylemore Castle and later the beautiful Gothic church to memorialise the tragic death of Mitchell Henry's wife who died in 1874 after contracting Nile fever while visiting Egypt. In 1922 the Irish Benedictine nuns arrived from Belgium, bought the property, and the castle became Kylemore Abbey.

Connemara's climate is not kind to buildings and over the years a process of erosion, due to the excess dampness, slowly invaded the church rendering it dangerous. Thankfully, since 1992, the nuns, with the help of the National Regional Development fund, the generosity of past pupils and many friends and benefactors, have been able to set about its complete restoration.

Being a lover of nature this is the bit that took my fancy. Restorations were reprogrammed when it was found that the main roof is a home to the largest known colony of Natterer's Bats in Ireland. During the early summer periods they give birth and nurse their young. Great care has been taken to ensure the bats haven't been disturbed and the colony has continued to breed year after year.

I was very pleased with myself for my spur of the moment decision to revisit Connemara and Kylemore Abbey. It will always be another of those special days that will remain in my memory till the day I move on or, God forbid, lose it.

I talked to some lovely people, did my sightseeing, and had a nice lunch. When I arrived back at the bed and breakfast house it was around seven o'clock. I thought I'd freshen up and go into the town for a meal and a few drinks. On my arrival in the town a pub called Currans had already caught my eye when I first drove into Galway, so I felt there had to be a reason for that being the person I am. So I got a good parking place outside and went in. After I finished my meal I decided to sit at the bar and finish my drink. Few people talk to you sitting at a table. You need to be at the bar where all the action is taking place.

Well, the bait worked. I got talking to a guy from

somewhere out of town and, boy, did he know how to talk! He had a flair for the art of conversation. He'd seen a lot of life. His tongue hadn't been laced with boredom like so many others I'd come across. I can't remember the story he related, but I enjoyed his company. Later he asked what brought me to Galway and I filled him in on a little of my life. He said, "You're about the most interesting man I've met in a while. Then he bought me a drink. He was an architect and was writing a book but the drink kept getting in the way, I cracked up laughing.

I must have spent about two hours in this guy's company before I took off. As I was leaving he said, 'I have some business to attend to tomorrow so I'll be back here the following day. I'd like to buy you lunch'. I said 'I'm sorry, but I'll have to refuse your kind offer. I'm off down South the day after tomorrow, but if you ever visit New Zealand here's my address and I'll buy you lunch!' He laughed as we shook hands and parted.

I had already planned to have one game of golf before I left Galway. So that same night I pulled out my golf location book and Carne Golf Course in Belmullet appealed to me. Mind you, I'd no idea if I was going to be able to get on the course, but seeing I was on a potluck holiday I was just going to enjoy whatever came out of the pot. A sensible person would have rung up to find out, sense is not a part of my character as you are well aware of by now.

The sun had already made its pleasure felt as I drove out, hopefully, to play a game of my up and down golf. I think golf for me, with a twenty seven handicap should be classed as an up and down game. That I believe makes it much more enjoyable.

Just before I arrived at the golf club I noticed the wind had strengthened and the clouds were starting to gather. That was bound to make my game a tough one. I went straight to the pro shop and asked if I could get a game. No problem, they said. We have a small group going out in about half an hour and you can join them. I went into the club rooms and made myself known, and a short time later we were heading off for the first tee. Well, I wasn't playing too bad for the first three holes when the rain joined the wind and the rest of the game became a nightmare for me. My three companions had no trouble with their game, and at one stage I felt as though they were thinking to themselves, what makes this fellow imagine he can play golf.

It was not only the wind blowing this golf course right on the coast that made it tough for me, but trying to strike the ball on the sandy and rough places I placed my ball in, was my complete undoing. I can't tell you how relieved I was when we finished the last hole and walked back to the club house. I was like a drowned rat with its tail between its legs and had seven balls fewer in my golf bag then when I started.

Christy O'Connor Snr, one of Ireland's famous international golfers had described Carne as a gem links. I guess I not only picked the wrong day, but also lacked the ability to become a real golfer. But at the very least people like me help to make up the numbers, and find my own sense of satisfaction from the game.

I was made to feel very welcome after I had changed my clothes and joined my companions in the club rooms. We had a few drinks and shared a few stories.

Next morning I packed my gear into the car, quite excited once again about the prospects of the next stage of the journey. The rapids of life are always waiting to test us but can't until we go out to meet them. The poet in me had no cry of regret as I tried to follow the Spiritual example of Christ. So far on this trip it had been fabulous, except for my golf experience. But if I was to win them all how little I'd learn. We are all victims in one way or another of the impacts and influences that come into our lives, whether it be from within us or from outside of us. How deeply we get scarred depends on the way we think and act when it comes to dealing with those influences.

THE BURREN, LISDOONVARNA, KILRUSH, DINGLE AND CAMP

As I continue with my story I'll not give you a day-by-day account of my actions as I have tried to do so far. The reason for that is because what I've told you so far remains so vivid in my mind. Over the rest of my trip I'll relate what I call the highlights, those wonderful experiences that jumped out from time to time and touched me where I needed to be touched. The main reason is that when you reach the age of nearly 87 the memory box has a lot more cobwebs to deal with. And also I have other things to write and I can't envisage myself rising like the Phoenix from the ashes to try and complete them.

After looking at my map I thought I'd head for Kilcolgan, then on to the Coast Road to take me to Kilrush to see If I could learn something of the whereabouts of my old friend Sean Brazil from my RAF days. That had been going through my mind since I decided to take this trip. A blast from the past is a gift that should never be overlooked. The days of our life are fragile, and they should be treated with both delicacy and courage.

As I drove out of Galway the sun gave me a big greeting smile.

What a beautiful day it was. So I drove at a very leisurely pace, stopping wherever my fancy took me, but there is no adequate description I can give you of the breathtaking beauty that was in front of me, or behind me, which of course had a lot to do with my happy frame of mind and the weather getting better all the time.

As I drove through the famous Burren in the county of Clare I stopped and walked up a gently sloping limestone landscape and lay down to take in the rugged beauty all around me. As it was a very clear day I could see the Aran Islands on the distant horizon. And as I lay there I could feel an incredible surge of tingling heat flowing through my body. I have no idea how long I lay there, but I have got to say it was one of the most marvellous experiences that has ever touched my soul.

I have been informed by a friend that The Burren in spite of its stone age appearance is the youngest landscape in Europe, and has suffered intense glaciation as recently as fifteen thousand years ago. There are estimated to be 50km of underground caves, which constitute the active river systems of the area, and the plant species grow in many varieties.

I had mapped out in my mind that I would spend one or two days in Lisdoonvarna which is famous for its matchmaking, besides its other qualities. Later that evening I made my way into Lisdoonvarna and found myself bed and breakfast accommodation. Next morning I had a late breakfast and took a stroll round the town. I can't remember the name of the building where the matchmaking took place, but I was very impressed with the layout, the pictures and the writing that adorned the walls. Then I wondered who'd found love and who'd found hell from its matchmaking.

About midday I spotted a quaint little pub with a number of people in it. What a stroke of good fortune that was. Shortly after I arrived I was treated to the best Irish dancing I've witnessed. For half-an-hour or more the publican's two daughters put on a breathtaking display of Irish dancing. Will I ever forget Lisdoonvarna? Not on your life.

An hour later I headed out to take in the Cliffs of Moher. This time they put on a magnificent display for me with no wind or rain but the sun bursting at the seams, and the Atlantic Ocean on its best behaviour. What a sight to behold. I'd never seen the water as calm as it gently played hide and seek with the rocks below. I found myself a little hollow at the cliff edge and must have stayed there for an hour or more, mesmerised by the mystical charm of all that surrounded me.

After some sandwiches and a drink I headed for Loop Head. By the time I had arrived the evening had started to make its presence felt, so I took a quick look around but found the scenery only second to what I had already tasted. On my way back I picked up a guy looking for a lift to Kilkee. As soon as we drove off I could tell from both the fumes and his actions that he had quite a few drinks under his belt. We hadn't gone very far when he said, 'You know I could kill you'. With all the sharp experiences of my new lifestyle I replied to his question as quickly as he'd laid it on me, 'can you drive?' He said 'no'. So I said to him, 'What's the bloody point?' He burst out laughing, put his hand on my shoulder and said, 'I like your style'.

We got to Kilkee with no more hiccups, he asked if he could buy me a drink in the pub he asked me stop outside. I thanked him, but said, 'no, I need to get back to Lisdoonvarna so I can be on my way early tomorrow morning'. He shook my hand and said, 'God bless you'. I thought to myself, 'He already has'.

Next morning with my next mission already programmed I headed for Kilrush. Good friends hold a long memory in my book, and Sean Brassel was one of them. He was born in Kilrush and lived there as far as I know till he joined the RAF in 1946 as I did. His reasons for joining were different from mine in some ways, yet maybe alike in others. I needed to get away from my old man, he from what he called the dreary prospects that surrounded him, plus the call of adventure. So I drove to Kilrush and booked into a small hotel.

That afternoon I latched on to this mission in earnest and struck gold at the first pub I went into. In a small towns most people know each other pretty well. I was given the address of Sean's sister and made my way there. When I told her who I was and my reason for knocking on her door the past came flooding back to her and she welcomed me in. After we'd exchanged feelings and emotions about the past and present she told me Sean was living in Leicester in England. She said, 'You can contact him by phone when you get back to where you're staying'. I can't remember her name, but she made me feel very welcome with her friendly personality and tea and scones.

When I got back to the hotel that evening I straight away rang Sean. Well, what went running through his mind when he realised it was me, only he could describe. He was completely flabbergasted. I've had a few top reunions in my life and this was certainly the beginning of another. Along with memories of the time we spent in each other's company there was also the gap to be filled in between then and now. We must have talked for a considerable time before he said, 'You're going to have

378 | Page

one hell of a phone bill'. And I said, 'Don't you remember our motto? Life's for living, not for worrying about'.

Just before we finished talking Sean asked if I could pay him a visit before I took off for New Zealand. He said Leicester was about a two hour drive from Watford. I said, 'Yes, I'd love to do that. I'll ring you before I come'.

Later I thought I'd go out for a drink before I hit the pillow. Wouldn't do to leave Kilrush without lifting my glass in memory of the town Sean was born in. Well it turned out to be a real fun night with plenty of music played on a piano and most of us singing along with it. And I was made more than welcome as one usually is in an Irish pub. Another lovely memory to add to the many others.

I was away early next morning to catch the ferry across the Shannon River. Little did I think I would crossing it by car for the second time, even though something in my mind said it was always a possibility.

After a peaceful crossing I followed the coast road south through Ballybunion, Ballyduff, Ballyheigue, Tralee and then into Dingle. I booked a room with a lovely view of Dingle Harbour and had an interesting chat with the proprietor, Joe. He showed me places of interest I might like to visit, and told me about the music scene and the drinking scene. I spent most of my three days cruising and taking walks around the Dingle peninsula with lovely weather to make it more enjoyable. I am not going into the pros and cons of those three days that Dingle offered me, but it more than satisfied my hunger for life and living. If you should ever go that way don't miss it. If you're open to simplicity and humanity it will more than fill your needs.

The big highlight for me was the last evening I spent there. I went into a pub around eight-thirty ordered a drink and sat behind a number of people entertaining us with their musical talents. I was quite close to a lady playing the violin and was humming away trying to keep in tune. Eventually, she turned to me and said, 'You've got a singing voice'. I said, 'I sing at a few folk clubs unaccompanied'. She said, 'will you sing a few songs for us?' I said I'd be delighted. What a fabulous night that turned out to be. Somewhere between midnight and one in the morning I was invited to a disco about ten minutes' walk from the pub. Once again I seized the opportunity simply because, like the last one, it will never come again. Well, I didn't do a lot of dancing, but I did relish touching base with some lovely, lively people, and enjoyed the spread they put on to fill our hunger and our thirst. About four in the morning I made my way back to my bed, and hit the sack completely exhausted, but more than satisfied.

After breakfast that morning I set my sights on the Ring of Kerry, then on to Killarney. I could have taken a shorter route South but something in my bones said take a look at Tralee as I had previously only passed through it without as much as a glance. The old intuition was beckoning me. Well, once again I drew an ace from the pack. As I was approaching a little place called Camp I spotted a man around my own age looking for a lift. I stopped and told him where I was heading. He said, 'That's where I'm going'. So off we went. He asked me what was I doing in this neck of the woods and I told him. 'God', he said, 'you're a breath of fresh air around here. You've got that crazy sense of intelligence that so many of us miss out on'. I said, 'I'll go along with the crazy part, but not the part about intelligence'.

As we drove into Camp he said, 'Can I buy you a drink? There's a lovely little pub there. I'd like to introduce you to some unusual characters'. Little did I know at the time that I was going to spend the best part of three days there. I parked my car outside the quaint little pub in the middle of nowhere and in we went. And once again I'm grasping at straws as far as names are concerned. Jim was the man's name I believe, but after that I will leave you. We were greeted by the landlord and his wife the moment we went in, and no sooner were we sitting down than we were joined by their two lovely children.

A stranger in Ireland can very easily become a magnet with children when curiosity raises its head. Mind you that can happen elsewhere as well because I've been there. In no time at all I felt I was accepted as part of the family. The children threw all sorts of questions at me and I responded in my own child-like fashion.

Later Jim suggested that we take a trip up to Tralee and meet some of his friends and have a nice meal. He said, 'I can also conclude my little business in less than half an hour, but in the meantime I'd leave you in good company', and he did.

I think Jim and I visited about three pubs before we sat down to a delightful meal with dessert to follow. I talked to a number of his friends, but as time progressed I got the feeling that Jim was not quite as popular as he made himself out to be. Since I'd ventured into my new life style of living my senses were more sharply tuned to my inner feelings, before putting any kind of reason to it. But I didn't let that affect the crumbs of experience that were being presented to me. Probably, one of my quotes fits in here. 'What do I know today? How well do I use it, and what kind of a future can I give it?'

As I needed somewhere to sleep along with the other necessities that go with it, I found a place just up the road from the pub called The Railway Lodge run by a lovely couple called Geraldine & Padraig O'Shea. I also enjoyed the company of their children.

Later that evening I dropped Jim off at his little cottage and was thankful he didn't invite me in. As a matter a fact he never did during our short acquaintance. I got the feeling he was a very private person who told you just enough to keep you reasonably satisfied. I believe he took to me because of my openness and craziness. I'd say like many others, he was a lonely person looking for a little human affection, and I fitted the bill. But I liked the old rogue. I found no real harm in him other than a few untruths that surfaced during my time with him. Like so many of us he was just trying to make ends meet wherever he could.

On my second-to-last night there I was treated to some wonderful music performed by two ladies. Afterwards I was invited to sing, so that really made my evening.

On my last evening a dark cloud developed. About eight o'clock a man in I'd say in his mid-forties introduced himself to me, quite slim and good looking. He said, 'I've heard quite a bit about you', so we got talking. He arrived with a group of about six or seven people who looked younger than he was. We talked for about fifteen minutes then he said, 'I mustn't neglect my friends. I'll catch up with you later'. By this time I was sitting on a bar stool talking to Jim and a few others. Later I glanced across to where this man was because he and his group were becoming very vocal. They seemed to be drinking faster than us old codgers or maybe we could hold our liquor better than they could.

The loveable rogue who took me under his wing

Not long after that this man came over to me and invited me to join him and his friends at his home. He said it wasn't far from where we were. Very quickly, in the best manner I could, I told him I'd have to decline his kind offer as I needed to be on my way early in the morning. That wasn't quite the truth, but I could see problems arising for me if I accepted the invitation, which was to prove right in a very short space of time.

By now this man was fairly drunk and my refusal must

have been a bitter blow to his ego. He looked at me, with his anger slowly getting the better of him, but when my gaze didn't falter, he staggered back to join his friends. I paid no more attention to him till he started to get really angry and once more made his way in my direction. But I didn't take any notice. I knew I'd always be in control as long as I kept my head. I'd been in situations like this many times with my father, and in other similar circumstances, so I'd a reasonable idea of how to take care of myself. The most important line of defence in dealing with someone who is intoxicated is never to let yourself be cornered. Just as he came up close to me waving his arms around and cursing, three guys grabbed him. He was dragged outside, followed by his friends.

A little later the landlord apologised for the incident. He told me that the man was gay and a troublemaker. He said, I think he thought you were gay and your refusal of his invitation, with him intoxicated, did the damage. Mind you it's not the first time I've been put in that locker, but not to those extremes. I guess I enjoy my own company at those needful times in my life which I realise can give off all sorts of different impressions to be taken up in all sorts of different ways. This sort of thing has been following me around since I changed my lifestyle around, and whatever difficulties it may bring me, I can either fall flat on my face, or find an even greater sense of satisfaction to rise above it all. And both of these I believe have as much to offer as the other. There is no special way to learn anything. It just is as it will be.

THE RING OF KERRY, KILLARNEY, GLENGARRIFF AND DURRUS

Next morning, with fond farewells to my hosts and their lovely children, I once again put the car through its paces, and hit out for the main road that would take me to Milltown, then on round the Ring of Kerry. As I approached the Ring of Kerry memories of my past visit to it conjured up all sorts of delightful visions in my mind. I felt my brother Gerald's presence more strongly here than any other part of my journey so far. When I first went back to Ireland in 1989 we did a lot of reminiscing about the Ring of Kerry, which had been one of the highlights for both of us. I actually talked to him as though he was there. And again who knows? And if it had not been for him, I would never had the good fortune to have taken this wonderful adventure that was to bring new friends and experiences my way. Thank you Gerald.

When I reached Milltown, the start of my journey around the King of Kerry, the weather was about to present in all its beauty. I stopped for refreshments at Glenbeigh. A big tourist bus was parked outside this pub I went into, so there were quite a few people having a leisurely time in it. I got talking to a few people off the bus, but can't remember the topic. But I do remember laughing a lot.

Then stopping every so often to take pictures, I slowly arrived at a place called Sneem. It was now about four or so in the afternoon, so I decided to take a secondary road that would connect me up with the main road to Killarney where I decided to spend a night or two.

When I arrived there I found a room in some kind of a hostel and decided to book in for a couple of nights. After something to eat I went back to my room and played some music on my cassette player. It had been a godsend item to me on my journey. My constant companion. Besides the other necessities that one needs to survive in life, God and music are my real survival kit.

Next morning I thought I would treat myself to a ride with one of the jarvies. Seeing that I had come this far I might as well enjoy the experience, and contribute a little something to those who make a small living from it. And I must say I did really enjoy the experience, plus chatting to the driver.

The rest of the day was spent walking around the beautiful gardens taking pictures and relaxing under the trees in peaceful slumber. Later I went back for something to eat, and played some music to enjoy the rest of the evening.

Around ten o'clock the following morning I was on my way to Glengarriff. Glengarriff had made quite an impression on me when I first visited it with my wife, brother Gerald and my sister-in-law Eileen in 1950, so it became a must on this journey. When I arrived at Kenmare I stopped for a cup of tea and a sandwich, then headed off again. Well, I'd only been on the road for a few miles when I spotted this guy looking for a lift. As I slowed down to stop I noticed how unsteady he seemed to be on his feet, so I more or less knew what to expect. As I wound down the passenger window he mumbled to me, 'I'm trying to get a lift to Glengarriff. I've been waiting here for an hour or so'. I said 'hop in. It's only a silly old bastard like me that's likely to pick you up'. So he got in, smelling like the arse end of the Guinness brewery, and started mumbling in the incoherent language people in his condition usually use. Luckily for me he soon fell asleep and I was once again able to enjoy the fantastic scenery before me.

When we arrived at Glengarriff I gave the guy a nudge and asked him where he wanted to be dropped off. As he got out of the car he nearly fell over himself trying to thank me.

A short time later I booked into a very pleasant hostel not far down the main road from the town centre. After I had freshened up after a spell on my bed, I strolled up to the town centre around seven o'clock for somewhere to feed my needs. Music, food and a few drinks. From what I can remember there were two pubs in the town. I no sooner walked into one of them when the guy I'd give a lift to spotted me and I became more like a celebrity artist than a stranger. He kept telling his mates what I'd done for him until I became quite uncomfortable. And no way was I allowed to put my hand in my pocket all the time I was there. The guy I had given a lift to had sobered up quite a bit. Amazing, I thought to myself, how a small unconditional gesture can sow so much goodwill.

A little later I got talking to a Welshman who'd come to Glengarriff for two weeks holiday and never left. He was well educated, and told me he had worked in some kind of family business. The family expected him to do the usual thing like getting married, having a family, and living the usual boring life that society lays out for people like him. But when he came to Glengarriff and saw how happy people were living their simple lives there he made he made a similar decision to the one I made, and found peace of mind beyond his wildest dreams. When he told his newfound friends of his intention to stay, and with little money to his name, they found him a little place to live, and put some odds and ends into making it comfortable. Then to sustain himself, he started doing odd jobs for people. He'd already been there close to a year when I met him, and a happier guy I'd yet to meet.

Around ten thirty I was told that the pub across the road had a musician playing there. As gracefully as I could I excused myself by thanking all those who'd been so kind to me and made my way across to the music. As soon as I entered the pub I ordered a drink and found a space close to where the guy was singing and playing a guitar. Very soon, through eye contact and my very obvious reactions to his music, a friendship developed between us.

I talked with him during one of his breaks, though I can't remember what we discussed, but he was one hell of a nice guy.

Later, a young man somewhere in his twenties approached me and said, I hear you're living in New

Zealand. I said, 'Yes, I emigrated there in 1965'. He said, 'I'm a Kiwi from Dunedin'. We became engrossed in conversation. The subject of golf came up and there the die was cast. Next morning with the sun shining down on us we teed off at nine hole golf course in Glengarriff. What a memorable game it was for me and my friend from Dunedin. And what made it even more fantastic was that we both finished on a 92. And as far as I can remember we had a drink in the clubhouse to celebrate the game and the companionship it brought us. I hope I'll never forget that game as long as I live.

That afternoon I took a drive to revisit a place called Healy Pass. It's a long winding road that runs up the side of a steep hill. I was very impressed the first time I cruised up its inviting curves, but unfortunately the weather hadn't been so kind then. But one is just about always rewarded in one way or another for perseverance. I got out of the car a number of times to gaze at the view and take photos. I must have been about two-thirds of the way up when I saw this guy parked in front of me also taking photos. I thought to myself, 'here's a chance to share some of the outstanding scenery as well as a little communication'. So when I stopped he wandered down to chat with me. Well we were deep in conversation when a touring bus had to stop because he hadn't closed his driving door. I was the first to notice it, and I told him. Well, we both laughed our heads off as he leisurely walked up to close it, with the drive of the bus smiling and casually waiting for him to do so. As the bus moved on we got a big cheer from some of the passengers. You could only get away with that in Ireland.

I spent my last day in Glengarriff paying a visit to Garnish Island. The island is reached by privately operated boats. Because of its sheltered location and the influence of the Gulf Stream the climate is almost subtropical and is acclaimed for its rich plant growth, for example, the rhododendrons and azaleas. I guess what took my fancy were the many attractive views I took in of the surrounding islands and the wildlife that inhabited them. And I must admit I was impressed with the Italian Gardens. It's a very inspiring place and I could well envisage George Bernard Shaw writing St Joan there in 1923.

A little later in the afternoon I was making my way round the water's edge when I came across a small group of people enjoying something to eat from a fairly large hamper. I waved to them, and then one of them called me over and offered me a glass of wine. Well, what a wild, joyous, crazy afternoon I spent with those lovely Scottish people, drinking their wine and eating their food, and sharing what some people might call their ridiculous view of life. Being a ridiculous person myself I completely understood where they were coming from. Oscar Wilde hit the nail on the head when he said, 'We're all in the gutter, but some of us are looking at the stars'.

On top of the world for a day at Glengarriff

Next morning, with some lovely memories of Glengarriff I was on my way again. I took out my map and thought I'd explore a little bit of the coastline that would take me through Durrus, and back on to the main coast road to continue my journey to Dublin. Once again I don't know what prompted me to take this out of the way route, but fortune was again smiled on me because of it. Someone once said 'the secret to a rich life is to have more beginnings than endings'. And I was certainly having plenty of them.

As I approached a place called Durrus I stopped by the side of road totake in some fabulous scenery. I walked across the road and leaned on a large gate to enjoy the view. A man on the other side of the gate spotted me and walked up his driveway and began talking to me. He told me about the people who owned an impressive piece of land beside his small farm. They were Germans and were farming their property in a big way.

After we'd talked for about fifteen minutes he invited me down to his cottage for something to eat and drink. John Bennett was one of those really nice people who bring a warm glow to your heart. What I call not only a real man, but also a genuine Irishman, no airs or graces attached to him, yet fully alive with a fine mixture of intelligence and simplicity. He made up some cheese sandwiches for both of us, and a mug of tea.

He told me that he'd worked on building sites in England but eventually got fed up with the hustle and bustle and returned to Ireland to get married. Sadly, his wife had passed away so now he lived on his own. He said he didn't enjoy the best of health, but didn't make an issue of it. There were some personal things he told me about his family that made me feel very sorry for him, but they'll remain private.

About an hour later, full of enthusiasm, John said, 'I'd like to buy you a drink and show you some of the beauty you don't see on the main road, if you don't mind driving both of us'. Well, you already know what my answer would be to that. So off we went on to a rough, ungraded road and, boy was he right about the God-given scenery. I don't know how many times I stopped before we reached the pub in Durrus. After introductions to the barman, or maybe the owner and a few others we sat down and knocked back a pint of Guinness each over three-quarters of an hour or so. John told me something of the history of Durrus, but history is not something that stays with me for very long because it's laced with all sorts of extreme differences both good and bad. It certainly has interesting values for us to learn a lot from, but I have a saying that touches on this: 'If all the justifiable actions of past history were held up for intense scrutiny, I wonder, I wonder, I wonder'.

When we'd finished our Guinness I asked John if he'd like another, but he said, 'No thank you, I don't drink much these days and probably wouldn't have had one today, only I met you'. With a grin I said, Yes I can be a bad influence at times" . 'On the contrary', he said, 'you've brought a sparkle into my life'. I thanked him for such a nice compliment.

When we got back to John's place he put together a small meal and we talked some more. He then said, 'I've got a spare room if you'd like to spend the night here', but I had to kindly refuse. The money I had was starting to burn a hole in my pocket, and the time factor was also built around that.

But to be completely honest there was another factor here. Apart from not enjoying the best of health John had an air of loneliness around him like so many others who lived remotely as he did. So the longer I stayed the harder our parting would be for him. In the short time I'd come know him I had very deep feelings for him. So I thought it wise to move on. And before I left he asked me to write to him, and I did. I got a reply but not from John. A lady friend of his wrote the letter to say thanks from John, but he was not well, and couldn't write. I guess the Good Lord just got us both together for a short time for His purpose, not so much ours.

WEXFORD, DUBLIN AND MILLISLE

Before I left John's place I felt a cold nagging away at me so I thought I'd try to get as far as possible before it set in. My sights were set on a visit to Northern Ireland before I hit back to Dublin to catch the ferry to Holyhead. Just before I got into Wexford I was feeling lousy, so I quickly found myself a place to stay. Next morning I made my way to a chemist close by and asked the guy behind the counter if he could recommend a miracle cure so that I could get back on my journey. He took one look at me and said, 'This is not Lourdes, but I'll do what I can for you'. So armed with the usual drugs of necessity I went back to my room, took my medicine and went to bed. Three days later I started to come alive again with little or no recollection how I got through it all. But I was certainly glad to be on the mend.

This unexpected delay had cost me time and money, so feeling weak but strong enough to drive, I made my way to Bray.

I took my time getting to Bray, taking in what I could of the coastline between Arklow and Bray. That also brought back its own memories as I used to take my wife and son Peter swimming around that area before the rest of our family arrived.

It was sometime in the afternoon when I booked a room in a cheap hotel, took a walk up Bray Head and found a spot to lie down and rest my weary bones in the sun. Once again the memories of my childhood came flooding back. I used to play cowboys and Indians here with my brother Gerald and a couple of friends and get into all sorts of childhood mischief. Once, the four of us nearly set fire to Bray Head trying to bake spuds in a hole we'd dug in the ground. That just came back to me rewriting my story. Lucky a few grown-ups spotted us and kindly waited till the spuds were cooked, then told us to put the fire out. And they really tasted good with some butter and bread my mother had given us. With my memories satisfied and my body more in tune I walked along the seafront till I felt the need to hit the sack.

Next morning I headed out for Northern Ireland. As I drove through Newry, the infamous borderline between the North and the South, there was no sign of welcome or harassment. I say that because I always like to give anyone or anything the benefit of the doubt. Mind you, I'd like to get that more often for myself, but then people like me who bring things to the surface must be prepared to live with the responsibility. As William James says, 'The art of being wise is the art of knowing what to overlook'.

I then took my map out and decided to stick to the coastline road which had been the original decision I made when I started this trip. When I got to a place called Portaferry I had an unexpected halt. The road had come to an end. What I didn't know was awaiting me was the water I had to cross with no bridge to convey me and my car to its far shore. But I quickly grasped the situation and embarrassment to its lowest level. Nothing worse than being embarrassed by another Irishman.

From what I can remember the crossing didn't take long and brought its own experiences. When I got settled on the far side I thought I'd give the coast road a miss. There would be water to feed my appetite, but with its own difference. When I arrived at the road that branched off in this direction I was stopped by two policemen. 'We're sorry, but there's a big dress rehearsal for the Twelfth of July parade taking place further up on this road and we've orders not to let traffic through. You'll have to take the coast road'. So I thought to myself God still has plans for you so stick to your original plan.

The two Police officers were very apologetic and we shared about fifteen minutes in conversation. One of them said, 'I envy you living in New Zealand'. And the other one said, 'I love Kerry, there's great fishing down there'. I laughed as I drove off and said to myself, 'well, fate obviously didn't want me to take the other road. Let's see what it's going to throw at me now'.

Just before I got into a place called Millisle I thought I'd better find somewhere to stay for the night. I kept my eyes open for bed and breakfast lodgings. Then, all of a sudden, as drove into this small town, I saw a group of Orangemen marching in front of me accompanied by a band playing something other than Waltzing Matilda. As I passed them I spotted a B&B sign on the side that they were marching. Not wanting to cause any kind of confrontation I drove a little way up the road and did a U-turn. I thought to myself one slip-up here and I'm dead meat. I could envisage the headlines in the Belfast newspaper, "Dublin man's life story comes to an abrupt end. Trampled to death by a ghost from the past".

Anyway I drove back and parked outside the bed and breakfast house with the idea of spending one night there, but that, like so many other plans I'd made before, would change. I rang the doorbell and the door was opened by a very warm-hearted man. He invited me in when I told him what my purpose was, then sat me down in the living room and invited his wife to join us. Very soon I was drinking tea and putting away the very tasty sandwich placed before me. I'd very much like to mention the names of these lovely people, but I lost their business card.

A little later I took my gear out of the car, had a shower and went for a walk. I took my umbrella with me as the weather was becoming changeable. I did enjoy my walk, taking in the effects of the sea on one side and the houses and nature on the other. When I got back about an hour later it was around nine o'clock. I was invited into the lounge and placed before me was a glass containing Black Bushmills whiskey. As you well know by now I had already been introduced to Bushmills, but Black Bushmills was a first for me, and I must admit I thought I could never become a fan of Black Bushmills, but that has changed over the years. I must say that these people knew how to give that extra touch of humanity to those who crossed their threshold. And I clearly remember relaxing in a cosy armchair while we all shared something to add a spice of value to life.

Next morning I arrived down at breakfast to find a very attractive lady already at the breakfast table. Soon I was engrossed in conversation with her. Betty lived in Belfast and was having a five-day relaxing holiday by herself. Well that completely changed my whole outlook for the day. I hadn't yet met a nice lady like Betty on my trip so my not-so-dead romantic mind began conjuring up all sorts of visions. So my decision to stay only one night went out the back door, and the fairy tales of Hans Christian Andersen crept in the front one.

I've always been childlike, shy and romantic so that fits the bill. But mind you, I'm not shy anymore. I can't afford that luxury.

I asked Betty if she'd like to spend the day with me taking in the sights. She agreed. I soon learned that this lady, like most of single women around her age getting close to mine, had been through rough walks of life, so she shared some of them with me, and I a few of mine. Since I changed my life around my new philosophy of being very open about where I was coming from enabled me to express all sorts of joy from within. I think back to the days I used to go to confession scared, yet so hungry for someone to listen to my real needs. But all I got were embarrassing questions on how my sex life was, and so forth. Then, if I was lucky, I was given ten Our Fathers, and ten Hail Mary's and a coating of absolution. I came out more confused than I went in.

I booked in for another two nights and told my host that Betty and I were going to spend the day together. He said, 'If you're interested there's a dance at the British Legion Club this evening', so I thanked him. I could be corrected for calling it the British Legion Club, but then I know I'll be well into that bracket before I've finished this book. I was never destined to become a writer, you may well agree, but at the very least I had the crazy ambition to try. But on the other side of the coin there is no such thing as a perfect story when it comes to human beings in my view. There are only interesting or uninteresting ones. As Caesar Pavese phrases it, 'We do not remember days, we remember moments'.

Well, after a great morning and afternoon in each other's company Betty and I decided to go to the dance that evening. When we arrived we were made welcome and were soon enjoying ourselves. Later we were invited to a table where a big man, around my age, was seated with his family and friends. I learned later it was more a royal command than an invitation. I was told that this guy owned a lot of property around the town. Word reached his ear that I was living in New Zealand and that is why he wanted to talk to me. After introductions the man started reminiscing about his trip around New Zealand in a campervan until we were exhausted with his self-opinionated descriptions. But the punishment didn't end there for we were both very cleverly conned into an invitation to visit him and his family the following morning. However the rest of the evening was very enjoyable as we did a lot of dancing.

We got in the early hours of the morning so there was no Bushmills that night. We did the usual kissing and cuddling in a quiet manner so not to wake anyone, then stole into our rooms. Next morning, not relishing the invitation ahead of us, we arrived at this man's house and were ushered into the lounge. The only thing I can remember, or maybe want to remember, were its two settees and a big armchair. It didn't take long to piece the picture together. He was one of those men who love to rule the roost. His wife and daughter sat very rigid, listening and nodding to what he had to say. It reminded me of one of those Victorian scenes from the past when so many women were restrained from questioning anything or showing their real emotions. In a way it took me back to my growing up years, little boys were to be seen and not heard, just used. Eventually, when this guy had more or less talked himself out, I discreetly brought my beliefs into play bringing a spark of enthusiasm to the eyes and, hopefully the minds, of his wife and daughter. We must have been there for close to an hour with no sign of a cup of tea appearing on the horizon. I said to myself, this is certainly a lost cause. Let's get the hell out of here. My God, what a difference between John Bennett and this individual, or our B&B people for that matter. I don't remember what I said to bring an end to this boring so called conversation, but it got us out of there.

We drove away and were both flabbergasted at not being offered just one lousy teabag. I said to Betty I could just visualise him opening up a B&B and expecting you to bring your own bed and food with you. We both had a good laugh over that.

Betty suggested we pay a visit to the seaside resort of Bangor so we spent the rest of the day there enjoying what it had to offer. That evening when we arrived back at our overnight sanctuary a Black Bushmills was placed on the table for me, and a glass of wine for Betty. After we had said our goodnights to our very generous hosts, Betty said she'd like to see some of the poems I'd written. So we went up to my room. While she was reading them I made us a cup of tea. After the poems we did our semi-passionate thing together and thanks to her strength, not mine, we parted not as lovers but as very good friends.

We'd touched each other's lives where they needed to be touched, and that way neither of us got hurt or tainted.

I wrote this poem a year later to touch base on my encounter with Betty and would like to share it with others who might have had a similar experience, or maybe even one that blossomed to an even greater level. You get a lot more understanding out of it than going into a confession box. I call this poem "Forgiveness in Themselves".

We lay upon the golden sands and shared
the things we'd done
Held nothing back in case we missed
where we were coming from.
The shadow of our distant past
like poems so clumsy written
and we the victims of them all
was all the excuse we had.
You turned to me with tender words,
You, too, had fallen from grace.
That every picture of what you saw
was hard to try and live with.
With all our secrets out in the open
a great wall had just come down.
Two loveable, confessional souls
found forgiveness in themselves.

I had breakfast ahead of schedule that next morning so as to make an early start, since I planned to be in Donegal before nightfall. I decided that would be my last main port of call before heading to Dublin to catch the ferry to Holyhead. Money was once more becoming a scarce commodity and I'd need something in my pocket to buy a cheap car when I got back to New Zealand. With breakfast tucked under my belt and my gear in the car, I bade farewell to my three lovely friends, and hit the road once more.

DONEGAL, ENGLAND AND LEICESTER

I had heard a lot about the Giant's Causeway so I thought that would be a must before I left Northern Ireland. As I passed through Larne it brought back memories of my teenage years, which I have already mentioned, and that brought a pleasant smile of satisfaction to my face. This time I could take in a better view as I was not that scared little rabbit anymore.

That afternoon I arrived at the Giant's Causeway and I've got to say without taking anything from it, I found it less impressive than my expectations had built it up to be. You can of course put that down to my over the hill sense of optimism which has deluded me on many occasions. I guess I'm a real Southerner. Give me the Cliffs of Moher with the wild or calm Atlantic gracing its shores. The beautiful Ring of Kerry, and the wide untamed scenery of Donegal. These are the places that touch the very depth of my soul. So as I said goodbye to Northern Ireland, I thanked it for the cherished memories it had given me.

Around eight that evening I arrived in Letterkenny, and booked into a small hotel for an overnight stay. Next morning I looked at my map and picked out a couple of places I'd visit before I set off for Dublin.

The next morning as I drove out of Letterkenny I saw a young man looking for a lift so I stopped and told him where I was heading. He said, 'If you could drop me off at a certain spot I can hitch another ride from there'. So off we went. He asked me about myself and quite openly I told him. He said, 'You're very easy to talk to', and opened up about some of his life. He said he'd become a born-again Christian after being through a lot of unpleasant religious experiences. He lived in Northern Ireland and was going to visit some relatives or friends in Donegal. He said that he was going with a young lady, but was having second thoughts about the direction that it was taking him. When we got to the spot where I was to drop him off I said, '"I'm in no hurry, let me take you to where you need to go'. He said he'd be very grateful as it had just started to rain.

When we reached the house he wanted to go to, we talked for a while before he took his leave. I pointed out a few things relating to his new set of beliefs and told him to tread very carefully as just about everything you think about, or think you see, is not what it really is. To try and understand life to whatever degree you are able to you must keep a very open mind about everything that is thrown at you. And when it comes to making choices, they must be yours and yours alone. Never be influenced by what's out there but by what's inside you, otherwise you'll get lost. He thanked me and asked if I would write to him. I said I would, and here is the answer I got from him.

"Thank you so much for your sweet words to me. It was as if an angel had written them. You spoke directly into my circumstances and assisted me in a difficult choice.

Basically, I had to choose whether to continue a relationship with a girl who also loved The Lord or break it off. My inner heart had been telling me this since the beginning, but I was attempting to live external guidelines which was not the word of God. You spoke of being true to one's self and to lead from the heart, enjoy life, to be creative. It confirmed many things that I felt. Basically, you gave voice to my feelings. C S Lewis said that two unhappy people in love would rather stay together than suffer the heartache of breaking up. I know now what he meant. It is so hard to separate from a female even if you are not totally compatible because of the emotions involved. I do thank God that He's helped me fill the void inside myself. The Scriptures say God is close to the broken-hearted and to those who are crushed. God has blessed me with regards to college fees so I I'd like to give Him the glory.

I presume the rest of your holiday went smoothly. I was glad to meet you. I told my friends all about you. You are a unique individual and a giver. I was refreshed for having spent time with you. You also come across as an intelligent guy on some profound course of life. I pray you continue to rejoice in life because God made all things for us to enjoy. Christ came to give His life and to give it to us more abundantly."

I'd say it's the little things we do for one another that

bring the most blessings into our lives. I think about that young man from time to time and pray he hasn't lost that beautiful sense of simplicity.

The rest of the day I just drove around taking in the sights that took my fancy, but the rain put a stop to a few other things I had in mind. But that was meant to be, I believe, otherwise I would have missed a wonderful night's music, and making some new friends that hailed from Scotland. As soon as I arrived back at my accommodation I was informed that there was music taking place in a pub down the road. What more could I ask for than to end my trip on a musical note.

The music had already started as I walked in the door and, seeing me on my own, a Scottish family beckoned me to join them. In no time at all they knew something about me, what I was able to tell them in the short time we spent together. I can't remember what part of Scotland they were from but I know they wanted me to visit them. As much as I would have loved to, money was the issue, not time. I could have easily have caught the ferry from Larne to Stranraer, stayed with them for a while, and then driven down to my daughter in Watford.

Fate, however, had other plans for me as I was to learn next day. But we had a great night and I sang a few songs for them.

WATFORD AND LEICESTER

Next morning I made my way to Sligo to join up with

the road to Dublin. That meant that I had covered as much of the coast of Ireland that was permitted to me. As I drove out of Sligo I saw a guy with one arm in a sling and the other arm holding a crutch. He had a lady with him thumbing a ride. So I stopped. They were looking for a ride to Mallow to stay with a friend while he was recuperating from surgery to his arm and knee.

I automatically knew fate hadn't placed him in my path for nothing so I said to myself, 'what's another detour here or there. I'm very used to them by now. I'll make Dublin before nightfall'.

Well, once again we travellers shared our ups and downs and got on like a house on fire. That guy had a great fighting spirit, and a wonderful sense of humour. There was no trace of pity in his voice and I was indeed privileged to be of service to him.

I got to Dublin that evening early and managed to make a booking to catch the ferry next day, then found myself a B&B.

The crossing to Holyhead next day was very pleasant with calm seas and good weather. I drove off the ferry and started my journey to Watford, little knowing that my sense of navigation was once more about to fail me. Just as well I never became a pilot in the R.A.F. I would still be up in the air.

One wrong turn found me in Chester, very lost and very pissed off. I said to myself, 'well, you've got a tongue in your head. Do what one usually does when one is lost, ask someone'. The first person, 'No'. The second person,'No'. But with the third person I struck gold. What a nice human being he was. He said, 'if I try to explain how to get out of here to reach the M6, I'm only going to confuse you and maybe even myself. You just follow me, and when I stop driving you keep going till you hit the M6 and that will eventually take you into Watford'.

I nearly went down on my knees to thank him, but he just smiled and said, 'We all get lost sometime or another'. I said 'yes, but isn't it nice when someone cares enough to do something about it'.

Well I don't know how many different streets we turned into before he pulled over and waved me on. But, boy, was I happy for him to put me on course. Another person I often think about.

I arrived in Watford just as darkness descended, very tired but very grateful to that that Someone who looks after me. I'd rung my daughter to say I was on my way. When I knocked on her door and she opened it in her night gown I said 'you go back to bed, and I will fill you in in the morning. We both need the sleep'.

The next morning I filled her in on the things I'd got into and up to and we had a good laugh. I told her I've got to go up to Leicester in a couple of days to catch up with one of my old friends from the R.A.F. When I come back I'll sell my car and head back to New Zealand. My windscreen had developed a crack in it when I was driving around Ireland, so I had it replaced. The guy came around the same day I phoned to have it done, and I was very pleased about that.

Two days later I was on my way to Leicester. I'd phoned Sean that I was coming and he gave me good positive directions on where to meet him at a big supermarket. Well, I had no trouble finding him but, boy was I in for a shock when he came over to greet me as I got out of the car. When we'd parted after we left the R.A.F. we were both in good shape, but I must say that the years in between had been a lot kinder to me than to Sean. He was carrying a lot of weight and had a walking stick. We hugged each other and he said, 'I never thought we'd meet again. I'm so happy to see you', and I responded. I drove him back to his house and we spent hours reminiscing over our days in the R.A.F. and catching up with the times in between. The difference between us was that he'd played for higher stakes than me and got his fingers burnt by so many so-called friends. I'm sure that will sound familiar to many of you. Then Sean said, 'You haven't let the grass grow under your feet, mentally or physically'. I said 'I just got lucky by changing my life around, otherwise I wouldn't be here enjoying your company'.

He said 'you can have my bed upstairs. Because of my bad knees I sleep in a bed down here'. Like me he was divorced and on his own.

During my four days with him I met some of his family, and played tennis with his grandchildren. In the evenings I took him to his local to have a few drinks and meet some of his friends. I must say I had a very enjoyable time while I was there, but I felt so sorry for him. I could see he was in a lot of discomfort.

Eventually, it was time to go so we did our farewell thing and I headed out once more for Watford. I thought to myself as I drove back, fate does play strange tricks in our lives. I used to look up to Sean in our Air Force days and now the boot is on the other foot.

The next day Alex placed a For Sale ad in the local paper for my car. Two days later it was sold. Then I had some special time with my daughter and grandson before confirming my air ticket to take me back to New Zealand. A few days later I was once more in the air, well satisfied with how I'd spent the money Gerald had left me and all the richness it had brought to my doorstep.

I felt somewhere in my bones Gerald would have loved to have done it himself, so instead I did it for him with a lot more of the ridiculous than he would have been capable of getting into. Every so often when I stayed with him he'd tell me what a crazy bastard I was, but there has to be at least one in just about every family.

Well, that concludes what I call the main story about my life and I hope you will enjoy reading it as much as I've enjoyed living it. The sequel to this story is on my blog up to a certain point. But I will carry on writing my blog till such time as I am not able to do it anymore for any reason.

Thank you one and all who have helped, inspired and encouraged me along the way.

Terry Robinson.

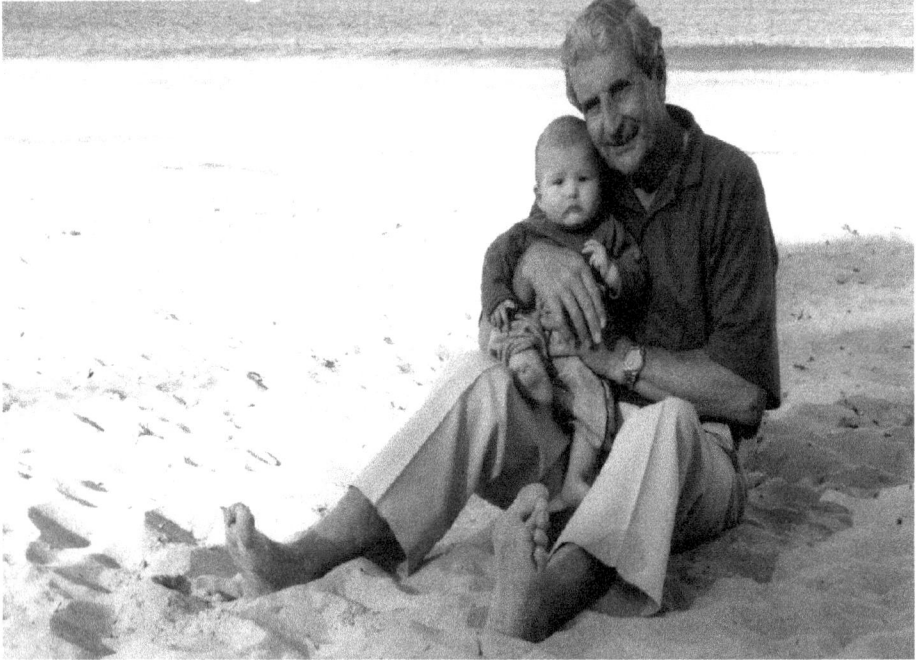

Conor and the 'old man' on Manly Beach

www.ingramcontent.com/pod-product-compliance
Lightning Source LLC
Chambersburg PA
CBHW072005270326
41928CB00009B/1551